Jack Sharkey

A Heavyweight Champion's Untold Story

By James Curl

Win By KO Publications

Iowa City

Jack Sharkey

A Heavyweight Champion's Untold Story

James Curl

(ISBN-13): 978-0-9903703-3-8

(softcover: 50# acid-free alkaline paper)

Includes footnotes, appendix, bibliography, and index.

© 2015 by James Curl. All Rights Reserved.

No part of this book may be reproduced, or transmitted in any form or by any means, graphic, electronic or mechanical, including photocopying, recording, taping, or by any information storage retrieval system without the written permission of James Curl.

Cover design by Gwyn Snider ©

Manufactured in the United States of America.

Win By KO Publications

Iowa City, Iowa

winbykopublications.com

Table of Contents

Acknowledgments	5
Foreword by Jack Sharkey III	6
1. Arrival	7
2. The Forging of a Fighter	12
3. Picking Himself Back Up, Sharkey-Maloney I	20
4. Weinert rematch and Jack Renault	26
5. Sharkey-Maloney II	34
6. Emilio "King" Solomon	40
7. Gorman and Risko	46
8. Sharkey-Maloney III	49
9. Staying Busy	53
10. The Black Panther	57
11. Homer Smith and Mike McTigue	67
12. Sharkey-Maloney IV	74
13. Sharkey-Dempsey, The Build Up	85
Photographs	94
14. Sharkey-Dempsey, The Fight	134
15. A Contender no More	140
16. Delaney	145

17. DeKuh, Tex and Christner	150
18. Stribling and the Phantom of Philly	157
19. Phil Scott	163
20. Sharkey-Schmeling I	168
21. The Toy Bulldog	175
22. Sharkey-Carnera I	180
23. Sharkey-Schmeling II, Winning the Title	183
24. The Passing of Ernie Schaaf	186
25. Sharkey-Carnera II	191
26. The "Fix" Question	197
27. The Kingfish and Loughran	202
28. Comeback	206
29. The Brown Bomber	214
30. Gone Fishing	217
Bibliography	222
Jack Sharkey's Record	223
Index	227

ACKNOWLEDGEMENTS

The following people deserve a special thank you for helping making this book possible. I would especially like to thank Jack Sharkey III for all of the great pictures he provided as well as the great stories and information about his grandfather. Dan Cuoco, director of the International Boxing Research Organization for helping with pictures, and information. Dan's help with my Walcott book as well as this one was invaluable. Adam Pollack for publishing the book, Joe Page and Mike Silver for taking the time to write their thoughts on the Sharkey-Carnera "fix" debate and editor Mike Valentino for looking over each chapter and giving me all those red marks.

There were many other people who contributed the making of this book in one way or another. I would like to thank them for their help. Tony Triem, Christine Lewis, Bob Yalen, Don Cogswell, Luckett Davis, Pat Coleman, Steve Lott, Dave Roake, Clay Moyle, Austin Killeen, Bill "Billy C." Calagero, Jim Carney, Larry Durst, John Gay, Dave Bergin.

If I have forgotten anyone, I sincerely apologize.

James Curl

FOREWORD

My grandfather, Jack Sharkey, was always an interesting figure in my life. He was not only my grandfather, but he was also the 1932 Heavyweight Boxing Champion of the World. He seemed larger than life to me. As a child, my family visited him and my grandmother in Epping, NH for holidays, summer vacations, and weekends. As one of several grandsons, I was privileged to be named after him, Jack Sharkey III. The "name" was very important to my grandfather as well as to my father, Jack Sharkey Jr. The poem, "Father's Family Name" was often quoted, and a plaque with the poem etched on it was later handed down to me. The last verse reads, "So make sure you guard it wisely, after all is said and done, you'll be glad the name is spotless, when you give it to your son." I was privileged to pass a clean name on to my son, Jack Sharkey IV. The name lives on!

When traveling with my father and grandfather as a boy, I always felt a sense of infallibility. Even as a child, I had a distinct impression of my grandfather's greatness, although I learned to appreciate it more as I grew older. Jim Curl writes in a way that kindles fond memories of my childhood. I can hear my grandfather's voice as if it were yesterday. In my mind's eye, I can see the way he took center stage in any setting, whether at home or in public. Wherever he was or whoever he was with, he commanded attention! Curl does an outstanding job writing about my grandfather's life, capturing both Jack Sharkey the family man and Jack Sharkey the fighter. During the fight scenes you will stay riveted to your seat, experiencing blow-by-blow action, as if watching his fights live. My grandfather achieved greatness during an era of greatness. It is my hope that you understand more fully this man. Jim Curl does a worthy job giving my grandfather, Jack Sharkey Sr., "The Squire of Chestnut Hill," the recognition that has been long overdue.

Regards,

Jack Sharkey III

CHAPTER 1
ARRIVAL

The huge steamship floated slowly into port at Ellis Island and came to a stop with a puff of white smoke and a jolting bump against the wooden docks. Dock workers quickly secured the iron giant with thick ropes as hundreds of Polish, Russian, Slovak and Lithuanian immigrants lined up along the rusty rails and excitedly peered over the side.

They were anxious to be off their makeshift home and away from the deplorable living conditions that they had suffered through to get to America. For nearly a month these immigrants had called the ship's steerage compartments home; rooms of iron and wooden framework half as long as the ship and just as wide. These quarters were jam packed with as many as a hundred and fifty people, and the "accommodations" were appalling. The ventilation was inadequate and the air was rank. The putrid smell of vomit from the seasick mingled with the stench of body odor and the filthy toilet rooms. During the voyage most of the immigrants lie down in their berths too miserable and sick to move about. Occasionally, during good weather they would go to the top deck for fresh air and to stretch out. However, when the sea turned violent the conditions worsened, sawdust had to be thrown down onto the floor to soak up the vomit. The cooks served food, basically soups, stews and bread, but most were too sick to eat much. As a result of the filthy living conditions many people became sick with infectious diseases like Typhoid fever and Dysentery. And it was not uncommon to find the occasional dead body, which was given a quick burial at sea, lest it spread more diseases.

Nevertheless, despite the miserable surroundings all was not gloom in the steerage rooms. There were those who tried to stay upbeat by playing cards, playing and listening to music and occasionally dancing, (when they were not too seasick), and the conversation about America and the future was endless.

With the ship secured the gangplank was lowered. Among the crowd of immigrants that made their way onto the docks was a young Lithuanian couple named Benjamin and Agnes Zukauskas.[1] They had given up everything and braved the danger of the steamship and the vast Atlantic Ocean to come to America. Once on the dockyard they were separated and a physician examined each of them for lice, disabilities and diseases. After

---

1 There are several different versions of Jack Sharkey's original last name that have been reported, including: Cukoschay, Cuckoschay and Zukoschay.

they passed the medical examination, they needed to answer a series of questions correctly, some of which were, are you a polygamist? An anarchist? They were then given their papers and cleared to go. Benjamin and Agnes were among the lucky ones. Many of the immigrants that were checked were found to have infectious diseases, which guaranteed them a hasty and miserable return trip home. The dreams and promises of America awaited Benjamin and his young wife Agnes; it must have been an exciting moment.

The year was 1900 when Benjamin and Agnes arrived at Ellis Island. Like most immigrants they had come to America for many reasons, some of them political, some of them religious but mostly they came for the opportunities that the land of the free offered; which meant they came to make money and have a better life. Like the majority of these early immigrants Benjamin and Agnes were probably illiterate and unskilled in any kind of work. As a result they took low-paying jobs and lived together in crowded dwellings just to make a living. Life was difficult for these early settlers. But, they were hard workers and incomparable at saving what little money they were able to earn. And what little extra they could afford was sent back home to relatives, most of whom were living in even worse conditions.

After staying in Brockton, Massachusetts for a while, Benjamin and Agnes eventually found a place to call home when they settled in Binghamton, New York. Binghamton, known as the Valley of Opportunity, attracted thousands of immigrants because of the abundance of factory jobs, most notably shoes and cigars. It was at a shoe factory that Benjamin eventually found employment, where he apparently worked for years. Agnes stayed home and took care of the boarders that the family took in to make a little extra money. Two years after their arrival Ben and Agnes were overjoyed by the birth of their first child, a baby boy born October 26, 1902. The happy parents christened him Joseph Paul Zukauskas. About three years later Joseph's younger sister, Mary followed.

Joseph grew up in the culturally diverse, impoverished neighborhoods of Binghamton. The children of Slavic, Polish, Jewish, Lithuanian and Italian immigrants provided a rich assortment of friends for the young boy. Because of the diverse ethnic mixture that Joseph grew up around, along with his Lithuanian parentage, he learned to speak a smattering of half a dozen languages and retained his ability to speak several of them his entire life. These neighborhoods of Joseph's early life were steeped in toughness. Growing up he learned to fight and to survive. Part of that survival meant having loyal friends that stuck together and for a time during his youth Joseph was the head of a neighborhood gang of rough and tough teenagers.

As a young boy Joseph walked three miles to St. Patrick Parochial school where he was taught by the good nuns. During lunch he sat alone and ate his sandwiches while everyone else walked home. At some stage in Joseph's eighth grade year his father became ill and was unable to work for a time; the family's meager savings were soon used up. Being from a poor family Joseph quickly realized that making money and keeping his family fed was more of a priority than an education; he had no choice but to quit school and get a job. To help support his family Joseph went to work at a shoe factory at the age of 12 tacking soles. By 14 he was part of a construction gang building a dike in Binghamton. It was hard work but it paid well and kept the boy outdoors where he liked to be. From there Joseph traveled around and did other jobs such as mixing concrete by hand and working as a brakeman for the railroad.

By 1917 Joseph was 15 and the world was deeply involved in World War One. Being patriotic the boy attempted to join the Navy but was rejected because he was too young. Not old enough for war it was back to work, shoveling coal on a barge. The work was brutally hard but the $15.00 a week was great pay, for a poor boy. By 17 Joseph was working in a glass factory as a glassblower. His sister Mary, who was 14 at the time, was employed as a cigarette roller.

At home things were less than great for the teenage boy. Joseph and his father, who had a temper described as violent, were not getting along. As a result of a particularly explosive argument, Joseph ran away. The young boy lived hand to mouth for about the next six months, sleeping at the YMCA, and working for Ringling Brothers circus in Bridgeport, Connecticut. It was a rough life for the recently emancipated teen. So, in October of 1920, when he turned 18, he wearily trudged across the Brooklyn Bridge with a scant five cents in his pocket and enlisted in the United States Navy. The well-built lad was quickly signed up and promised an annual salary of $350.00. Within a few days Joseph was wearing Navy blues at the training station in Newport, Rhode Island. After eight weeks of basic training, he was shipped off to the sweltering Caribbean where he was stationed aboard the *U.S.S. South Carolina*.

"They called it the Banana Fleet," said Joseph of his stint. "We used to go ashore with another company of Marines and a cannon and put down uprisings."[2]

Joseph adjusted surprisingly well to the harsh regime of the military life. In fact, his time in the Navy became one of the best times in his life, as he would later recollect. There was action, camaraderie, a warm bed and three square meals a day. And it beat the hell out of living as a starving runaway. It was while in the Navy that Joseph got his first taste of boxing. "Aboard the ship we'd hit the heavy bag until we were blue in the face. We also did a

---

[2] "The Story of Jack Sharkey, Boxing's Tragic Figure," by Jim Brady, *Boxing Illustrated.*

little road work." Joseph also gained a reputation as a real tough guy when he witnessed a fellow recruit stealing ice cream bars from a child vendor. Confronting the thief the two boys quickly came to blows, with Joseph handing the fellow a solid whopping. A slightly different version of the story has Joseph being the victim of thievery and it was his bowl of ice cream that was stolen; the outcome of the fight being the same.

Word of Joseph's prowess spread quickly among the fleet and reached the ears of the Naval Athletic Director. Since the fellow that Joseph had given a shellacking to was an amateur middleweight boxer, the director was impressed to say the least. The two eventually met with the director suggesting that Joseph join the boxing team. Initially, the young sailor was a bit apprehensive about fighting and showed little interest. It was his friend, Ensign Mickey O'Reagan, once light heavyweight champion at Annapolis, who eventually persuaded Joseph to pull on a pair of gloves. In no time, Joseph Paul was lacing up the leather and learning the rudiments of the jab, hook and straight right hand. Eager to show off his newly acquired skills a match was arranged against a behemoth of a man, described as being as big as Popeye's nemesis, Bluto. Joseph won the fight by decision and in his own words, "I got to be king of the walk."[3] A different account has Joseph fighting a black fighter named Green and winning by a first round knockout.[4] For the next four years Joseph fought in every tournament that he could under the name "Battling Ski" and eventually won the fleet championship, for which he was awarded a belt.

It was during his time in the service that Joseph met and befriended a young recruit by the name of Ernie Schaaf. The two became fast friends and spent time together aboard the *U.S.S Denver*. In no time Joseph's interest in boxing rubbed off on Ernie. As the story goes Joseph and Ernie were matched for a fight. Joseph, being six years older and a lot more experienced gave Ernie quite a beating. Nonetheless, the two remained close friends for years. Ernie, like Joseph showed a lot of promise early on and continued to box while in the service. After his discharge in 1926 Ernie followed Joseph's lead and embarked on his own boxing career.

While on R&R in Boston in 1924 Joseph, now fully bitten by the boxing bug, wandered into one of the city's many fight clubs. During the 1920s boxing shared a place next to baseball and horse racing as the most popular sport in America and there were hundreds of fight clubs across the country. These brutal battlegrounds were filled with thousands of cauliflower ears and broken nosed dreamers. The matches held in these dim, smoky clubs were usually unsanctioned and had very few rules. The fights played out in

---

3 "Underrated Sharkey, Now 79 Recalls Ring Experiences," *Houston Chronicle*, April 4, 1982.
4 "Jack Sharkey Jumps From Sailor to Fistic Threat," *The Ogden Standard Examiner* July 20, 1927.

front of cigarette smoking, fedora-wearing crowds that screamed for blood and knockouts. Here it was truly survival of the fittest where only the strong survived.

"When we got liberty, I went ashore and roamed the city. So I saw a fight club and I walked upstairs. There was a scruffy little guy behind a desk. He said, 'what do you want?'

I'm a sailor in the Navy. I boxed some, I said.

'Don't bother me,' he said. I started for the door. 'How many fights?' he asked me.

About thirty, I won all but one.

'I'll give you a $100 for four rounds.' I would have fought the Navy for a $100. Then he asked me my name. I told him, Joseph Zukauskas.

'Where the hell did you get a name like that?'

I had visions of the $100 flying away. I walked around the block several times thinking of a fighting name. Knockout so and so…kid so and so…No, that won't do. Dempsey was my idol and the great Tom Sharkey had been called sailor Sharkey. I put the two together and I came back."[5]

With no official amateur background besides the fights he'd had in the Navy, Joseph took the $100 that was offered and disposed of one Billy Moulden on January 29, 1924, inside of a round. The paper the next day described Sharkey as possessing everything a coming champion would need. "The sailor, stationed aboard the *U.S.S Denver*, jabbed technically and crossed his mighty right with precision, sending Moulden down three times before referee Jerry Moore stopped the one sided affair."[6]

With a win under his belt and a proper fighter's name put together, Joseph, who would now and forever be known as Jack Sharkey, was about to embark on a journey through the often contentious but always exciting world of professional prize fighting. During the next 12-years he would know incredible success and terrible lows. He would be involved in some of the most controversial fights of all time and battle some of the most legendary fighters to ever step into a ring. And in the end he would leave his own unique mark on boxing's colorful history.

---

5 Jack Sharkey, *Yankee Magazine*, September, 1983.
6 "Sharkey Shows a Wallop," *Boston Globe*, January, 30, 1924, pg.8.

CHAPTER 2
THE FORGING OF A FIGHTER

Shortly after his first fight Sharkey found a suitable gym to call home and began training earnestly at Kelly's Boxing Gym in Boston. It was at Kelly's that Jack met Johnny Buckley, the man who would manage and guide him throughout his career. John Francis Buckley, a short heavyset man with a round happy looking face, was born to James and Nellie Buckley on May 22, 1889 in Massachusetts,[7] and was of Irish descent, his grandparents having emigrated from Ireland in the early 1800s. Buckley, together with his younger brother Jerry, had been involved in the fight game for sometime as managers, trainers and promoters. By the time Sharkey came along Buckley was already successful and had a stable of promising young fighters. Even so, Buckley was always on the lookout for new talent, especially heavyweight talent; he found it in Jack.

Seeing that the young sailor was eager to train and get into the ring, Buckley wasted no time in setting up a fight, and introducing Jack to his first trainer, "Battling" Jim McCreary. Buckley also helped the young boy obtain an honorable discharge from the Navy, after serving four years.

With a suitable team assembled, the now ex-gob, (gob being a slang word for sailor) went into serious training for his second fight under the watchful eye of McCreary. Jim McCreary, an African-American, was born in North Carolina sometime in the late 1890s. Jim was a veteran heavyweight with over a 100 fights and still active as a fighter when he and Sharkey began working together. In fact, McCreary often acted as Jack's sparring partner. Jack was also fortunate enough at this time to be exposed to the knowledge of middleweight Jack "Twin" Sullivan who filled in as co-trainer for several of Jack's early fights. Sullivan, like McCreary, was a seasoned battler who had 156 recorded fights and over 20-years of experience. The wisdom that these two master boxers imparted on the young boy was beyond measure, and no doubt had a big impact on his style and rapid development.

On February 8, 1924 Jack climbed into the boxing ring at the Mechanics Building to take on Pat Hench. Pat or "Battling Hench" as he was known in the Army claimed to have participated in over 30 amateur bouts and by all accounts was a tough guy who could give as well as take punishment. Having just began his professional career his record was only 1-2. Jack, however, proved to be too much for the tough ex-soldier.

---

7 Ancestry.com.

Sharkey knocked the awkward Hench down near the end of the first round and three times in the second. After going down two more times without being hit, Pat was disqualified by the referee.

With only a couple of fights to his credit it was already apparent that the 6', 195-pound fighter was anything but ordinary. Jack was naturally athletic and gifted with exceptionally fast hands, punching power and a solid chin. In addition, he had plenty of courage, as he would show throughout his career by stepping into the ring with anyone. And he never drew the color line, taking on black fighters as well as white ones. Along with his natural athleticism, Sharkey had handsome, chiseled features, slick black hair and vibrant blue eyes. The 22-year-old fighter looked as if he belonged on the big screen alongside Douglas Fairbanks in some swashbuckling thriller.

Although at this early stage of his career Sharkey was a crude brawler, later on he would develop into a more technical boxer because of his fragile hands; early on he tried to emulate the style of his idol, Jack Dempsey. Dempsey, known as "The Manassas Mauler," was the reigning heavyweight champion of the world when Sharkey started his career and was an extremely popular champion. Dempsey's aggressive, bob and weave style was imitated by many an aspiring young fighter dreaming of fistic glory. However, this tear away style led to Sharkey having multiple fractures in both of his hands during his early career, thus the eventual change from slugger to boxer.

It was fortunate for Sharkey that he happened to start his boxing career in Boston. Boston along with New York, Philadelphia and New Jersey was a major boxing metropolis during Sharkey's career. The city was famed for giving rise to John L. Sullivan "The Boston Strong Boy." Sullivan, the son of Irish immigrants was born in 1858 and fought his way from the poor streets of Boston to win the heavyweight title in 1882. By capturing the title John became recognized as the first heavyweight champion of the "gloved area." Sullivan was the most important sports figure of his time and did more for prizefighting during his 10-year reign than anyone before him. Sullivan revolutionized how the sport was conducted and helped bring boxing to the collective consciousness of mainstream America.

"The Boston Strong Boy" wasn't the only great fighter to come out of Boston. Several of the greatest fighters in history were either born there or adopted Bean Town as their home. Sam Langford "The Boston Tar Baby" got his start in Boston. Joe Walcott "The Barbados Demon" and Welterweight champion was born in Barbados but grew up in the South End. The only undefeated heavyweight champion in history, Rocky Marciano, was born in Brockton, Massachusetts. And the Marvelous one, Marvin Hagler also came from Brockton. From the time of John L. Sullivan to the modern era, Boston has enjoyed a rich boxing history.

Due in part to the influence Boston fighters had in the 1920s and 1930s boxing's popularity rivaled that of baseball and horse racing and just about every kid in America wanted to be a fighter. Such was boxing's impact that during the early twentieth century it has been said that if one was to see two boys fighting on a street corner in America they would be jabbing and hooking correctly. For poor kids boxing was seen as a way out; a way to make something of oneself. An example of this would be Jack Dempsey. He went from traveling hobo to the most popular sports figure in America during the 1920s. Dempsey's fame equaled that of Babe Ruth. And he made a lot more money.

Next up for Sharkey was Dan Lucas on February 26, 1924 at the Mechanics Building. The fight was ended by an easy second round knockout after Jack landed a crushing right that left his opponent asleep on the canvas.

McCreary and Sullivan had their hands full getting their young apprentice ready for his next fight. Jack, showing the kind of fearlessness that would follow him throughout his career, took a big step up in competition when he agreed to meet Canadian fighter Eddie Record on March 18, 1924 at the Grand Opera House in Boston. Although never more than a journeyman fighter, Record was much more experienced than Jack and was by far his most dangerous opponent to date. Coming into the fight Eddie was 13-8-1 with 12 knockouts and a newspaper decision loss.

With just under a month to prepare, McCreary and Sullivan spent every available moment tutoring their young fighter. "Battling" Jim and Sharkey sparred dozens of rounds. During these sessions McCreary worked on refining Jack's foot-work, balance and feinting techniques as well as teaching him how to bob and weave to avoid punches. By fight night Jack Sharkey was a finely tuned fighter.

The fight turned out to be a thrilling battle and was reported to be to be one of the best heavyweight clashes in many a moon. The excitement began in round one when Jack knocked Eddie over the top rope and out of the ring with a smashing right to the jaw. Eddie quickly made his way back into the ring, but Jack controlled most of the round and cuffed Record at will with left hooks and hard rights to the body.

Eddie took round two by a slim margin and was seen as having a slight edge in round three by boxing effectively. Rounds four through seven were all Sharkey's. Eddie won round eight by knocking Jack down twice with dangerously low blows; the first one Eddie apologized for. But, before the round ended Jack was back in command. In round nine Jack again knocked Eddie out of the ring when he landed a terrific right hand that sent Record through the ropes and into the lap of a surprised spectator. Round ten saw Jack boxing beautifully and landing jolting rights and lefts at will as he finished the fight strongly.

Clearly thinking he won, Jack, along with most of the audience was shocked when Eddie was awarded the decision. Hearing the result over the loudspeaker the crowd roared its disapproval loud and clear. It was reported in the *Boston Globe* the next day that Sharkey had won at least seven of the ten rounds and should have won easily.[8] After the fight an angry Sharkey voiced his outrage and called for an immediate rematch. Eddie, feeling that he had won the fight fair and square, readily agreed.

The rematch was fought just over a month later on April 25, 1924 and was the main event of the evening at the Boston Arena. This time Sharkey made sure that there would be no questionable decisions.

From the opening bell Jack was aggressive and forced the action. The ex-sailor proved to be the superior of Record and out boxed Eddie easily in round one. Eddie came on strong in round two and was effective with his jab and finding a home for his right hand. Not wanting to let his opponent get the upper hand, Jack came out with bad intentions in round three. Bobbing and weaving, Sharkey constantly came forward unleashing a whirlwind of punches that battered Eddie throughout the round. Round four was much the same as three with Jack landing flurries of punches that had Eddie on the defensive. In the fifth round Sharkey changed his point of attack from Eddie's head to his body. The ex-sailor viciously attacked Record's mid-section, driving him around the ring with hard lefts and right. During the sixth Eddie took a terrific shellacking to both his ribs and head that had everyone wondering how he stayed on his feet. In the seventh, sensing that the end was near, Jack tore out of his corner and attacked his foe with a series of fast punches. Eddie weathered the first attack but was too weak to survive Sharkey's second assault. A precision right cross to the jaw dumped Eddie to the canvas and put an end to the fight.

The impressive victory over Record, along with his other wins, was getting Sharkey a lot of ink in the local papers. As a result of the growing recognition Jack began to get a big head. "Oh I thought I was a real big shot, a real big shot,"[9] said Sharkey in an interview 60-years later.

With his early success the cocky young fighter, just barely more than a boy really, felt supremely confident, enough so that he and his manager Buckley agreed to a fight with Floyd "The Auburn Bulldog" Johnson on June 23, 1924. Taking on Floyd was an enormous step up in competition. At 24-years-old, Floyd had been fighting for four years and had defeated such notable fighters as "K.O." Bill Brennan, Fred Fulton and Quinton Romero Rojas. He had also been in the ring with former heavyweight champion Jess Willard. It was reported in the papers leading up to the fight

---

8 "Maybe His Failure to "K.O" Record Cost Sharkey Award," *Boston Globe*, March 19, 1924, pg.16A.
9 "The Story of Jack Sharkey, Boxing's Tragic Figure," *Boxing Illustrated*, by Jim Brady.

that Angel Firpo, the big Argentinean who had come out on the losing end of a three round slug fest with heavyweight champion Jack Dempsey, was afraid to fight Johnson. Coming into the bout Johnson weighed 198 and had a record of 36-4-8 with 22 knockouts, along with two newspaper decisions: wining 1 and drawing 1. Sharkey weighed 181 and had a far less impressive record of 4-1 with 3 knockouts.

On the night of the fight Boston fight fans crammed into the sold out Grand Opera House to see boxing's latest rising star. It had been a long time since a fight, or fighter, had generated this much interest. For this fight Sharkey brought his new bride, Dorothy and sat her ringside. The two had met while Jack was still in the Navy and were married on June 16, 1924. It would be the first and last fight his wife ever attended. Years later Jack would say, "She didn't like nothing about boxing, except the recognition it got me."[10]

Despite facing a fighter that was immensely more experienced, Sharkey's natural abilities carried him through to what turned out to be an exciting, yet easy victory. "He took me for a softie," Jack would later say. By all accounts Sharkey boxed circles around his more experienced foe and feinted him into knots, while landing lefts and rights almost at will. In the second, Jack nearly ended things when he floored Johnson for a short count with a well-placed right hand. However, Jack showed his inexperience after Johnson regained his feet by becoming over anxious, and trying to finish Floyd off quickly. "The Auburn Bulldog" used his vast ring experience and was able to survive the round because the excited young fighter missed more punches than he landed. Jack made the same mistake in the fourth when he had Johnson in distress from a big right hand, but, in his excitement he wound up missing the opportunity to end matters again.[11] For the remainder of the fight both Sharkey and Johnson boxed well. But, it was Sharkey who dished out most of the punishment. When it was over, Jack was awarded an impressive and well deserved 10-round decision, having won eight out of ten rounds.

If Jack had been full of himself before, his head was now the size of a hot air balloon. The headline in the *Boston Globe* read, "Last Night's Bout Shot Jack Sharkey into the Fore Ranks of Heavyweight Boxers."[12] Another article read, "Meteoric Rise of Sharkey in the Ring Game Leads Some to Believe Boston Will Produce New Champion."[13]

---

10 "The Story of Jack Sharkey, Boxing's Tragic Figure," *Boxing Illustrated*, by Jim Brady.
11 "Last Night's Bout Shot Jack Sharkey into the Fore Ranks of Heavyweight Boxers," *The Boston. Globe*, June 24, 1924, pg.19A.
12 Ibid.
13 "Meteoric Rise of Sharkey Leads Some to Believe That Boston Will Produce New Champion," *The Boston Globe*, June 23, 1924, pg.7.

To put in perspective just how impressive Sharkey's rise was, by July of 1924 with only six professional fights to his name Jack was already being touted as a future opponent for heavyweight champion Jack Dempsey and was being called "The new John L. Sullivan." Buckley was receiving a flood of offers from promoters who desired the services of Sharkey.[14] But, the portly manager was in no hurry to rush his charge. Instead, his plan was for Jack to develop over the course of the next two years while slowly increasing his level of competition before tangling with any elite fighters.

Consider this. Jack's first 10 opponents had a combined "official" win-loss record (does not include newspaper decisions) of 141-63, and Jack went 8-2. It was truly amazing that a fighter with only six professional fights had beaten Homer Smith, a fighter that had over 50 professional fights. In addition, at this early stage Jack was already being considered as a possible opponent for a number of top contenders.

Sharkey racked up three more wins starting with Homer Smith. Smith, who was born in Kalamazoo, Michigan in 1893, began boxing at 18 and was paid $0.75 for his first professional fight. He was another far more experienced fighter with an "official" record of 36 wins, 14 losses and 27 knockouts, as well as dozens of newspaper fights. Up to this point, Smith had been in the ring with everyone including Jack Dempsey, for which he was paid $218.00, Harry Greb, Billy Miske and Jack Johnson. Admittedly, Smith lost most of his fights against top level opposition and was probably on the slide at 31-years-old and having over 100 fights when he faced Sharkey. Held at the Braves baseball stadium on July 15, 1924 in Boston, the fight was a clear cut 10-round decision win for the ex-gob.

Just eight days after his fight with Smith, Al Roberts became Sharkey's next victim. Al was yet another far more experienced fighter with a respectable record of 26-9-1 with 16 knockouts. He also had six newspaper fights: winning 2, loosing 3 and drawing 1. Moreover, he had shared the ring with some great fighters like Gene Tunney, Harry Greb and Billy Miske. Jack won a 10-round decision in what was called a slow fight and earned a forced vacation when he broke his left hand and bruised his right; he was expected to be out of the ring for several weeks while they healed.

With his hands on the mend, Jack spent some time attending fights. On July 29, he was at the Jimmy Maloney-Wolf Larson match and watched as Maloney, a popular up and coming Boston fighter defeated Larson. Little did either fighter suspect at the time that they would become involved in a fierce four fight rivalry that would last for four years.

---

14 "Jack Sharkey, Boston Heavyweight Touted as Rival for Dempsey," *Oakland Tribune*, July 18, 1924, pg. 7.

Three weeks later with his hands healed Sharkey was back in the ring with "Young" Jack Johnson on August 20, 1924 at the Fair Grounds Auditorium in Maine. After six tame rounds that amounted to little more than a glorified sparring session, Jack was awarded the decision. The crowd, which had booed their dissatisfaction throughout the bout, booed even louder at the fight's conclusion.

With his latest victory Jack's career shot to new heights. The *Boston Globe* ran an article that read, "From Crude Boxer to Title Contender in Nine Months,"[15] and called Sharkey's rise "Sensational." And then disaster struck and Jack's pugilistic meteor began to sputter and fizzle and his career came rocketing back to earth with a resounding crash. One of Sharkey's major flaws, his inconsistency, was about to show itself.

The cause of Sharkey's quick fall started with a bout against Chilean boxer Quintin Romero Rojas, known as "The Cuban Hercules." Quintin, who was originally from Santiago, Chile, carried a record of 11-4-2, 4 by knockout, but like many fighters from his era his early record is uncertain and he may have had many more unrecorded bouts. At 6'1" and 195-pounds "The Cuban Hercules" was only slightly bigger than Jack, but by all accounts was very tough and muscular. The fight was held on August 29, 1924 at the Mechanics Building in Boston and was said to be a tremendous give and take battle.

The first round opened with Sharkey boxing smartly. He circled his opponent, feinting and shifting until the Chilean would drop his gloves. At which point Jack would land quick jabs to the face and hard rights to the ribs of his slower opponent. Romero opened up some in the second and landed some short wicked uppercuts to Sharkey's jaw. Jack tried to bob and weave to avoid the heavy blows, but only managed to dodge a few. Sharkey answered with two sharp lefts to Quintin's stomach that had the Cuban wincing in pain. A hard uppercut split Quintin's bottom lip and had him spitting blood. Romero came on strong in the third with some big bombs that had the ex-sailor covering up. Sharkey tried to return fire but only managed to land light jabs with no real power behind them. It was suspected at this time that Jack had possibly broken his right hand, but as the round neared its end Sharkey surged back and turned the tide of battle back to his favor by landing some hard left hooks to Romero's rib cage.

Quintin rushed forward in round four landing rights to the kidney and vicious uppercuts to Jack's chin. Sharkey showed his gameness by fighting back and landing quick jabs and sharp uppercuts until he was visibly winded.

---

15 "From Crude Boxer to Title Contender In 9 Months Is Ex-Tar's Meteoric Record," *The Boston Globe* August 26, 1924, pg.11A.

The minute rest between round four and five did the tiring Sharkey a world of good. Refreshed, Jack came on strong in the fifth. He drove the Cuban to the ropes with jabs, a left hook and a hard right to the stomach that caused Romero to grimace in pain. Jack then boxed magnificently at long range landing lefts and rights that rocked the Chilean. The ex-sailor continued having success in the sixth with superior speed and boxing ability as Romero appeared to be fading. The burly Cuban swung the battle back into his favor in the seventh by getting in close and landing solid uppercuts and rights to Sharkey's chin. The punches visibly weakened the tiring Sharkey.

Jack tried to take the play away from Romero in the eighth but the exhausted fighter had nothing left on his punches and couldn't keep the big Cuban off. It was clear that both of his hands were giving him trouble as Romero was walking through his punches and engaging Jack at close quarters. A hard left hook by Romero caused blood to flow freely from Sharkey's smashed nose. Jack retreated to the ropes where he was all but powerless to stop his opponent's barrage of leather. Sharkey did however, manage to box his way off the ropes, but a succession of hard blows to the stomach and jaw took the last of Sharkey's remaining strength as he pitched face forward onto the canvas. The bell rang loudly a moment later saving Jack from a knockout.

Jack's seconds rushed out and dragged their dazed fighter to his corner. Quickly some smelling salt was shoved under the young fighter's nose, but it had little effect bringing Jack back to reality. Someone then grabbed a bucket of water and doused Sharkey's head, the shock of the cool liquid woke Jack up just in time for him to hear some quick instructions from "Battling" Jim and the ringing of the bell signaling the start of round nine.

Standing unsteadily, his corner men pushed their man forward. Bravely, Jack staggered out and vainly tried to lift his arms for the inevitable attack, but it was no use, he was a beaten fighter. His head dropped first, then his knees buckled as he fell forward and sprawled on the canvas, down and out. Romero, to his credit, made no move to attack his opponent as Jack crumbled to the canvas. The Cuban simply stepped aside as the referee called a halt to the fight. Years later Sharkey recalled the end of the fight saying, "I was tired, so damn tired."

Buckley along with "Battling" Jim lifted Sharkey and carried him back to his corner. A ringside physician examined the semi-conscious fighter and suggested a trip to the local hospital, fearing a concussion. However, after a few minutes Jack's head cleared and he left the ring under his own power. The young fighter was driven home to his new bride in Binghamton. Every bump that the car hit jolted his aching body and was a reminder of his defeat. Jack's fast rising career had fallen and it had not yet hit the bottom.

CHAPTER 3
PICKING HIMSELF BACK UP
SHARKEY-MALONEY I

It took several days for Jack's bruised body to heal after the beating he had taken at the hands of "The Cuban Hercules." But, being young, he healed quickly. However, the mental part of the loss, and the blow to his inflated ego took a lot longer to recover from. Sure, he had lost once before to Eddie Record, but that was a questionable decision and most felt that he had won that fight. The loss to Romero was different. Jack had been beaten and left a crumpled heap on the canvas; there was no question that he had been defeated.

Nobody would have blamed Jack if he had taken an easy bout after his loss to Romero. But, the ex-sailor was never one to take an easy fight just because he had suffered a loss. So it came as little surprise when he signed to fight one of Boston's best and most popular young fighters, "Dynamite" Jimmy Maloney. This fight would mark the start of a great four fight rivalry between the two that would last for the next four years.

In a time in America when the Irish were disparaged as "Mick's," Italians as "Wops" and the Jews as "Kikes" the Sharkey-Maloney fights were mini Armageddon's. It wasn't going to be an easy fight for Sharkey. Jimmy was no soft touch. He was a well-schooled, pressure fighter that carried a wallop in either hand.

Jimmy Maloney was born on April 28, 1903 and was of Irish descent. He grew up in South Boston and started his career in 1924, the same time as Sharkey. Right from the start the 5'10", 200-pound slugger was a fan favorite. During his ten-year career Jimmy was beloved by his fellow Bostonians and had a large and fiercely loyal fan base. "Dynamite" Jim was seen as a true dyed in the wool, blue collar fighter. Even though he made some very good money during his fighting days, he continued to work as a fish peddler throughout his career.

Leading up to the fight it became apparent that the two boys didn't like each other. Sharkey added fuel to the fire when he was quoted in the local papers saying that there never was an Irishman who could beat him. Of course the fans in Boston, a distinctly Irish town, were furious when they read Jack's words. Because of the dislike between the two fighters and Sharkey's abrasive remarks, fan interest was high. Reservations for seats came flooding in and tickets sold quickly.

Both fighters were taking this fight very seriously. Maloney was reported as being in the best shape of his short but successful career and invited fans to attend his open workouts at Kelly and Hayes Boxing Gym. Across town, Sharkey was training just as hard. In the morning Jack did several miles of road work around the Brooklyn Reservoir. At 3 o'clock in the afternoon he worked out at Jim Toland's gymnasium where he would shadow box, hit the heavy bag and exercise with dumbbells. Sharkey would then finish up by boxing two fast rounds with Jack "Twin" Sullivan and four three minute sessions with "Battling" Jim McCreary.[16] Just days before the fight, Sullivan reported that Jack was an apt pupil and had taken in everything that he had been taught, and added that Jack would be a hundred percent better than in his last fight.

With television years away from being a common household item and pay-per-view still 60-years away, there were only two ways to follow a fight in the 1920s. A person could listen to a radio or buy a ticket and watch the bout live. Most fans preferred to watch live fights. As a result boxing matches in Boston drew huge crowds and the Sharkey-Maloney fight was no exception.

On November 5, 1924 the fans at the Mechanics Building were keyed up and the place was filled to capacity with thousands of people, the majority of which were Maloney supporters. They came to see Jimmy give the boastful ex-sailor the shellacking of his life. The Sharkey fans came to see if Jack could make a successful comeback after his devastating loss to Romero. Coming into the fight Jack was 8-2 and weighed 184. Jimmy, a little less experienced, held a record of 4-1 and weighed 197.

Sharkey's return to the ring was anything but triumphant. Possibly feeling a little tentative after his loss to Romero, Jack seemed unwilling to carry the fight to Maloney or mix it up. Instead he was content to stay on his toes and box cautiously at long range. Uncharacteristically, Maloney was also a little hesitant and showed a healthy respect for Jack. But, the Boston fighter was a little more willing to throw punches. As a result of their careful attitudes the fight turned out to be a tame affair and offered only intermittent action. Jack did become more aggressive in round eight and even taunted Maloney when he hollered, "Why don't you come out and fight." Jimmy only smiled. In the end Maloney was awarded a majority decision by a score of six rounds to three with one even; Jack was handed his second loss in a row. The crowd, unsatisfied with the fight booed loudly.

Brushing aside the Maloney loss, Sharkey was back in action a month later at the 113th Regent armory in Newark on December 15, again taking on a fighter that had a ton more experience. Charley Weinert, known as "The Newark Adonis" was from Australia and considered to be a very good "scientific boxer." He had put together an impressive "official" record of

---

16 "Maloney-Sharkey Bout Has Fans Keyed up to High Pitch," *Boston Daily Globe*, October 31, 1924, pg.18A.

32-7-1, with 19 knockouts. In addition Weinert had 17 newspaper decision wins and 10 losses. Charley also had some notable wins over Quintin Romero Rojas, Louis Angle Firpo, "Battling" Levinsky and Ed "Gun Boat" Smith. When he retired in 1929 Weinert had an overall record of 40-10-1, 27 by knockout. He also had 45 newspaper decision fights: winning 31, losing 11 and drawing 3.

Sharkey, now with a record of 8-3, came into the fight at 193-pounds, Charley at 184. For Jack, it turned out to be a terrible night. The still developing and inexperienced young fighter was badly over matched. From the opening bell it was clear that the veteran Weinert was too experienced for Sharkey. As a result, Jack was out boxed for eleven of the twelve rounds, and was only credited with wining round six.

During the first three rounds Charley dished out a painful beating to the ex-sailor, scoring well with stinging jabs and hard rights to the face and body. By the mid-point of round three Sharkey was a bloody mess. His left eye was split open and nearly swollen shut and he was bleeding from his nose and mouth. Showing his gameness, Jack tried to fight back, but Charley would tie the ex-sailor up whenever he would get inside and nullify the young fighter's attack. Jack did, however, manage to land a few solid wallops to Weinert's jaw in round three, but Charley took the blows and fought back harder. In the fourth Charley displayed some clever boxing when he shot a left and right to Jack's body. The blows forced Sharkey to drop his hands to guard his midsection. With his face unprotected Weinert quickly drove home two smashing lefts to Jack's bruised and blood covered jaw. In the fifth Weinert made Jack look like an amateur and had him missing repeatedly.

Angered, frustrated and behind on points, a desperate Sharkey came roaring out for the sixth and banged a hard right to Charley's face followed by two rights to his midsection. Jack did enough to win the round, but near the end of the session Charley had resumed command.

From the seventh round on, Weinert's impressive boxing skills were on full display as he carried the fight to Jack and gave him a thorough boxing lesson. Sharkey was able to land a few hard shots here and there during the last four rounds, but Weinert would just step back and smile, or tie Jack up. When it was over, Charley was awarded the newspaper decision.

Newspaper decisions were common when Jack fought and were usually done to curb gambling on a fight. If both fighters were still standing at the fight's conclusion and there were no knockouts, a no decision was rendered and neither fighter was declared the winner. However, this did not stop the ringside reporters from giving a consensus result amongst themselves and printing a "newspaper decision."

With three losses in a row Jack's stock fell sharply. Now when his name was mentioned in the papers it was usually followed or was preceded by something like, "once a title aspirant" or "former prospect." Nevertheless, for Jack boxing was a job and he had to work to earn a living. It was announced on December 23, that promoter Sam Wallace had secured a match for Sharkey against Jack De Mave, in New York. This fight would mark the first time that Jack would be fighting in New York. De Mave, known as "The Golden Boy" (some 80-years before Oscar De Lahoya) because of his blond hair was a prominent heavyweight in the 1920s. His big moment of fame, which came after his fight with Sharkey, was his impressive one round knockout of highly ranked Bob Lawson in 1925. During his busy career De Mave fought many of the leading heavyweights of his day and was a very solid fighter. Coming into the Sharkey fight it was reported that De Mave had won 21 fights in a row.[17]

With the start of 1925 Sharkey was hoping to get back on track for a shot at the heavyweight title. He went into serious training for the De Mave fight at Toland's gymnasium and once again "Battling" McCreary was responsible for getting Jack into fighting shape.

On January 8, 1925 Sharkey made his New York debut at the Manhattan Casino; he did not disappoint. Apparently the sage teachings of McCreary and Sullivan were starting to have an effect. It was reported that Jack had returned to form and was a much-improved boxer. The ex-sailor earned a solid 10-round decision by boxing masterfully in what was called a sensational fight. Although Jack won nearly every round De Mave showed his willingness and attacked with bulldog like courage, but was simply out classed in every way and was lucky to escape without being knocked out.

Sharkey's New York debut was a hit! So impressive was Jack's showing that New York promoter Tex Rickard wanted to sign Sharkey to a two-fight deal. Rickard at the time was matchmaker for Madison Square Garden and boxing's most dynamic and powerful promoter. Born George Lewis Rickard on January 2, 1870 Tex rose to prominence in the 1920s and helped usher in "the golden age of boxing." In 1921 Rickard promoted the Jack Dempsey-George Carpentier fight. The fight became the first title fight to be broadcast on radio as well as the first fight to generate a million dollars in ticket sales. Due in large part to Rickard's influence, boxing was brought to the forefront of American sports. Tex helped elevated the sport from the smoke filled arenas and made it fashionable.

Despite an offer by Tex, Jack refused. Instead, he wanted to redeem himself in Boston and have rematches with two of his conquerors, Weinert and Maloney. But first, Jack had to get by the hard punching James "Sully" Montgomery of Fort Worth, Texas. At 6'2" and in excess of 200-pounds "Sully" was a big Irish heavyweight and very athletic. In college he excelled

---

17 Boxrec.com lists De Mave's record at 9-3-1.

at football as a center and was a star player. Aside from boxing, "Sully" also played two-years of professional football in the National Football League with the Chicago Cardinals in 1923 and the Frankford Yellow Jackets in 1927. "Sully's" rise as a fighter was comparable to Sharkey's. Like Jack he rose quickly and defeated some good fighters. The ex-football player achieved national fame when he defeated Sharkey's nemesis Quintin Rojas. Champion Jack Dempsey ventured an opinion after watching "Sully" fight saying that Montgomery was "one of the most promising of the young crop of heavyweight championship aspirants."[18]

Jack had a big advantage going into the Montgomery fight in that his trainer Jim McCreary had fought Montgomery, losing by a 10th round knockout the previous November. However, McCreary had learned a lot about "Sully's" strengths and weaknesses during the fight and was only too happy to impart his knowledge onto his young apprentice.

The Montgomery fight was seen as a chance for Jack to climb back to the pugilistic heights he'd once held. And by all accounts he was taking the match very seriously. A report of his training sessions in the papers said that Jack was becoming a more refined and skillful boxer. And that he was fast, precise with his punches and feinting masterfully. Obviously the teachings that "Battling" Jim was imparting on the young boy were continuing to have an effect.

Just days before the fight Jim was asked to give his prediction. "Let me say here that I am not saying that Sharkey is going to win just because Montgomery beat me. I'm no sore head and I've been too long in the game to try to mislead anybody into believing as I do, but I am saying that Jack Sharkey will defeat "Sully" Montgomery because Jack Sharkey is a vastly improved boxer than when I worked with him last. The only chance Montgomery will have to win is to score a knockout and I honestly don't believe he can land the big punch on Sharkey. Jack's too fast on his feet, feints and ducks and weaves and rolls too well for the big boy to get over his Mary Ann. And one punch won't win the bout for that Montgomery baby. How many boxers have knocked Sharkey out? One, Romero Rojas. And Rojas didn't put him down until he had landed a hundred punches on Sharkey, who was all in and helpless. And didn't Sharkey take plenty? I'll say he did. Who else has ever stopped him? Nobody."[19]

McCreary's prediction turned out to be dead on. The contest started with Sully forcing the action in round one, but from then on, with the exception of rounds seven and nine, Sharkey was in command. Jack, who

---

[18] "Sully Montgomery Will Have Chance to Show Fistic Ability," *The Boston Globe*, November 20, 1924.

[19] "Sharkey Will Win From Montgomery, Opinions Battler," *The Boston Globe*, January 15, 1925, pg.A21.

was outweighed by 13-pounds, easily out pointed his lanky opponent and showed that he was becoming a much more "scientific boxer" by feinting, weaving and ducking. The full arsenal of his improving boxing skills was on display as he showed speed, cleverness and ring generalship and gave the awkward Montgomery a methodical boxing lesson.

Sharkey's win over Montgomery had once again established Jack as a legitimate contender. The papers the next day read, "Jack Sharkey's comeback places him once more firmly on Dempsey's Trail." Sharkey was now set to try and avenge one of his defeats; a rematch with Charley Weinert.

CHAPTER 4
WEINERT REMATCH AND JACK RENAULT

With his recent victories Sharkey had once again placed himself firmly back into the title hunt and earned himself a rematch with "The Newark Adonis" Charley Weinert. This rematch was a highly sought after bout with several prominent promoters vying for the opportunity to make the fight. Tom Goodwin, Frank Flournoy and Tex Rickard all wanted the fight, but it was Boston promoter, Tom Goodwin who snatched the bout from the grasp of Rickard and signed the two fighters to a February 10, 1925 date.

For Sharkey the fight was one that he literally begged for. He was eager to avenge his loss to Charley and was confident that he could win. In fact, he predicted to win in a way that would leave no doubt as to whom the better fighter was. For the fans of Boston the fight promised to be a good one and they were anxious to watch the two scientific boxers battle it out.

Preparing for the fight, Jack was between trainers and decided to follow his own training routine, which may not have been the best recipe for victory. Nevertheless, on February 10, 1925 at the famed old Mechanics Building, Jack climbed into the ring with Weinert and looked to be in great shape. Charley, who at this time was ranked third in the world, was a 10-8 favorite to beat the ex-sailor, again.

Anxious to prove he was the better fighter Sharkey started round one by tearing into Charley and landing several hard rights to the body followed by quick jabs. Weinert returned with a few of his own body shots but was content to lay back and try to out box Sharkey. Throughout the round Jack was the aggressor and forced the action by constantly boring into Charley and concentrating his attack on Weinert's body. By the round's end Jack's aggressive attack and Charley's lack thereof had won him the round.

Sharkey kept it up in round two and continued to press the action. He landed a number of telling left hooks to Charley's face and got the better of the infighting as well. Weinert though, used his ring-craft to survive Sharkey's early assault and turned the tide of battle in round three. Thoroughly warmed up, Charley took the play away from Jack and scored well throughout the round with stiff jabs and hard body shots.

The two combatants battled on fairly even terms throughout rounds four and five. Jack was successful with his quick shifting attack and hard left hooks, while Charley scored well with jabs and counter rights. "The Newark Adonis" found his groove in round six, frequently finding a home for his long lefts and thudding rights to the body. When the bell sounded Charley had captured the round with superior boxing skill and cleverness.

Sharkey came on relentlessly in round seven and repeatedly landed hard counter rights to Charley's jaw. For a while it looked as though Jack was on his way to a sure victory as his opponent began to show signs of tiring. By the round's end Jack was again in the lead.

Whatever momentum Sharkey had built in round seven was lost when he decided to slow down in rounds eight and nine. Maybe thinking he was ahead or maybe because he was starting to get a little arm weary, the ex-gob seemed content to loaf. As a result, Charley snatched rounds eight and nine, resuming command and the lead.

Round ten was a whirlwind of action with Jack fighting doggedly and scoring well with left hooks and right crosses early in the round. Weinert worked his jab and after a particularly solid one, Jack's left eye began to swell rapidly. Ignoring the pain from his damaged eye, Sharkey fought back hard. He missed a left hook but caught Charley with a right to the ear. The ex-sailor followed with a left hook to the stomach and a left uppercut that stopped his adversary in his tracks. Charley pumped in a right to Jack's belly and Sharkey landed an uppercut that had Weinert's head bobbing. The two then exchanged hard punches in close with Jack getting the better of the infighting. Charley backed off and landed hard jabs to Jack's jaw. As the two came into a clinch the bell rang ending an even round and a very close fight.

Throughout the 10-round bout both fighters had shown terrific boxing ability. Jack had the better of the infighting and landed the harder punches, but Charley carried the better jab and landed the cleaner shots. In the end, Weinert walked away with a very close, disputed decision. Sharkey's choice to loaf in rounds eight and nine was seen as the reason he had lost the fight. But there were plenty of dissenters in attendance and at ringside that yelled their disappointment at what they felt was an awful decision.[20]

The loss to Weinert did little to Sharkey's career in terms of lowering his stock. In fact, the papers called it the swiftest and most scientific battle ever waged in a Boston ring. And that Jack had boxed "the most brilliant battle of his career"[21] and had only lost by the most infinitesimal margin.

If Jack was disappointed over his loss to Weinert he didn't have a lot of time to dwell on it. At home his wife Dorothy was in the final stage of pregnancy and just a week after the fight she gave birth to the couple's first child on February 17, a healthy baby girl they named Dorothy. By all accounts Sharkey was completely smitten with his daughter and even turned

---

20 "Boston Heavyweight Can Blame Self For Losing to Weinert, Loafing Cost Sharkey the Victory," *Boston Globe*, February 11, 1925, pg.9.
21 "Sharkey Lost But Little Prestige in Weinert Go," *Boston Globe*, February 11, 1925, pg.A19.

down a March bout with Ad Stone because he was too wrapped up in his daughter to train seriously.[22]

After taking the better part of a month off Jack finally agreed to an April fight with the highly ranked Canadian fighter, Jack Renault. Renault was a talented boxer and real tough guy. He had been hardened by serving as a member of the Canadian Northwest Mounted Police and said that the job had left him immune to fear. Renault was considered one of the most skillful of the big men and carried a solid wallop in his right hand. Up to the point of taking on Sharkey the Canadian had amassed an impressive record of 45-5-1 with 15 knockouts and was currently on a 25-1 streak. In addition, he was also coming off an impressive win over one of Sharkey's conquerors, Quintin Romero Rojas. At this point Sharkey's record was 9-4 with 3 knockouts.

There were those who questioned whether or not Sharkey should have taken the fight. Some felt that the young fighter was being unfairly over matched, especially coming off of a loss. Renault, like Weinert was a top fighter and ranked number four in the world. However, for Sharkey the fight was seen as chance to get into the elite of the heavyweight division, an exclusive club that Renault was part of. Even though Sharkey was taking on yet another fighter with a lot more experience he was confident, saying, "I have had only about 16 months experience in the ring, but I feel without boasting that I am just as fast, just as clever, and punch just as hard as Renault."[23]

On April 3, 1925 Sharkey and Renault squared off at the Boston Arena. Right from the start the fight was a fast paced, action filled battle. Both boxers, realizing that a victory would elevate their career, went at it as soon as the bell rang. Jack was cunning in round one and put his jab to good use, which was much faster than his opponents. Renault centered his attack on the ex-sailor's head but found that Sharkey was an elusive, bobbing and weaving target and was good at blocking punches. The two exchanged blows several times during some hard infighting; it was during these close exchanges that Renault excelled and edged out the round.

Jack boxed well in round two and more than held his own against his much more experienced opponent. By virtue of his faster footwork and jab Sharkey won the round.

Round three started with the two fighters working furiously on the inside. During the violent infighting things turned rough and both boxers were guilty of throwing low blows and elbows. The referee quickly stepped in and issued a warning to stop the rough-house tactics. A moment later

---

22 Gossip of the Boxers, *Boston Globe*, February 21,1925, pg.A6.
23 "If Sharkey Beats Renault, it Will be a Long Step Toward Chance at Title," *Boston Globe*, April 3, 1925, pg.A23.

they were again battling at close range. Each scored well with thudding body shots and ripping uppercuts, but it was Renault who edged out the round.

Jack came out boxing on his toes in round four and had Renault missing badly. The Canadian managed to get inside a few times and land some smashing body shots but Jack stayed mostly on the outside. Putting on a fine display of boxing skill and working behind an effective jab Sharkey took the round by a large margin.

Renault took rounds five and six by forcing the action and out fighting Jack in-close with hard clubbing shots and head-snapping uppercuts.

The seventh saw Sharkey come alive. After taking several foul blows to the back of his head and neck he was visibly upset. Enraged, Sharkey sprang into battle with a flurry of punches to Renault's body. He then whipped over a fast right that crashed into Renault's jaw and sent him staggering into the ropes. Renault fought back but Jack came in bobbing and weaving under his opponent's punches. He landed a precisely placed right to the jaw that buckled the Canadian's knees and had him woozy just as the bell put an end to a round that belonged to Sharkey.

Having recovered after the minute rest, Renault attacked Jack's body to start round eight and was having some success until Sharkey landed some heavy lefts and rights that forced Renault up against the ropes. From then on Sharkey took the play away from his opponent and thoroughly out boxed the Canadian for the remainder of the round.

Showing that he was as tough as he claimed to be, Renault battled back in the ninth. By using an unrelenting body attack, that had Sharkey wincing whenever a blow landed, Renault took the round.

Coming out for the final round, Jack started by working behind his jab. Renault shot rights to Sharkey's head and body only to be met with power lefts. The two fighters spent most of the round fighting in-close and trading short rib shaking body blows. The round ended with both men swinging away at close quarters and Jack having a slight edge.

A loud cheer went up when it was announced that Sharkey had won the decision. It had been another extremely close fight, but Sharkey's harder blows, all around work and ring generalship gave the young fighter an advantage and earned him a hard fought victory.

The win over the highly ranked and respected Renault put the relatively inexperienced Sharkey into *Ring magazine*'s top ten rankings and sent his stock skyrocketing. With just over a year and a half experience and only 15 fights Jack sat alongside the elite big men of the heavyweight division, which included Harry Wills, Gene Tunney, Jimmy Maloney and Tommy

Gibbons.[24] For Renault, the loss was a devastating blow to his career and one that he would never fully recover from. Even though he was a talented fighter and ranked as high as number three in the world, he would never receive a shot at the heavyweight title.

Just a few days after his big win the fight fans of Boston were clamoring about a Sharkey-Maloney rematch. Alex McLean, one of the city's local matchmakers was trying to put together a huge charity/carnival boxing event at Braves Field for early June and wanted Sharkey and Maloney to headline the show. There were even rumors that Jack and his manager Johnny Buckley had met with Maloney's manager, John McGrath, and had signed papers for a June 5 rematch. Each fighter was supposedly guaranteed to make $7,500.

In response to the rumors McLean came out with a statement on April 30, claiming that the fight had not been signed. "Not that I have not been trying to get the big fellows," said Alex. "But up to date I have not been able to have the managers of the two heavyweights agree. I still hope to, for a Maloney-Sharkey bout would be the greatest attraction in New England."[25]

With the Maloney fight still in negotiations, team Sharkey went ahead and agreed to meet Australian fighter George Cook on May 25, at the Mechanics Building. This fight was to take place just eleven days before Sharkey was supposed to take on Jimmy Maloney. It was a risky move. Either Jack was confident of an easy win, or as many felt, this was a bad bit of managing by Buckley. If Sharkey lost he would be out of the fight with Jimmy, a match he really wanted, and Cook would replace him.

A few days later on May 6, 1925 the rumors turned out to be true. It was reported in the papers that rivals Jack Sharkey and Jimmy Maloney had formally affixed their signatures to contracts and agreed to box 10-rounds for the Endowment Fund of the American Legion at Braves Field on June 5, 1925. Since Maloney was recognized as the New England heavyweight champion the fight would be for Jimmy's title and belt. All profits from the boxing show, billed as "The Big Noise," would go to help widows and orphans of World War One veterans. But first Sharkey had to get by George Cook.

George Cook, who was born in Cobraha, Australia was all of 27-years-old and had been fighting as a professional since 1916. Despite standing only 5'9" he weighed a rock-hard 190-pounds. Because of his height and short arms Cook preferred fighting in-close as opposed to long range boxing. Throughout his career George had barnstormed all over Australia,

---

24 "Boston Heavyweight Aspirant Adds to Prestige by Scoring Clean-Cut Decision Over Canadian," *Boston Globe*, April 7, 1925, pg.13.
25 "Not Signed Yet, But Trying Says McLean," *Boston Globe* April 30, 1925, pg.12.

Europe and the United States and was a fearless fighter that would take on anyone. Because of his willingness to face any and all opponents, Cook had compiled a less than glamorous record of 16-17-4. Despite his terrible record Cook was viewed as a good fighter.

Throughout the fight's build up it was apparent that Jack didn't think much of Cook's abilities and held him cheaply. A 10 to 3 betting favorite, Sharkey came into the fight extremely confident. He began the first round aggressively by driving a hard left to Cook's body. George responded with his own body shot, as Jack missed a right to the jaw followed by a hard uppercut that landed. A second later the two clinched. Sharkey then missed a left aimed at Cook's jaw. George jabbed with his left and crossed a right to Jack's chin and worked in rights and lefts to Sharkey's mid-section. In close Jack let loose a left to the body that Cook blocked but connected with a right to the jaw. Cook then surged forward and forced Sharkey into the ropes with a hard jab and a number of body blows. With his back to the ropes Jack shot a hard right to Cook's heart but took a left jab to the mouth and nose and a left hook to the body as the round ended.

Jack came out with a swagger to start round two. It was obvious that Sharkey was cock-sure and felt he could end the fight whenever he chose. From the start of the round Jack boxed well on the outside and opened a deep cut over Cook's left eye with a counter right cross. The blood, which flowed freely down Cook's face, seemed to worry the Australian fighter. Bloodied but unyielding, George was able to block some of Jack's punches and force him into the ropes where he landed hard blows to the ex-sailor's body. Fighting his way off the ropes Jack kept his smaller opponent at bay with his jab and superior long-range boxing ability until the bell signaled the end of the round.

The third round, the slowest of the fight, was characterized by both fighters blocking and looking for openings. Sharkey kept looking to get over a right hand aimed at George's bleeding eye, but Cook was able to block most of Jack's attempts. Sharkey eventually landed a hard left to Cook's body and the two went into a clinch. A second later Jack wrestled Cook to the canvas. Once up both fighters were warned by referee Joe O'Conner to knock off the rough-house tactics.

Cook opened the fourth by missing a left and taking a hard right to the side of his head. After blocking a left from Sharkey he planted a solid left to Jack's belly. Sharkey swung a right for the jaw but Cook deftly blocked the blow. Sharkey then landed an uppercut as the two came to grips and exchanged on the inside. Pushed apart by the referee, Cook rushed in and landed a straight left but took a right uppercut to his chest as the two tied up. The crowd, displeased with the holding and wrestling booed and stamped their feet. Coming out of the clinch George connected with a left hook to the side of Sharkey's face followed by a swift left to the body and a right to the head. Jack gave back an uppercut as the two again fell into a clinch and the bell ended the round.

The fifth round was the most spirited of the fight and Jack could be credited with a slight advantage. He repelled a quick attack at the beginning and landed his favorite right uppercut to Cook's chin. George landed his own right to Jack's ribs and sent in two lefts to Sharkey's belly as the two clinched. While in close Jack slammed a left to Cook's face followed by a right to the nose. Two quick jabs, a right cross and a left hook completed Sharkey's attack. Cook retaliated with three swift lefts to the body. As the two fighters continued to hold and wrestle they wailed away throwing wild lefts and rights with little regard as to where the blows landed. Battling furiously, Jack slowly forced Cook to give ground only to have his opponent come back with a stiff jab to the face just as the bell rang.

George forged ahead and held an advantage in rounds six and seven. He boxed well using his jab to great effect, despite being at a physical disadvantage, and landed frequent right crosses. During some vicious infighting Cook bombarded Sharkey's ribs and came out on top of several brisk exchanges. Jack connected with a few of his uppercuts but was mostly busy trying to protect himself to do much execution.

By round eight Sharkey's cockiness was gone and he knew he was in a desperate fight. The Australian seemed to have figured out Jack's feints and was easily blocking his left hooks. Sharkey did manage to catch Cook a few times with well-placed jabs. But George came back with a vengeance and drove Sharkey into the ropes with a terrific right to the stomach. Sharkey fought back with a lead right that missed as George pounded away with lefts and rights to Jack's ribs. Again Jack tried to fight back throwing hard lefts and rights at his opponent's head but was once more out worked by George who continued to pound away at his midsection.

The ninth saw Jack regain some ground. The ex-sailor was on his toes and moving swiftly. He scored well with fast jabs to the nose and mouth and digging left hooks to Cook's ribs. George tried to get in close and continue his body attack but Jack was just too fast when he elected to box at long range.

Sure of a victory Cook opened the tenth with a big left to Jack's body but took a right to his face in return. George then landed three successive rights to Jack's stomach before the two clinched. During the clinch both fighters were guilty of landing blows to the back of the head and were warned by the referee. Coming out of the clinch Sharkey threw a one-two that George blocked followed by a right that George ducked. George came back with a one-two to the head followed by a left, right to the body. He quickly continued with a jab and right cross that caught Sharkey flush on the chin. Sharkey, willing to stand and mix it up, planted a right uppercut to the body as George tore in with two lefts to Jack's stomach. Jack missed with a straight right hand lead as both swung away wildly with George landing a hard jab on the point of Jack's nose just as the bell rang signaling that the fight was over.

When the decision blared out over the loudspeaker that Jack had won the fight, George along with his manager Charley Lucas and everyone in attendance was shocked. Sharkey, who had only moments before displayed a dejected attitude as he awaited the decision, was visibly flabbergasted as he realized he had won. The announcement of the decision was followed by a loud, hostile uproar from the fans that was said to "have never been paralleled in Boston." For a full ten minutes the crowed voiced their disapproval over the result and threw trash into the ring. Showing himself a good sportsman George went over and shook Sharkey's hand. The Australian was man enough to realize that the bad decision was not Jack's fault. He then went over to his crestfallen wife and gave her a kiss and murmured words of encouragement to her as team Sharkey quietly headed towards their dressing room.

The following morning the *Boston Globe* read, "Sharkey Gets Award Although Outfought."[26] So awful was the decision that talks of a full investigation were ongoing for days. However, despite the uproar the Sharkey-Maloney fight was still a go. And everyone quickly forgot about the controversy as the much-anticipated rematch between two of Boston's fiercest rivals approached.

---

26 "Crowd Receives Big Shock When Decision Goes to Sharkey in Battle With Australian heavyweight," *Boston Daily Globe*, May 26, 1925, pg.12.

CHAPTER 5
SHARKEY-MALONEY II

Following his battle with Cook, Jack spent two days resting at his wife's parents' home in Epping, New Hampshire. On the third day he started training at Toland's gym to get ready for his big fight with Jimmy Maloney. For this fight Sharkey once again called on the wise knowledge of "Battling" Jim. McCreary brought in ultra fast light heavyweight Archie Skinner as a sparring partner to help sharpen Jack's reflexes and footwork. Together the two boxed several rounds daily and apparently the sessions paid off. It was reported just a day before the fight that Jack looked to be in tremendous shape, without an ounce of superfluous weight showing anywhere on his body. When asked about his thoughts on his upcoming fight with Jimmy, Sharkey said, "I am going to show New England the best Sharkey they ever saw at the Braves ball grounds that night. I know what I can do and what I can't do, and I know that I can whip Jimmy Maloney. I've been waiting for this chance for almost a year. I know that he is a good fighter and a hard hitter, but while I don't want to appear egotistical, I think I can hit just as hard and can box a great deal better. I'll do my talking in the ring, however."[27]

Just a few days before the fight Jimmy was visited by a delegation of newspaper men who came to watch him go through his paces in preparation for Sharkey. When asked about Jack, Jimmy said that he was at the Sharkey-Cook fight and came away convinced that he could beat Jack once again. "It was just like college football games," said a grinning Maloney. "He knew I was 'scouting' him and he was supposed to remain 'under wraps,' if he had anything in wraps, I'll rip the wraps off a week from Friday night."[28]

Although Maloney was exuding an air of confidence and was being a bit boastful, he was not underestimating Sharkey. "Dynamite" Jim knew that Jack was one of the most talented fighters in the heavyweight division and respected his rival's abilities. This was evident by the seriousness he showed in his preparation for the match, as he skipped rope, punched the heavy bag and sparred several fast rounds with Joe "Hambone" Kelly all under that watchful eye of his trainer, Harry Kelly. Jimmy also knew that a win here would be huge, and would place him in a position for a match with Harry Wills and then a possible shot at champion Jack Dempsey.

---

27 "Jack Sharkey Back at Training," *The Boston Globe*, May 29, 1925, pg.10.
28 "Jim Maloney Allows He Will Rip the 'Wraps' Off Sharkey," *The Boston Daily Globe*, May 25, 1925, pg.20.

On June 5, 1925 fight fans all over Boston were excited. Thousands of people flooded the American Legion hoping to get a ticket before the event sold out. At 12:00 noon a fleet of World War One biplanes flew low over Boston Common and dropped down written orders for tickets to the event. The lucky finder could turn the order in at the headquarters of the Crosscup-Pishon American Legion post at 250 Washington Street, and get into the event for free.

At 6 o'clock the gates to Braves field were opened to the public. There was a lot to see and do. At 6:30 there was a concert in the boxing ring by the "7-11" company which included singing and dancing. At 7:00 there was a brief military procession including the ceremony of "Retreat" by detachments of soldiers, sailors and Marines, followed by an aerial display and staged dogfight that amazed the crowd of over 30,000 that had crammed into the stands.

At about 7:30 the boxing portion of the event kicked off with the national salute which was fired from a battery of French 75 millimeter guns and the lowering of the colors. This was followed by a moment of silence to pay respect to the brave men who died in World War One while "Taps" was played.

The first bouts of the evening began promptly at 7:45 and started with George Manolina out pointing Chick Canavan in six fast rounds. Next up, Boyo McCormick stopped Jack Lyons in the third round when he split Lyons' lip and the fight had to be stopped. Al Mello, a member of the U.S. Olympic Boxing Team, stopped "Scoops" White in the sixth round after giving him a terrible beating to his body. And in the semi-final bout George "Kid" Lee earned a technical knockout over George Eagle when Eagle's left eye swelled shut and his corner called it quits.

With the pre fights out of the way it was now time for the featured bout of the evening. At 10:00 on a warm clear night, Team Sharkey made their way into the brilliantly illuminated ring. As they did so they were welcomed in with loud whistles and cheers. A few moments later Team Maloney followed. The popular South Boston fighter was likewise received warmly by thousands of screaming fans.

Called to the center of the ring the two fighters were given their prefight instructions by referee Johnny Brassil. Once done, both teams returned to their respective corners and disrobed. Jack, weighing 183-pounds looked fit and ready to go. Maloney at 194-pounds looked as hard as steel. A few seconds later the bell resounded loudly above the roar of the fans and the battle was underway.

Eager to even the score, Jack rushed from his corner, feinted and threw a big left hook that Jimmy deftly blocked with his glove. The two held briefly but were quickly separated by the referee. Maloney threw a left jab that Sharkey avoided with quick head movement and then slammed a hard left hook into Sharkey's jaw. The two then exchanged jabs with Sharkey connecting to Jimmy's mouth and missing a left hook that Maloney ducked. Jimmy swung his own left hook that found its mark on the side of Jack's face followed by a jaw rattling uppercut that landed squarely under Sharkey's chin.

Momentarily shaken up by Jimmy's powerful blows Sharkey grabbed hold of his opponent. Coming out of the clinch Jack shot out a fast left to the head and a right to the body followed by a hard right to Jimmy's ear that drove the South Boston fighter into the ropes. Pressing the attack, Sharkey jabbed and then drove in another hard right and stiff jab to Maloney's head as he skillfully blocked a counter left hook from his opponent. Maloney in turn blocked a hook to the body and landed an uppercut to Jack's throat. Sharkey countered with a jab and right cross to Jimmy's jaw as the two embattled rivals continued to swing away for a few seconds after the bell sounded. It was a good opening round for both fighters and left the crowd screaming for more.

Maloney began round two by jabbing and driving a straight right to Jack's ribs. Sharkey shot back a jab to Jimmy's face but Maloney retaliated and turned Jack around with a clubbing right to the side of his head. The two then fought in close through a series of rapid exchanges, with Maloney getting the better of it. Backing off, Jack rushed back in and missed an uppercut as Maloney landed an uppercut of his own. Jack then pushed forward and forced Jimmy into a corner with a left hook. Maloney however, slugged his way out with a right to the stomach and a left, right combination to Jack's head. Sharkey, angered by the punches countered with a left that landed hard on Jimmy's face. The two then circled each other trading jabs and looking for an opening. Seeing his chance Jimmy shot in a left to the body that was low. A split second later he drove a straight right and left hook to Jack's belly. Sharkey came back with a left hook to Maloney's jaw followed by a fast right that landed cleanly on Jimmy's face just as the bell rang.

The third clearly belonged to Jimmy. He jabbed well and cleverly bobbed and weaved out of range of most of Jack's jabs and hooks. Jimmy was also effective at maneuvering Sharkey into the ropes several times and unloading some bruising shots to Jack's stomach.

Realizing he had lost round three, Jack changed his strategy in the fourth. Instead of slugging with Jimmy, Sharkey decided to box. Moving quickly on his toes and using his jab to great effect Jack soon found a rhythm and began to take over with his superior boxing abilities. During the first half of the round Sharkey repeatedly landed stinging jabs and right crosses. Jimmy, finding his bobbing and weaving opponent an elusive target, missed with most of his punches. Midway through the session Jimmy landed a hard right to Sharkey's neck but was repaid in kind with a short counter left hook to the side or his face. Jack then backed Jimmy into the ropes with a flurry of hard body shots. As Jimmy crouched to avoid taking punishment Jack hit him with two rabbit punches in the back of the neck. The two then exchanged combinations of furious punches in close. Jack came out on top of these exchanges and finished the round strong by boxing circles around Jimmy and landing head snapping jabs as the bell rang.

Throughout rounds five and six Jack showed his impressive boxing abilities. With the skill of an artist Sharkey landed accurate jabs and left hooks to Maloney's face while displaying great skill in blocking and ducking Jimmy's sweeping hooks. During the rounds Jack gave Maloney a terrible beating and at times made him look like a novice. By the end of the sixth Jimmy was groggy as he headed to his corner and the crowd, loving the action, was roaring for more.

Showing that he was in tremendous condition, Jimmy recovered quickly from the pounding he had taken in the last two rounds. He fared better in the seventh and held his own by staying in close and concentrated his attack on Jack's body. Jack, perhaps taking a breather decided to forgo the boxing and elected to fight Jimmy's fight. And then came the eighth.

Maloney, knowing that he was behind came out for the eighth looking to keep his seventh round momentum going. He opened the round aggressively with a huge left hook that caught Jack high on the head followed by a right that had bad intention written all over it. The punch would have ended matters right there if Sharkey hadn't skillfully dodged the blow. The two then clinched and wrestled in a corner. Separated by the referee Jack jabbed and landed a clubbing right to Jimmy's head. Visibly angered, Maloney tore after his opponent like a mad bull and threw a left hook aimed at Jack's stomach that landed a little low. Down went Sharkey, plummeting to the canvas, and up came the crowd cheering and screaming. Jack rolled onto his stomach with a look of agony on his face as he yelled out foul to the referee. Shaking his head no in response to Shakey's cries, Brassil began the count. When he reached nine Jack was back on his feet in a bent over posture and was plainly in pain. Maloney charged in with the ferocity of a tiger but Jack covered up and then fought back stubbornly trying to hold off his maddened foe. A left hook to the pit of the stomach followed by a right to the jaw sent Jack sprawling back to the canvas. The crowd's noise level rose to a deafening roar as once again Brassil began his count. When he reached nine Jack rose and braced himself for another impending attack. He was scarcely up when Maloney drove in a hard shot to the pit of the stomach that put Sharkey down for the third time. Showing his grit, Jack pulled himself up and again Maloney landed a hard shot to the ribs, putting the ex-sailor back on the canvas; again Jack forced himself up at the count of nine.

Maloney, now completely consumed with the fighting madness could almost taste the knockout. As he steadied himself to deliver one final crushing blow and the fans of Boston yelled until they were hoarse, Sharkey suddenly burst to life. He rushed in swinging wildly and threw Maloney off balance. In doing so, Jack went into the ropes and sprawled over the middle strand for a moment and went down to the canvas for the fifth time, without being hit. Not seeing that Sharkey had went down without taking a blow, Brassil started the count. Exhausted and virtually out on his feet Jack took full advantage of the count to try and clear his head. Not until Brassil's count reached nine did Jack rise up. A few seconds later the bell rang saving Jack from another barrage of leather.

Adrenaline charged, Jimmy burst out for round nine looking to put an end to the fight. He caught Jack with two vicious left hooks to the head, the second one dropping Jack for a count of four. Rising unsteadily Jack braced himself as Maloney slammed a hard right to his jaw that again sent him back to the canvas, this time for a count of three. Tottering to his feet, Jack looked as though he was just about beaten. However, after a quick check by the referee the fight was back on. Maloney surged in carrying Jack to the ropes and blasted him with a barrage of ripping rights and lefts to the head. Jack bobbed and weaved while attempting to avoid the avalanche of leather coming his way. Suddenly Jimmy changed his attack to Sharkey's body. As the two engaged in ferocious infighting Maloney was letting his punches fly. In doing so, several of his blows landed directly on Jack's groin and sent him to the canvas clutching himself in visible agony.

Seeing that the punches landed low referee Brassil jumped in and pulled Jimmy away, sending him to a neutral corner. Some expected Brassil to start his count as an intense silence fell over the place. But instead, Brassil reached down and lifted Jack's right arm in the air denoting that he had awarded Jack the fight on a foul. It was the right call to make even though the blows were without question unintentional. Brassil displayed good judgment and courage in disqualifying Maloney, a popular idol with a large following in Boston. However, his decision turned out to be a dangerous one.

In an instant the ring exploded into chaos. Maloney started to yell his protest to Brassil as Sharkey's seconds and Manager leaped into the ring to help their injured fighter. At that point Maloney's corner also made an appearance in the ring with one of his corner men rushing Brassil and taking a swing at him. Jimmy, still yelling at the referee, came to his senses and grabbed his enraged corner man and tried to calm him down. In another instant there were police and boxing officials everywhere. Everyone was yelling and screaming trying to restore order. Finally, after a few tense moments a small riot was avoided and everyone was calmed down and the ring was cleared. The controversial ending, however, was not without its ramifications. Both fighters and their respective handlers were upset. Maloney and his team were arguing that the stoppage was unfair. Sharkey and his group were mad that Maloney would not concede defeat and hand over the New England championship belt. After some heated arguments everyone agreed to a meeting. At that time it would be decided if the stoppage of the fight on a foul was going to be up held or if a different ruling would be handed down.

In all it was an unsatisfactory ending to a great boxing show and an exciting fight that saw Jack boxing well. In spite of the controversial ending the event was a huge success bringing in more than $60,000 and over 30,000 spectators. At the time it was the largest and most successful boxing event in New England history. If there was one positive to take away from the fight it was a guarantee that these two embittered rivals would soon meet again.

CHAPTER 6
EMILIO "KING" SOLOMON

Two days after his fight with Maloney, the Massachusetts State Boxing Commission held a meeting to discuss Brassil's decision to award the fight to Sharkey on a foul. Both fighters and their managers were present at the meeting. Also in attendance was master of ceremonies Major Paul H. Hines, attorney for the charity boxing event, Joseph Hurley, Referee Johnny Brassil and chairman for the American Legion, George Wiswell. After a lengthy debate which heard arguments from everyone involved, the commission decided to uphold Brassil's initial decision. The verdict didn't go over too well with Maloney and his manager; in fact, it only added more fuel to the Maloney-Sharkey rivalry. To add insult to injury Maloney was also forced to relinquish his New England title belt. Afterwards, both sides declined to be interviewed; team Maloney stormed out of the meeting. George Wiswell announced afterwards that Jack would be presented with Maloney's $1,000 gold mesh championship belt at a ceremony to be held later in the week.[29]

On the evening of June 12, 1925 Sharkey and his team arrived at the Olympia Theatre in Boston for the official belt presentation. In an introductory speech, Major Paul Hines thanked everyone for the success of the charity boxing event which brought in a profit of over $25,000 for the Endowment Fund. At 7:30 sharp, Hines called Jack and Buckley up to the stage and presented Sharkey with the New England heavyweight championship belt. Sharkey in response declared that he was very happy to receive the belt as a token of his victory. Buckley stated that the belt would never be at stake when Jack boxed since it was a gift, with no stipulations attached.[30] After the official ceremonies everyone sat back and enjoyed dinner, musical entertainment and a showing of the fight.

A few days after the belt ceremony Johnny Buckley wrote a letter to the New York State Athletic Commission suggesting a tournament between Harry Wills, Jack Sharkey, Gene Tunney and Charley Weinert to determine an opponent for champion Jack Dempsey. It read, "In view of recent ring happenings I believe the NYSAC should stage a heavyweight tournament before naming the chief contender for a bout with Dempsey. Harry Wills was recently recognized as the leading challenger, but I believe that Gene

---

29 "Question Right of Brassil in Award to Sharkey on a Foul," *The Boston Daily Globe*, June 8, 1925, pg.9.
30 "Sharkey Presented Championship Belt," *Boston Daily Globe*, June 13, 1925, pg.10.

Tunney's recent knockout of Tommy Gibbons and Jack Sharkey's defeat of Jim Maloney creates a new situation.

"Sharkey has eliminated Jack Renault, Jim Maloney and Sully Montgomery from Tex Rickard's list of ten leading heavyweights, while Tunney disposed of Gibbons and Stribling put Rojas off the list. This leaves Dempsey, Tunney, Wills, Weinert and Sharkey. Either Wills or Weinert will be eliminated on July 2, when they meet at the Polo Grounds. I would suggest that Tunney be asked to meet Sharkey and that the winner of this tussle be pitted against the victor of the Willis-Weinert contest. The survivor of such a series would be recognized by the American sporting public as the logical contender for a bout with Dempsey. If plans for this tournament are formulated at once it will be possible to stage a battle for the heavyweight championship of the world by the middle of September."

"You will find Sharkey willing to fight any of the leading contenders. He will box once every two weeks if necessary. During the last six months he has engaged in seven battles, meeting Charley Weinert twice and clashing once with Jack Renault, Jim Maloney, Jack DeMave, George Cook and Sully Montgomery. Sharkey has fought more often in six months than Dempsey has in his six years as world's heavyweight champion. Sharkey, like the immortal John L. Sullivan, believes that the proper place for a heavyweight to do his fighting is in the ring against the best available opponent. May I not hear from you on this matter?"[31]

Just a couple of days after writing his letter there was talk that a fight between Sharkey and Gene Tunney was in the negotiation stages. This was the fight that Sharkey really wanted and he and his team pushed hard for it. However, since Gene was already signed to fight "Italian Jack Herman" the fight never made it past the talking stage. Sharkey maintained throughout his life that Gene had ducked him and that he could have beaten Tunney. 60-years later in an interview Sharkey said that Gene "couldn't crack an egg" and "couldn't have hit me in the ass with a handful of tacks." He then added, "If there was ever a guy who needed a beating it was Gene Tunney."[32]

Unable to secure a fight with Tunney, team Sharkey was forced to look elsewhere. They quickly found a willing opponent. In late June, news surfaced that Sharkey would be returning to the ring to take on Emilio "King" Solomon on July 31, 1925. Solomon, a fighter from Panama was in the U.S trying to make a name for himself. Since his arrival in May of 1925 Emilio had won four fights in a row, including a big win over Sharkey

---

31 "Suggest Tourney to Name Opponent For Dempsey," *Boston Daily Globe,* June19, 1925, pg.A18.
32 "The Story of Jack Sharkey, Boxing's Tragic Figure," by Jim Brady, *Boxing Illustrated,* pg.82.

conqueror Quintin Rojas. The popular young Panamanian was looked on as a rising young contender and had shown that he was a talented boxer. After four wins Emilio felt confident enough to take on Jimmy Maloney. The match took place on July 13, 1925 just eighteen days before his fight with Sharkey. The fight marked the return of Maloney since his disqualification loss to Sharkey. Despite a supreme effort that showed Solomon display speed and clever boxing ability, Jimmy came away with a hard fought 10-round decision. The loss, however, did nothing to tarnish Emilio's reputation as an up and comer. In fact, his effort against Maloney endeared him to the boxing fans of Boston.

Jack was taking his title of New England Heavyweight Champion very seriously. According to Buckley, Jack had never trained so conscientiously before. He even went as far as to rent an apartment for a short time on Nantasket Beach. He felt that living near the ocean and away from Boston would help him relax and offer fewer distractions.

Once settled in, Sharkey began to train with zeal. To achieve peak conditioning Jack was up at the crack of dawn running between five and eight miles along picturesque Jerusalem Road. During his runs the winding road offered a spectacular view of the early morning ocean and breathtaking sunrises.

After his roadwork Jack either motored over or took the boat to Boston where he put in a strenuous workout at Toland's Gymnasium. When interviewed after one of his workouts, Sharkey said that he had watched Solomon-Maloney and felt sure he could beat Emilio. "If this fellow Solomon thinks he's going to box circles around me, he's just plaine daffy. He'll find that I can step around some myself. And as for him keeping his left glove in my face, well nobody has been able to do that yet."[33]

Solomon prepared for battle at Marty Fitzpatrick's gym in Boston. Having been ringside at the Sharkey-Maloney fight, Solomon and his manager George Lawson were of the opinion that Jack could not take it to the body. Therefore their strategy was simple; Emilio would concentrate his attack on Jack's rib cage. This strategy led Emilio's manger to state the following when interviewed just days before the fight. "A chain," said Lawson, "is only as strong as its weakest link. No matter what he or his manager claim, Sharkey cannot take punishment to the body. Regardless of the merits of the alleged foul that gave him the New England heavyweight title in his last battle with Maloney, he displayed a striking weakness when hit in the stomach. But I knew long before that contest that he doesn't like it about the body; in fact, that anybody who directs his fire at the ex-sailor's mid-riff is almost sure to slow him up. It must not be forgotten that I

---

[33] "Both Ready Now For Battle Tomorrow," *Boston Globe*, July 30, 1925, pg.11.

brought Quinton Rojas to Boston to fight Sharkey more than a year ago. Rojas was instructed to keep battering away at his body and what was the result? He knocked Sharkey out in the eighth round, although he tried to respond for the ninth. Now, I don't claim to be a wizard, but I claim that I was the first to discover Sharkey's weakness, and Rojas was the first to check Sharkey's winning streak. Jack Sharkey has other weak spots and I am sure Solomon will uncover them next Friday night. You can bet we wouldn't send Solomon against Sharkey unless we were pretty sure that he will whip the Boston man."[34]

Two days before the fight a fit looking Sharkey radiated confidence when he said to a group of visiting reporters, "Just say that I am about ready for Solomon and that he will find that his vaunted speed will not prevail against me Friday night. I never map out a campaign before any bout, but I guess I've doped out a way to beat this Solomon person, and I'll beat him by a far greater margin than Maloney did."

Dark clouds hung low over Braves Field and threatened to soak the 11,000 excited fans that had turned out to watch Sharkey and Solomon trade punches. They came expecting a thrilling fight between two crafty boxers; they were not disappointed.

The evening began with George "Kid" Lewis defeating Tony Julian in a ragged one sided fight. Sharkey's sparring partner Archie Skinner came next and knocked out Clemente Saavedra in the third round of an action packed, free swinging slug fest. As a light rain began to fall there were some talks of having the main event before the semi-windup. However, it was decided that Al Melio and Frankie Quill would go ahead and fight at their scheduled time. Luckily, the fight was a short one, ending in just four rounds.

At about 9:30 Jack and Solomon met at ring center and received their instruction from referee Johnny Brassil. Both fighters looked to be in terrific shape. Jack, having added a few pounds with the intent of increasing his punching power was a muscular 190. Emilio, lithe limbed and slightly taller than Sharkey, came in at 196 with a record of 14-3, with 4 knockouts.

From the opening bell the contest held the rapt attention of the crowd despite the sprinkling of rain which had started to fall. Sharkey came out on his toes bobbing and weaving with his hands held at about waist level. Just a few seconds in, the ex-gob whipped over a hard left hook to Solomon's temple. The crowd roared in glee as Emilio danced out of range. Jack immediately went after his opponent and threw another left hook that landed high on the Panamanian's head. He followed quickly with a right to the heart that had Solomon clinching. Pushing Jack away, Emilio suddenly came to life snapping a hard jab to Jack's chin while swiftly ducking a right.

---

[34] "Fast Battle Due Friday," *Boston Daily Globe*, July 29, 1925, pg.A16.

Solomon then countered with a hard right to Jack's face. Sharkey fired back with a right uppercut that lifted Solomon's head. Emilio returned the favor by landing two jabs but was hit in return by a right hand to the ribs. Solomon jabbed again but once more Jack planted a hard right to the stomach and landed a well-aimed left hook to the jaw. A second later the bell rang. It was a good round for Jack.

Solomon seemed to find his rhythm in round two. He began by jabbing and boxing in his own unique style. Sharkey tried a left hook but missed as Emilio moved out of range with the skill of a ballet dancer. The Panamanian then ducked and slipped a right and left from Jack but took a hard right to the stomach as the two tied up. Breaking from the clinch, Emilio landed three rapid fire jabs to Sharkey's face while Jack tried to use quick head movement to avoid the punches. Emilio then drove in a hard right to the body, and Jack countered with a short right to Emilio's ribs. Sharkey then missed with a looping right and took a hard left hook to the neck. He fired right back with a left to Solomon's jaw, but took two hard lefts to the body, a right to the neck and a straight left to the mouth. It was a solid round for Solomon.

Emilio kept up the good work in round three and had a decisive advantage. His left, right combinations were in perfect working order and kept Sharkey off balance and on the defensive. Jack tried to stop his whirlwind foe with a concentrated body attack but was only able to land a few rights to Emilio's breadbasket.

"The King" was again out in front in round four. His speedy attack, quick jabs and left hooks gave Sharkey fits and seemed to have the ex-sailor perplexed. Jack came on more aggressively in round five but was again out boxed by Solomon and had a hard time landing an effective punch.

Aware that he was waging a losing battle, Jack stepped it up in round six. He made up some ground when he started to catch Solomon with rights to the body and solid right hooks to his opponent's face. Sharkey continued to be effective in round seven with a sustained body attack that was noticeably slowing the Panamanian fighter down. The eighth saw Solomon make a stand as he out fought Jack by landing quick jabs and left hooks to the body.

Knowing that the fight was close, Jack took command and set the pace in round nine. He repeatedly landed hard right hooks to the body and teeth rattling uppercuts to Emilio's chin. Despite all of the talk from Solomon and his manager about concentrating on a body attack, it was Jack who was the more effective body puncher. Solomon boxed valiantly but could not stop Sharkey's rib shaking attack.

The crowd was on its feet cheering during the last three minutes of the fight. Solomon opened the round by landing two quick jabs that aroused Jack's ire. Swiftly, Sharkey leaped in and landed a smashing shot to

Solomon's rib cage followed by a right cross to the jaw and a right to the heart. Solomon tried with a left but missed. Jack then landed a crushing right to the Panamanian's body that caused him to bend over and grimace in pain. So hard was the blow that the impact was said to be heard all over the field. Sharkey kept up his vicious attack by landing another left to the stomach and a right to the kidneys. The blows had Solomon hurt and holding on. Nevertheless, Emilio fought back gamely. He connected with a left to Jack's mouth but took another hard right to his body in return. Jack then landed a left to the stomach while Emilio hooked a left to Sharkey's head. The two then exchanged a series of fast punches as the bell rang, signaling the end of a close, exciting fight.

Moments later the fighters were brought to ring center and stood anxiously awaiting the decision. Both men knew it was a close fight and felt that they had done enough to win. Seconds later the decision blared out from the loudspeaker and Brassil raised Sharkey's hand in victory. His fans cheered loudly, while Solomon's fans raucously voiced their disapproval. Although it had been an extremely close fight it was Sharkey's rally in rounds nine and ten along with his fierce body punching throughout that had won him the battle. Moments later as Solomon followed Sharkey out of the ring both fighters were given a loud, standing ovation for their efforts.

CHAPTER 7
GORMAN AND RISKO

Jack's win over Solomon had him in high spirits. Just a few days after the fight he readily agreed to meet tough guy Bud Gorman, on August 17, 1925. Jack, who seemed to thrive on fighting hard opponents, was confident of a victory, perhaps too much so.

Bud first came into the public eye as a sparring partner for Tom Gibbons in 1923, when Tom was training for his fight with heavyweight champion Jack Dempsey. The 6', 200-pound Wisconsin native showed his talent and toughness day after day by hanging in there with Gibbons, a master boxer. The young fighter, hardly more than a boy at the time, displayed a lot of raw talent, toughness and heart, essential qualities for an aspiring young fighter.

During the two years since his time with Gibbons, Bud had kept a busy schedule and developed into a solid, well-schooled boxer. When he signed to fight Sharkey, Gorman had a professional record of 14-1 (not including newspaper fights) and had defeated some outstanding competition such as "Young" Bob Fitzsimons and Jack De Mave. In his last fight Bud had suffered his first "official defeat," a razor thin decision loss to one of the finest pugilists of all time, William Stribling. Because Bud put up such a good showing again Stribling the loss actually helped elevate his career and get him the fight with Sharkey.

By all accounts the Gorman fight should have been a victory for Jack. However, Jack's biggest flaw, his inconsistency, reared its ugly head. Jack, who could look like the best heavyweight in the world when he was on, could also look like nothing more than an average journeyman when he was having an off night. The ex-sailor came into the bout overconfident and undertrained. Although he looked fit at 184-pounds and was a 2 to 1 favorite, Sharkey didn't think much of his opponent's abilities and it showed in his performance.

Even though it wasn't one of Sharkey's best efforts the fight was still described as a fast paced battle fought at breakneck speeds and a sensational victory for Bud. Gorman displayed rare boxing ability from the onset and carried the fight to Sharkey throughout. As the bout moved along his judgment of distance and his ability to step out of range and dart in again improved perceptibly. Throughout the fight Bud was consistent with stinging jabs and accurate right hands. It was Bud's sharp boxing ability and determined, concentrated attack that was responsible for his victory. During the latter rounds Sharkey became desperate and fought with purpose, but it was to no avail. Bud was not to be denied a victory. Even though Jack was outpointed by a wide margin and credited with wining only two rounds, he put up a stubborn battle and never stopped trying. From what was written in the papers, Bud apparently fought a near perfect fight, while Sharkey appeared to be a trifle off his usual boxing form.

Sharkey's loss to Gorman took away little of the ex-sailor's prestige. Jack had been fighting for less than two years and an occasional loss was to be expected. After all, he was still developing and learning.

Anxious to get back in the ring, Sharkey had a match lined up in no time. Buckley announced that he had signed Jack to a September fight with hard punching Johnny Risko, "The Ohio Iron Man" It was reported that Risko said that he had come to Boston for the express purpose of making a name for himself by knocking out Sharkey.

At just 23-years-old and having fought professionally for only three years Johnny had already engaged in 75 fights winning 50 by knockout. However, like a lot of fighters during the 1920s the majority of these victories were newspaper decisions. Coming into the fight Risko had an "official" record of 14-1 and was know as a "spoiler," because he specialized in making young, upcoming prospects look bad.

Johnny arrived in Boston about a month before the fight and set up camp at Kelly's boxing gym. During an interview after a workout session he expressed a ton of confidence and predicted a victory over Jack saying, "I don't think I'll have any trouble with Sharkey. I understand Sharkey is a fast clever, boxer. My body punches will slow him down. I have been tipped about Sharkey's body weakness and it is my purpose to play for that weakness continually wearing him down to a walk and then over will go the finishing blow. Romero Rojas stopped Sharkey here in Boston. He was supposed to be at the height of his career then, but two weeks after he disposed of Sharkey I met him in Cleveland and had him on the floor a couple of times."[35]

Sharkey was reported to be taking his fight with Risko a lot more seriously than his last fight. Having been warned about Risko's punching power, Sharkey was taking no chances. It was said that he was putting in some serious workouts at Tolland's gym and looking very sharp. The ex-sailor declared that he would be in much better shape than in his last effort and blamed his defeat by Bud to overconfidence and a lack of discipline in his training. Sharkey promised that he would never be caught napping again and guaranteed a much better performance. Furthermore, he knew that if he could get by the hard punching Risko a big money third fight with

---

[35] "Risko Just the Type of Boxer to Bring Out the Best Sharkey Has to Offer," *Boston Daily Globe*, September 16, 1925, pg. A19.

Maloney was almost a sure thing. He was also aware that another loss could derail his career for good.

Exactly one month after his fight with Gorman, Sharkey and Risko met at the Mechanic's Building on September 17, 1925. For all his vaunted punching power and talk of taking the fight to Jack, "The Ohio Iron Man" did not live up to the hype. The fight turned out to be a relatively easy 10-round decision win for Jack. However, even in victory Jack's performance was a little disappointing. Although he won the fight by a wide margin, the fans were at times let down by his lack of aggression. There were periods when Jack seemed to loaf and let opportunities to land punches escape him.

In the opening round Jack appeared somewhat lazy. As a result, Risko was able to land body shots that a more animated fighter might have blocked or avoided. Then again there may have been a method to Jack's madness. After all the talk of his weakness for body punching, Jack may have taken a few just to prove to his opponent that he could take it.

Jack came alive in the second and brought into play his vaunted footwork and cleverness that he was known for. From the second through the fourth Jack was on his toes boxing. He jabbed well and crossed straight right hands and jolting left hooks that landed flush on his opponent's jaw.

Johnny held his own in the fifth as again Jack seemed to hold back and get a bit lazy. The Clevelander found Jack's body more than once with hard lefts and rights, but if Sharkey had a weakness to body shots as Risko had claimed he certainly did not show it. Risko's fifth round surge was short lived. Jack took the play away from Johnny in the sixth and continued to dominate through round seven and eight with his masterful footwork and boxing ability.

The last two rounds were close because of Risko's dogged aggression and Jack's lack thereof. Johnny tore after Sharkey, but found his fleet footed opponent a hard target to get to. Every time Johnny would bore in, Jack would either bounce out of the way or stop Johnny's onslaught with well timed one-two combinations. Nevertheless, Johnny kept up his relentless attack occasionally finding Sharkey's ribs. However, what body blows Risko was able to land were offset by Sharkey's cleaner, well-timed punches. In the end there was no question about the justness of the decision; the crowd though was a bit fickle. Some of the fans booed their disappointment about the fight because it was too tame, while Sharkey's fans cheered loudly for their man as his hand was raised in victory.

With his win over Johnny Risko, Sharkey would embark on a thirteen fight win streak that would include a much anticipated third fight with his nemesis, Jimmy Maloney and lead to an immensely controversial fight with Jack Dempsey.

CHAPTER 8
SHARKEY-MALONEY III

Jack's much anticipated third fight with his great rival Jimmy Maloney was set for November 30, 1925. Because of the bad blood between the two and the fact that the fight was for Jack's New England heavyweight championship, interest was high the moment promoter Tom Goodwin announced the match. Fight fans throughout New England were riveted on the approaching bout. The conflict between the two Boston fighters had developed into more than just a neighborhood rivalry; it was now a big-time show. And each boxer was eager to prove his superiority.

Because Jack was fighting to keep his title he trained meticulously. To help get him into shape Sharkey hired heavyweight Tom Kirby and former opponent George Cook for sparring partners. Together the three spent weeks grinding through rigorous sparring sessions that were said to be closer to real fights than sparring matches.

For this fight Jack wanted to increase his speed and footwork with the hopes of being able to out box, and out point Jimmy. By increasing his speed Jack was also hoping to be able to stay away from the free swinging, rushing Maloney. To accomplish this Jack worked with former bantamweight fighter Abe Friedman, a master boxer with over a 100 fights. Under the guidance of Abe, Jack improved his timing, feinting and all around speed. After several weeks Abe had sharpened Jack into superb physical condition.

On the other side of Boston, at Kelly and Hays's gym, Maloney was training with a vengeance. "Dynamite" Jim needed no incentive to get in shape. Feeling that his title and belt had been taken away unfairly, Jimmy had only one goal, defeating Jack Sharkey. Maloney's plan of attack was to be aggressive and bring the fight to his rival. Since Jimmy was more of a slugger than a boxer, his goal was to get in close and unleash a vicious body assault. To help assist with his plan Jimmy sparred three rounds a day with New York heavyweight Carl Carter. Knowing that Sharkey was extremely fast, middleweight Jimmy Amato White was called in as a second sparring partner. Together, Maloney and Jimmy sparred dozens of rounds with the intention of increasing Maloney's footwork and hand speed. By all accounts, after weeks of hardcore training, Jimmy got himself into great shape and was straining at the leash to get his gloves on Sharkey.

By Thanksgiving the two fighters were nearing the end of their training. So dedicated was each fighter to their strict training routine that both kept the feasting to a minimum, especially when it came to dessert.

On November 28, both men completed their final workouts. The official weigh in was scheduled for 12:00 noon on Monday, November 30, the day of the fight. However, when it came time for Jimmy to step on the scale, much to everyone's surprise, he was a no show. Word soon came that Jimmy was at home, sick with a cold and fever. The Massachusetts Boxing Commission immediately dispatched Dr. Mackey to Maloney's home. Dr. Mackey confirmed that Jimmy was indeed sick and in no condition to be fighting.

Upon learning that Jimmy was unable to fight, Tom Goodwin sent a telegram to the papers and radio stations throughout New England so that they could broadcast that the fight had been canceled. Despite getting the word out a large crowd of fans gathered around the doors to the Mechanics Building only to be turned away with the disappointing news that the fight was called off and rescheduled for next Saturday the 5th of December.

As soon as the fight was postponed the smack talk leapt into high gear. Supposedly harsh remarks were hurled from Sharkey's camp in the direction of Maloney's camp with the intention of ridiculing Jimmy's claim of sickness. Some reports said that Jack and his team were questioning whether or not Jimmy was really sick. Others reported that Sharkey thought that Jimmy was hiding behind the claims of a head cold because he was afraid to face him. And yet others said that Jimmy had deliberately run out of the fight. In his own defense, Jack, who was viewed as an honest sportsman, maintained that he never questioned Maloney's sickness and alleged that the press had contrived the stories. Having fought Jimmy twice, Jack knew that Maloney was no coward and had no reason to question Jimmy's integrity.

By December 2, Jimmy was back in the gym. He appeared to be in great shape and fully recovered. He was however, furious over the implications and insinuations that were made towards him concerning his illness. Maloney, a fighter through and through, had never had his courage questioned before. Even in defeat Jimmy had always been brave and given his best.

Although Jimmy appeared to be fully recovered and looked ready to go for the December 5 showdown he relapsed and began to feel ill again on the evening of December 2. On December 3, he was examined again by Dr. Mackey and Dr. Klein at his home. The two doctors found Jimmy in bed, drawn and pale with indications of bronchial troubles. The next morning a formal statement was written by Dr. Mackey and delivered to the Massachusetts Boxing Commission that read, "In view of the low pulse and subnormal temperature I deem it inadvisable for Maloney to resume training at present. Furthermore, I would suggest he be examined by a heart specialist before resuming boxing in any way"[36] Once again it was announced that the fight would have to be postponed.

As suggested, Jimmy was checked out by a specialist, Dr. Catis Phipps. His findings were nearly identical to the other two doctors. Jimmy had a slight case of bronchitis and a cold. However, there was nothing wrong with his heart. The doctor suggested that after a few days of rest Jimmy could resume training on Monday, December 7.

Following the doctor's examination a short meeting with promoter Tom Goodwin and the Massachusetts Boxing Commission was held. A new date of Friday, December 11 was agreed on followed by an official announcement on the local radio stations and the next day's papers.

By Monday Jimmy was back at Kelly and Hays and looked good as he sparred three fast rounds with Jimmy Amato and punched Carl Carter around the ring with power and drive. The session gratified his trainer.

Since television had not yet been invented the only way to follow a fight in 1925, was to watch it live or listen to it on a radio. Given that the fight was of such interest nearly everyone who couldn't get a ticket tuned their radios to WNAB at 9:30 to hear Charles Donelan give a blow-by-blow account of the contest.

10,000 fans crammed into the smoky Mechanics Building on the evening of December 11, to watch Jack take on the pride of South Boston. In light of Jimmy's recent illness, Jack came into the fight a slight favorite to retain his New England title even though Jimmy's trainer claimed that his fighter was fully recovered and eager to swap leather.

Sharkey, weighing a well-built 193-pounds entered the ring first and was greeted by a salvo of cheers from his fans, which gradually changed to raucous boos and cat calls from the Maloney supporters. Moments later Jimmy at a solid 194-pounds slipped through the ropes to a massive roar from his adoring fans.

For Jimmy and his fans it turned out to be a rough night. Obviously feeling the effects of having been sick and having his training routine disturbed, Jimmy was not the "Dynamite" Jim of yore. Sharkey, firing on all cylinders, was able to easily out point his ever weakening and erratic opponent over the course of the 10-round bout. In rounds two, four, seven, eight and ten Jack's margin of victory was seen as overwhelming. That Maloney escaped without being knocked out in the final frame was due to Jack getting over anxious trying to put his rival away. Jack caught Jimmy with a left hook midway through the tenth that wobbled Maloney and nearly sent him down. Quick as a flash, Jack, with his teeth set grimly, sprang forward and drove in a right uppercut cleanly to the point of

---

36 "Maloney Not Fit to Fight," *The Boston Daily Globe*, December 3, 1925, pg.24.

Jimmy's chin. Back and sideways tottered the pride of Boston but Jimmy stubbornly stayed on his feet and fought back gamely. Even when Jack landed another smashing right cross that had Jimmy's fans on their feet and screaming, Jimmy continued to fight back wildly and managed to hang on till the final bell.

Moments later Johnny Hallahan announced what everyone already knew; Sharkey had won the fight easily. A score of the fight showed that Jimmy had won two rounds, the first and fifth. A few of the newspapermen at ringside thought that Maloney may have won the third as well. Even though Jack had won nearly every round the fight it was still described as "one of the more spirited heavyweight contests witnessed in the city for a long time."[37] And even though Maloney looked bad he fought tenaciously and never stopped trying.

Upon hearing that Jack had won the huge crowd erupted into an uproar. Jack's fans cheered and Maloney's fans booed. The two sides began throwing trash at each other as well as verbal insults. For a moment it looked as though the large mob might turn violent. However, after a few tense moments things eventually cooled down and nobody was hurt.

Sharkey exited the ring happy and victorious. Jimmy left a fallen idol. With his left eye swollen shut and his right eye half closed the bruised and battered pride of South Boston made his way to his dressing room. Unable to look at his concerned father who sat ringside, Jimmy passed by with his head held low. Despite his poor showing, however, Maloney was far from through. Although he announced his retirement after the fight, Jim would quickly miss the smell of resins and the cheering of his fans. Six months later "Dynamite" Jim would make a comeback. He would rebound with an eight-fight win streak and he and Sharkey would meet for a fourth and final decisive showdown.

---

37 "Sharkey Easily Whips Maloney," *Boston Daily Globe*, December 12, 1925, pg.7.

CHAPTER 9
STAYING BUSY

Sharkey's dominating win over Maloney placed him firmly at the number three spot in *Ring magazine's* top ten rankings for 1926. After two years of boxing, the young pugilist had finally come into his own. At only 24 the ex-sailor had developed into a world class boxer and was just entering his prime. His style was fully developed and with 22 fights under his belt against a lot of top-notch competition, Jack had gained a wealth of hard-earned experience.

1926 would prove to be a good year for Jack and a year of note for boxing. To start things off Jack scored two easy wins, a second round knockout over Mexican Joe Lawson on January 18, and a 10-round decision over Eddie Huffman on February 12, which saw Jack boxing cleverly and handing Huffman a neat boxing lesson.

After his fight with Huffman, Jack returned home from New York. Buckley soon had a match lined up with Pat McCarthy on February 18. The fight would be for Jack's New England heavyweight championship. Preparations for the fight went smoothly, until Jack injured his thumb two days before fight night. An examination found that his thumb was discolored and severely swollen. The match was immediately cancelled. Furthermore, it would be two to three weeks before Jack would be able to get back into the ring.

Unable to fight, Sharkey took the next couple of weeks off to let his thumb heal. By late March word came out that he was well enough to continue and would be taking on Emilio "King" Solomon. Jack and Emilio had fought seven months prior with Sharkey taking a 10-round decision over the colorful Central American fighter.

The rematch turned out to be, by all accounts, easier for Jack than his first meeting with the "King." Knowing that Solomon was no mean foe, Jack took the fight seriously and fought with a purpose. The day after the fight the write up read, "The Sharkey of last night was a rip, tearing, vicious fighter, who kept continually after his man, varying his assault from a vicious attack to the body to swift left and right hooks to the jaw."[38]

The papers went on to further describe the beating that Solomon took as "the most crushing defeat that 'King Solomon' had experienced in his five Boston appearances."[39] That Solomon escaped without being knocked

---

[38] "Sharkey Decisively Out Points Solomon," *Boston Daily Globe*, by Lawrence J. Sweeney, April 2, 1926, pg.1.
[39] Ibid.

out was a testament to his courage and stamina. Two times Jack had "The King" out on his feet, once in the seventh and once in the ninth, but Solomon held tough and managed to finish the fight on his feet; although losing a lopsided 10-round decision.

Two weeks after his fight with Solomon, Jack was up early doing road work in preparation for his rescheduled fight with Pat McCarthy. As he neared his apartment building where he and his wife were living, Sharkey noticed dark smoke pouring out from the basement. Acting quickly, he sprang to action. Following the trail of smoke Sharkey found the basement enveloped in flames. A few seconds later, Jack ran into the building frantically pounding on doors and yelling "fire!" All told Sharkey woke six families including his wife and child. His discovery of the fire got everyone to safety and the fire department on scene quickly, saving the building from being destroyed. His bravery earned him the title "the hero of the Brighton blaze."

On April 19, 1926, Sharkey and Pat McCarthy finally met at the Boston Arena. When the fight was over there was no question as to who had won. Jack, boxing brilliantly, took every round from Pat who was said to have boxed timidly. The only thing that stopped Sharkey from scoring a knockout was Pat's continuous holding and wrestling tactics. In the third Jack found Pat's jaw with a straight left and whipped over a right cross that put Pat onto the canvas. Again in the sixth, after a rare spirited exchange from Pat, Sharkey dug in a vicious left to the body that forced McCarthy to the canvas where he complained to the referee that the blow was low. So one-sided was the bout that a large portion of the crowd started to leave by the sixth round.

Jack's next outing was scheduled for June 25, against previous opponent, Bud Gorman. Bud and Jack had met once before back in August of 1925, with Jack losing a 10-round decision. The ex-sailor was eager to avenge his loss and promised not to underestimate Bud like he had done in their first meeting. As an added bonus, ex-heavyweight champion James J. Jefferies and ex-contender Tom Sharkey (the man from whom Jack Sharkey adopted half of his ring name) were in town and would be acting as Seconds. Tom Sharkey would be working Jack's corner and Jefferies would be helping in Bud's corner. At one time Tom and James were the greatest of rivals and had fought two titanic battles. The first being a 20-rounder and the second a 25-rounder; Jefferies won both by decision. Now, the once great ring warriors were on tour together as part of a vaudeville show; putting on a boxing exhibition and comedy act.

Stepping into the ring Jack was said to be in a vicious mood and anxious to get at Gorman. As soon as the bell rang Jack, weighing in at 190 rushed out to meet Gorman who weighed 200. The two combatants met at ring center and proceeded to mix it up at a fast and furious pace. After approximately two minutes, Jack suddenly sank to the canvas, his face pasty white and a mask of agony from a solid blow that landed well below the belt line. Most of the 5,000 in attendance never saw the punch. However, referee Johnny Martin had clearly seen the foul and immediately awarded the fight to Sharkey.

Following his fight with Gorman, Jack went right back into training. He had an important bout lined up with top contender, George Godfrey, "The Black Shadow of Leiperville." At 6'4" and between 220 and 260 George was a big heavyweight for any era and represented one of the most dangerous opponents Jack ever tangled with.

Born Feab S. Williams in Mobile, Alabama on January 25, 1897 Feab later changed his name to George Godfrey after George "Old Chocolate" Godfrey, a black Canadian boxer from the bare knuckle era. George's first known fight was in 1919; however he probably had many more before that date that went unrecorded. During his career George battled a number of notable fighters and had some impressive wins over the likes of Jimmy Maloney and Paulino Uzcudun. George's greatest accomplishment may have been a 10-round draw with Sam Langford, "The Boston Tar Baby" and quite possibly the greatest fighter to have ever tied on a pair of gloves. However, a few fights later George was knocked out in the second round by Sam who was incidentally 8 inches shorter and some 50-pounds lighter. Sam repeated the trick again a few months later in quicker fashion when he knocked George out in the first round.

During his career that spanned from 1919 to 1937, George won the world "colored" heavyweight title twice as well as the International Boxing Union world heavyweight title. Coming into the Sharkey fight George was ranked number six according to *Ring magazine's* ranking and was being touted as one of the best heavyweights in the country. Furthermore, George was said to carry a punch that was on par with Jack Dempsey's.

Jack's fight with Godfrey was originally scheduled for September 3, 1926. But, just a few days before the match George wrenched his knee in training and the fight was canceled and rescheduled for September 23. Being in great shape and not wanting to waste his training, Buckley quickly found a replacement opponent for Jack; relatively unknown Orlando Reverberi.

Although the fight was put together on short notice it turned out to be an exciting battle. After being floored in the first round by a wild right hand swing that had Jack more surprised than hurt, Sharkey roared back and battered the Italian all about the ring. In the second round the wild brawl continued. At one point during a fierce exchange Jack crashed over a right to the jaw that sent Orlando to the canvas. Up at five Orlando gamely fought on and lasted out the round.

Out from his corner in a flash, Jack tore into his opponent to begin round three. A stiff jab followed by a right to the point of the chin drove Orlando to the canvas; but he was up quickly. Moments later the two threw caution to the wind and were swinging away with powerful blows. Sharkey, dodging a right hand bomb, countered with a clubbing right that shook Orlando and drove him to the canvas. Up at the count of three but obviously hurt, Orlando floundered around the ring with Sharkey in hot pursuit. A smashing right hand to the head followed by a flurry of blows once again sent Orlando sprawling onto the canvas. It was at this point that the referee stepped in and stopped the beating.

Eight days later on September 23, 1926, Jack and George met at the Mechanics Building in Boston. Even though the fight had been canceled fan interest had remained keen and thousands turned out to watch the battle. Coming into the fight Godfrey weighed a solid 220-pounds and at 29-years- old was at his peak of his powers. With a 33-pound weight advantage and a powerful punch George was a 10-8 betting favorite. Jack, at 187-pounds was unconcerned with George's physical advantages and was as usual confident of a victory.

From the opening bell Sharkey was the aggressor and brought the fight to George, who was noticeably slower. After a few minutes of fighting it became evident that Godfrey was not willing to mix it up. Instead he was content to wrestle and shove Jack around the ring. Because of George's tactics the large crowd began to boo. The booing continued throughout the fight as round after boring round dragged on. By the end George was credited with winning only two rounds and landing less than a dozen meaningful punches. Jack on the other hand had tried to make a fight of it. He was effective at landing his right hand and tattooed Godfrey's body with vicious power punches throughout. After 10 dreadful rounds, Jack was awarded an easy decision victory.

A day after the Sharkey-Godfrey fight, Boston fight fans and fans all over the world were in a daze. In what turned out to be a massive upset, Jack Dempsey, the man that nearly everyone thought was unbeatable, lost his crown to Gene Tunney. Over 120,000 people had showed up to watch the battle, making it the most watched sporting event outside of auto racing and soccer. Afterwards, in his dressing room, Dempsey uttered the now famous words to his wife, Hollywood starlet, Estela Taylor, "Honey, I forgot to duck." With Dempsey beaten, team Sharkey immediately turned their attention to getting a fight with Tunney. But first he would have to face "The Black Panther.

CHAPTER 10
THE BLACK PANTHER

Born in Louisiana on May 15, 1889, Harry Coleman Wills is truly a fighter of legend. Known as the Black Panther, Harry stood 6'3" and was covered with 220-pounds of lean muscle. In a time when fighters knew nothing of performance enhancing drugs and did very limited weight lifting, Harry's size and athletic ability was all-natural.

It isn't known exactly when Harry began fighting. Like a lot of fighters during his era his early fight record is yet undiscovered or lost to history. The Panther's earliest known fight was against Kid Navarro when he was approximately 21-years-old. However, it's more likely that he began fighting at a much younger age. What's known for sure is that Harry had a career that spanned at least 21-years. During that time he fought some of the greatest and most renowned fighters of all time.

During the years when Harry fought the controversial "color line" was in full force. At times the color line kept white and black fighters from fighting each other. It also made it extremely difficult for a black fighter to get a shot at a title, especially the heavyweight title. Because of the color line, Harry and the other black fighters were forced to fight each other multiple times to make a living. This resulted in Harry fighting Sam Langford (arguably, pound for pound, the greatest fighter ever) 18 times, winning 15, losing 2 and drawing 1. Eight of Harry's wins were newspaper decisions. Harry also battled Sam McVey, another outstanding black fighter five times and the legendary Joe Jeanette twice.

Since black fighters had such a difficult time getting a title fight they were forced to come up with "colored" versions of the titles, such as the "colored heavyweight championship." Wills won the colored heavyweight title from Sam Langford on May 1, 1914. However, the decision was disputed as both boxers claimed victory.

In 1925 Harry was the terror of the heavyweight division as well as the number one rated challenger for champion Jack Dempsey's crown. Despite the color line, Harry kept after Dempsey and repeatedly petitioned for a shot at the heavyweight crown. However, Tex Rickard, Dempsey's promoter wanted nothing to do with a mixed-race fight for fear of race riots if Wills defeated Dempsey. In 1910 Rickard had promoted the famous Jack Johnson-James J. Jefferies title fight in Reno which resulted in several deaths after Johnson, the first black heavyweight champion, defeated Jefferies, "the great white hope." Years later, when Dempsey spoke about the fight, he said, "I would have fought Wills, but nobody would promote it."

Nevertheless, Wills kept at it and his persistence nearly paid off. With mounting pressure from the public and the New York State Athletic Commission to defend against Wills, promoter Floyd Fitzsimmons stepped up and agreed to promote a Dempsey-Wills fight. In September of 1925 Wills and Dempsey traveled to Benton Harbor Michigan and signed for a 1926 title fight. Unfortunately, the fight never happened. Issues over money caused Dempsey to pull out and people were forever left with the question of, what if?

Instead of a fight with Harry, Dempsey defended his title against Gene Tunney on September 23, 1926, and lost his title. After talks of retirement Dempsey decided to continue his career. To get a rematch with Gene, Jack would have to face Sharkey, who was also trying to position himself for a title shot against Tunney by taking on Wills. The two would eventually meet in 1927 in one of the most controversial heavyweight fights of all time.

Jack's fight with Wills was seen as a golden opportunity; a fight that would "make him" if he were to win. Moreover, a win here would likely get Jack a shot at Dempsey's conqueror Gene Tunney. Wills was seen as Jack's most formidable challenge to date even though he was 37-years-old and had not fought in a year. Still, there were those who felt that Jack was being over matched. Harry was a seasoned veteran who outweighed Sharkey by 26-pounds and carried a massive power punch.

Despite the disadvantages that Jack would be facing, it was actually Sharkey that had sought out the fight with Wills. Promoter for the fight, Jack Fugazy, explains how it happened. "Six months ago Jack came to me with his manager and begged me to get Wills. At first I didn't give him much of a tumble. Of course I knew he was a good fighter, but I didn't think of matching him with Wills. Sharkey's insistence, his unfaltering confidence in himself led me to make the match. He told me how he could whip Wills. While I don't care to commit myself, I want to say that you've got to admire a fellow with such confidence in himself, he has been to my office two and three times a week to further impress me that he will win. He won't be turned back on that notion. I never saw a big man who impressed me more than he did and I'm certain that I have made no mistake in selecting a boxer who will give Wills the battle of his life."[40] Jack wasn't the only one who was confident. Buckley had no doubt that his man would win. When asked by William Muldoon the New York boxing commissioner if he expected Jack to knockout Wills Buckley replied, "No, he won't knock Wills out, I don't believe. But he will positively out point him."[41]

---

40 "Sharkey Sought Match With Wills," The *Boston Daily Globe*, October 8, 1926, pg.26.
41 "Jack Sharkey Full of Confidence As Night of His Supreme Test Draws Near," *Boston Daily Globe*, October 9, 1926, pg.A8.

The Sharkey-Wills fight was set for October 12, 1926 at Ebbet's Field, home of the Brooklyn Dodgers. With the fight being held in New York, Sharkey and his team decided to relocate to the Big Apple a few weeks beforehand and train at the world famous, Stillman's gym. At the time Stillman's was the center of the fistic universe. Between the years of 1920 to 1959 anybody who was anybody in terms of professional boxing came to train, visit or conduct business during its day.

Stillman's was owned and operated by the irascible Lou Stillman, a gun toting ex-cop who sat atop a raised chair under a time clock. From his vantage point Lou kept an eye on the gym and barked out orders or insults from a loudspeaker. Typically something like, "get out of the ring you bum, you call yourself a fighter?"[42] Always dressed in a tweed jacket, even on the most humid days, Lou ruled with an iron fist. Carrying a loaded .38 in his waistband, the tyrannical Stillman was not adverse to getting in the face of the baddest fighter or throwing out a visiting celebrity. Despite Stillman's dictatorial personality the place was constantly sought out as the premier gym to train at by great fighters like: Benny Leonard, Sugar Ray Robinson, Jack Dempsey, Primo Carnera, Joe Louis, Jersey Joe Walcott, Rocky Graziano, Willy Pep and Beau Jack, to name but a few. There wasn't a direction you could look where there wasn't a legend working out.

The fame of Stillman's went beyond the great fighters that trained there. Movies stars frequented the place as well. At any given time one might spot Frank Sinatra talking with Sugar Ray Robinson or Dean Martin and Jerry Lewis hanging out at ringside chatting with Rocky Marciano. Marlin Brando and Paul Newman became regulars and soaked up as much of the atmosphere as they could when each played fighters in their respective movies: "On the Water Front" and "Somebody up There Likes Me."

Not only was the gym famed for its clientele, it was also well-known for its filth. Lou absolutely refused to clean the place or even so much as open the grime-covered windows to allow in a little fresh air. The public, as well as many of the fighters, smoked in the place and after years of being closed up the gym reeked of stale sweat, mould and cigarette smoke. Soggy chewed up cigar and cigarette butts littered the dirt encrusted hardwood floors and competed for space with the numerous cockroaches. The unsanitary condition of the gym prompted Lou to say, "The Golden Age of prize fighting was the age of bad blood, bad air, bad sanitation and no sunlight. I keep the place like this for the fighters' own good. If I clean it up they'll catch cold from the cleanliness."[43]

---

42 "Stillman's Gym, the Center of the Boxing Universe," by John Garfield.
43 Wikipedia, Lou Stillman.

In the center of the grimy gym stood two rings known as ring 1 and ring 2. The once white canvas floors were long ago stained an off white from countless sparring matches and a million droplets of sweat and blood. Ring 1 was reserved for the best fighters while the rest were relegated to ring 2. Sitting on chairs and rickety wooden benches in front of the rings was a collection of fight managers, promoters, trainers, reporters and an assortment of bashed nose tough guys. Behind the rings some of the most legendary trainers like Charley Goldman and Ray Arcel taped up fighters and got them ready to spar as the world's elite boxers jumped rope or shadow boxed right next to them.

It was in ring 1 that Jack worked himself into fine trim. To help get Sharkey accustomed to fighting a larger, heavier opponent, Buckley hired 6' 6", 235-pound "Big" Bill Tate as a sparring partner. Tate was a leading black contender who had fought Harry Wills twice and was one of Jack Dempsey's primary sparring partners. Jack also sparred with little flyweight Frankie Genaro to help increase his speed. On October 6, Jack displayed his skills to a group of visiting reporters and looked impressive. It was reported the next day that Jack was approaching peak form and had shown a lot of punching power when he knocked down Nick Fadil twice and pummeled heavyweights Jack Stone and Martin O'Grady severely.

On the day of the bout the atmosphere and excitement of a big fight had taken hold of New York. A few hours before the gates were opened a huge line had formed that snaked around Ebbet's Field and went down the block as far as the eye could see. As people continued to show up traffic all over Brooklyn was a mess and parking for the fight was almost nonexistent. By 9:30 p.m. over 40,000 excited fans had crammed into Ebbet's Field taking up every available seat.

A slender crescent moon hung brightly in the clear sky when Sharkey climbed through the ropes. He walked to the center of the brightly illuminated ring with a broad smile on his face and waved to the huge crowd as they filled the cool night with loud cheers. If Jack was nervous in any way he showed none of it. Sharkey was then asked by one of the radio announcers to say something to all the fans listening at home. "Hello everybody this is Jack Sharkey speaking. I'm going to beat Wills tonight as sure as hell."[44] Two minutes later Harry entered the ring wearing his familiar faded blue robe and received a warm welcome from his many fans. Wills was also invited to say a few words to his fans listening on the radio, but refused, saying, "I'm superstitious. I'll speak after the fight is over,"[45] and promptly went to his corner. Once the fighters were settled in their

---

44 *The Chronicle Telegram*, October 13, 1926, pg.11.
45 Ibid.

respective corners, Jimmy Maloney was introduced and issued a challenge to the winner. Moments later the fighters met in the center of the ring and were given their instructions by referee Patsy Haley. Soon after, the bell rang loudly signaling the beginning of the action.

Sharkey began round one bobbing and weaving and dancing on his toes. He fired a fast right that crashed into Harry's jaw and the two fell into a clinch. Wills landed a hard right to the jaw as Sharkey drove both hands to the body and forced Harry into the ropes. Halfway through the round it was clear to everyone that Jack, at 188-pounds, would have a huge speed advantage over Wills, who weighed in at 214½. Throughout the remaining minute and a half Harry was out speeded and unable to do much with his quicker opponent. Sharkey presented "The Black Panther" with an ever-moving target and landed blindingly fast combinations and jabs at will. His speed was said to be amazing as he landed punches upon any spot between stomach and jaw. Round one would be an omen as to what would come.

With his success in round one, Jack's confidence rose. The ex-sailor tore into Wills in round two, unafraid of his larger opponent. Early on Sharkey fired both hands to Wills' head forcing him back into a corner. Jack then unloaded a number of thudding body shots. Trapped in the corner Harry started using one of his old tricks. He began to hold with his left around Jack's neck and pound Sharkey to the body and face with his powerful right hand. Jack immediately began to complain to the referee that he was being fouled. In response, referee Patsy Haley grabbed Harry's arm and give him a warning for the illegal move. However, twice more Harry hung his left glove around Jack's neck and pounded away with hard right hand punches. Harry's continued holding and hitting eventually brought loud boo's from the crowd as well as another warning from the referee just as the round came to a close.

Wills shot a right to Jack's head and took a right to begin round three as the two fighters mixed it up at a lively pace. Harry manhandled the smaller Sharkey in the clinches but took a hard right hand smash as they came out of a clinch. Wills jabbed nicely during the round and seemed to be adjusting to Jack's greater speed. However, Jack was successful several times rushing in and landing hard body shots. For the most part the third round was fought on fairly even terms. It ended with the two flailing away with both fists as the bell sounded. Going back to his corner blood was dripping from a small cut over Jack's right eye; "The Black Panther" had drawn first blood. Harry would find though, that his ability to compete with Jack on even terms would be short lived.

With the speed of a lightweight Jack came out for round four. He opened up with a furious two-fisted attack that staggered Wills and drove him into a corner. Harry countered with several body blows but the punches had no effect. Sharkey wove under a Wills jab and shot over two hard blows. The punches found their mark on Harry's head and the Black Panther was again momentarily shaken up and forced into the ropes. Escaping from the ropes, Harry began to box cautiously as Sharkey bobbed and weaved and rushed in. Jack planted two hard lefts to Harry's body followed by a hard left and right to the chin. Midway through the round Jack caught the Panther with five clean punches to the face that again sent him into the ropes and had the huge crowd on its feet cheering. Bleeding from his mouth after Sharkey's attack Harry once more started to hold and hit. Frustrated by Harry's fouling tactic Jack pushed Wills away and slammed a hard right to his jaw just as the bell rang. Back in his corner Sharkey said to Buckley, "I've got him, Johnny, I'll knock him out in the next round."

"You'll do nothing of the kind, Jack," replied Buckley. "You'll do as you agreed to do, fight carefully."[46] With that Jack reluctantly agreed to fight carefully as previously agreed.

Jack opened round five with a long right to Harry's head as the two came together and fought at close quarters. Harry landed a short left, right to Jack's head but took a hard left to the body in return. Separated by the referee Jack came right back with a hard overhand right that caught Wills flush on his face. The punch caused Wills to grin broadly although it had clearly hurt him. The two then began to wrestle about the ring and referee Patsy had a hard time keeping them separated. Just as the bell sounded Jack drove in a left to Harry's nose as Harry hooked a clubbing left to Jack's body.

The sixth saw only intermittent action from both fighters. This was largely due to the fact that Harry continued to clinch and maul Jack every time the two would get close. When not wrestling with his opponent Jack boxed well on his toes and was effective with his rapid jabs and left hooks, while Harry looked for an opening and occasionally fired his right hand.

By the seventh Harry was starting to get busted up and Jack had in effect clipped the Panther's claws. Early in the round Jack landed a powerful left hook that opened a deep cut above Harry's right eye. Feeling the warm blood stream down his face Harry again began to hold and Jack complained. Separated by referee Patsy, Sharkey danced out of range. As Wills charged in Jack caught him with a vicious right to the head that sent blood splattering across the ring. The two then fought in close and Jack more than held his own during the bruising infighting. Both fighters landed hard hooks to the head and body, but it was Harry who eventually relented. With his left eye cut and starting to swell shut Wills could do little to keep

---

46 "Buckley Insists of Carrying Out Plan of Careful Fight," *The Boston Daily Globe* October 16, 1926. pg.B32.

the relentless Sharkey off of him. At the round's end Sharkey unloaded a series of quick head shots that had Harry holding and spitting blood at the bell.

Both fighters connected with hard rights to the head to begin round eight. Jack caught Harry with a hard uppercut as the two clinched. A smashing left to the face in close had Harry spitting blood again. Wills then fired a four-punch combination that Jack avoided with slick head movement. Sharkey returned fire with several hard rights to Harry's head. One of the punches opened a cut under Wills left eye adding more blood to his already bloody face and chest. Not able to cope with Jack at long range Harry went back to fighting his faster opponent in close; which included holding and hitting. The two finished the round trading punches in close.

Harry opened fire with both hands and drove Jack to the ropes to start round nine. With Sharkey up against the ropes Wills unloaded a combination of bruising body shots. Jack fought his way off the ropes and had Harry backing up from a barrage of head punches. Wills clinched to stop Jack's attack but was quickly separated by the referee. Jack then attacked with a series of rapid lefts and rights to Harry's head. With no return punches from Harry, Jack continued his assault. Sharkey drove Wills across the ring with a crisp right and worked both hands to the head and body. Another hard right drove Wills into the ropes just as the bell rang.

A looping overhand right smashed into Harry's face early in round ten. The punch jarred Wills and had him shaken up for a moment. A follow up left hook drew blood from Harry's nose. Fighting in close Sharkey caught Harry with a terrific right and some rapid-fire body blows. Harry covered up and looked to clinch as Jack missed a left hook swing. Jack, bobbing and weaving came in low and landed a number of hard body blows. Harry fought back, swinging wildly as the bell signaled the round's end.

Harry dug a left into Jack's ribs to begin round eleven but took a hard left to his head in return. Wills began to box cautiously as Jack looked for an opening. It was at this point that Sharkey came rushing in carelessly and Harry caught him with a pulverizing punch that nearly ended the fight. Interviewed after the fight Sharkey had this to say about the blow. "The punch jarred me and made me dizzy, and I was not myself until the round was almost over."[47] Realizing that the dying Panther could still deal a deadly blow, Sharkey was cautious. The two circled each other jabbing and went into several clinches. Both fighters seemed to be a little weary as the pace slowed. Coming out of a clinch Sharkey sent in a hard uppercut that nearly

---

[47] "Sharkey Says Sailor Boy is Ready for Marine," *Boston Daily Globe*, October 13, 1926, pg.14.

sent Harry through the ropes. Jack followed up with two quick rights to the head just before the bell.

A clinch started round twelve. Once the two fighters were separated Harry landed a hard right hook to Jack's chin followed by two stiff jabs. Weaving his way under Harry's long jab Jack forced Harry to the ropes with a flurry of hard blows to the head and a right to the belly. The blows had Harry holding, again. Pushing Harry away, Jack leaped in with a left jab followed by a smashing right to Will's rib cage. Again Harry found refuge by holding. Covered in blood and tiring badly the Panther continued to clinch until the bell sounded.

By the thirteenth round Harry was a beaten fighter and he knew it; he had been in too many fights to be fooled. Having nothing left to fend Sharkey off with, Harry started to foul once more. He again held Jack behind the head and flailed away with his right hand. Referee Haley was quick to warn Harry, but the warnings went unheeded. Jack, trying to end the fight unleashed a series of fast punches to Harry's head backing the Black Panther to the ropes. Wills, taking a vicious body attack again held Jack around his neck. This time though instead of hitting Jack with straight right hands Wills backhanded Jack across the face several times. 60-years later in an interview Sharkey told of the moment. "I was going to knock him out. Well, in the old days when you knew you were going to get licked, you could foul yourself out. That's what Wills did in the thirteenth round to keep from getting stopped."[48]

As soon as Harry delivered his backhand blows to Jack's face, referee Haley jumped in and separated the two fighters, calling a halt to the action at .40 seconds into the round. He grabbed Harry's arm and led him to his corner where he was promptly disqualified. Haley then went to Jack's corner and raised Sharkey's hand in victory. A few moments later the official announcement came over the loudspeaker. The often mercurial Sharkey was overcome with emotion and began to cry.

Ten minutes after the fight, Jack was back in his dressing room along with his father, who was beaming proudly, his sister, her husband and Buckley. Along with Sharkey's family the dressing room was further crowded with half a dozen reporters, all scribbling madly in response to questions and snapping photos. After a question from *Boston Globe* sports writer, Roger Batchelder, Jack had this to say about the fight. "I'm so happy that I can't talk," said Jack. "Boston had much to do with it, I felt every minute tonight that Boston and the rest of New England was behind me. It was funny, but when the yells came from the crowd I could distinguish 40

---

[48] "The Story Of Jack Sharkey, Boxing's Tragic Figure, by Jim Brady, *Boxing Illustrated*, pg.88.

voices that I knew from the old hometown. One has to have support at a time like that. I was glad to find that when I went into the ring, I got a good hand from the boys and I was also glad when Harry went through the ropes that the crowd was cordial towards him. I should have felt badly if they had started in handing the razz to Harry as they gave it to him later."[49]

"Were you ever hurt?" asked Batchelder.

"Once in a while" responded Sharkey "We weren't playing marbles you know and no one likes a good sock unless it was to help him to do better work. But as soon as I had taken my chair in my corner and had a good squint at him I knew the fight was over. I had him licked good and plenty while the band was playing 'The gang's all here' and I noticed that his eyes didn't meet mine squarely for long. They shifted and I out looked. That's always good dope. If you can out stare the other boy, the battle is won. I don't mean to say that Harry was afraid of me, for he stuck it out with much physical courage, but I think that when he saw me looking at him he could hear the last bell tolling."[50]

"What made you cry like a baby when you were awarded the decision?" asked Batchelder.

"Because just then I felt like one," Sharkey replied frankly. "I had been getting set for a knockout but Harry kept fouling and I could not show the crowd what I could do. The result was inevitable, of course, for the crowd wouldn't have stood longer the low punches and the jabs during the breaks. I fought the best I could tonight, but I didn't have the chance to show what I could do against a clean and open fighter like Tunney. But that is another matter, isn't it, John?"[51]

Buckley's only reply was a proud smile on his portly face followed by, "We'll tell the world."

The win over Wills was an impressive victory and one of the most important wins in Jack's career. As far as Wills was concerned, because of his fouling the Panther received a 30 day suspension, which prompted him to say, "I guess I'm through." Harry was far from through. He would fight sporadically for the next five years and end his career with a four-fight win streak in 1932. After retirement Harry invested his money into real estate and became a successful businessman.

Sharkey was now firmly on the doorstep of fistic fame. In terms of rankings he was now behind Jack Dempsey and hot on Tunney's tail. Prior to the fight Jack's critics had questioned the Boston fighter's courage, punching power, and desire to win. Beating Wills, the man who had terrorized Jack Dempsey and the heavyweight division for the better part of

---

[49] *The Lima Ohio News*, October 13, 1926, pg,16.
[50] Ibid.
[51] Ibid.

seven years, erased most of those doubts. The fight also earned Jack one of his many nicknames. Because he had cried after the fight the press dubbed him "The Weeping Warrior."

Sharkey was now looked upon as a viable challenger for Gene Tunney's newly acquired championship. The victory prompted Jack to say, "I am ready for Tunney, a sailor boy is always anxious to meet those leathernecks."[52] However, to get to Gene, Sharkey would have to face one of the most fearsome fighters the world has ever known, Jack Dempsey, "The Manassas Mauler."

---

52 "Sharkey Says Sailor Boy is Ready For Marine," *Boston Daily Globe*, October 13, 1926, pg.14.

CHAPTER 11
HOMER SMITH AND MIKE MCTIGUE

Jack and Dorothy returned home from New York on Friday, October 15. Once home, Sharkey planned to relax through the weekend and do some fishing while recovering from his fight with Wills. Rest was what he needed because he was scheduled to box an exhibition match against one of his regular sparring partners, Rocky Stone the following Monday. Jack and Rocky were scheduled to be the main event at one of Boston's most famous theatres, the Howard Athenaeum, or as it was affectionately called, the "Old Howard." Fans were treated to a fine display of boxing skill by both fighters and each was given a tumultuous round of applause when they finished.

Just a few days prior to his exhibition match, David F. Egan of the *Boston Globe* was sent to Jack's house to get the scoop on the hot young contender that everyone was talking about. Egan arrived at 16 Stone Avenue, Chestnut Hill and spent most of the day talking with Jack and his family. Egan found that Jack was anything but the stereotypical cauliflower eared boxer.

Sharkey along with his wife Dorothy and their two daughters, Dorothy and Marilyn, lived in a white two story California-type bungalow. Egan discovered that Sharkey was a real homebody and loved to be with his family. "He's wonderful to me and the kiddies," said his wife Dorothy. "He wants to spend all his time here, he wants his family all to himself, and in making his plans he always thinks of his little family first." Dorothy's grandmother, Mrs. Mary Van Keuren Pike, whom was visiting during the interview, added that, "Jack gets up in the night and looks after the babies, you know how babies fuss, and Jack never misses it in the least."[53]

Further talks revealed that Sharkey enjoyed an occasional cigar but never drank. In addition, Jack and his family attended mass at St. Mary's church, in Brookline every Sunday. Egan found that the young heavyweight was also a great lover of music and did a little strumming on the tenor banjo and ukulele as well as some singing. However, there was a difference of opinion between Jack, Dorothy and her grandmother, as to how well Jack sang and played.

Inevitably the conversation turned to boxing. Sharkey was frank when he confessed to Egan that he really did not like professional boxing. As a sport he loved it, and from a scientific point of view he considered it a

---

[53] "Real Sharkey Is Family Man, Washing Dishes and Tending Baby," *Boston Globe*, October 17, 1926, pg. c7.

healthy form of exercise. But he did not like the slugging and the heartlessness and cruelty connected with the sport. As far as pastimes Jack pointed out that he loved to go camping, fishing and hunting.

It was near twilight when Egan wrapped up his interview with Sharkey. After spending a day with Jack, Egan had found that he was likable and intelligent. Egan also found that Jack was not the swell-headed, boisterous, braggart that his reputation had suggested. In his own words David had this to say about Jack. "Despite the fact that he is a professional pugilist he is as far removed from the usual conception of a prize fighter as Harry Wills is removed from the world's heavyweight crown. He is no swaggering pirate, no roistering rounder, no blustering bully. He is a quiet, likeable 24-year-old boy, completely wrapped up in his attractive wife and two small babies."[54]

Four days after his interview, Sharkey and Buckley filed an official challenge with the New York Athletic Boxing Commission for a shot at Gene Tunney's heavyweight title. Gene responded by saying that he stood ready to box any contender named by Tex Rickard when the promoter says the word. While waiting to see how things would play out with Tunney, rumors started to surface on October 27 about a possible Sharkey-Maloney fight. Reports were coming out that Maloney was anxious to meet his old rival again. Just a day later more news reached the public that Sharkey was offered $150,000 by Chicago promoter William Clements to fight Jack Dempsey. Buckley confirmed the news, saying talks for a fight next year in Chicago were ongoing, but as of yet nothing definite had been done. Dempsey was reported to have said that he was in no hurry to climb back into the ring after his loss to Tunney. He wanted to return to his home in California and start training. "If I find that I haven't gone back too far to give a suitable account of myself I will attempt to regain the title."[55] Tex Rickard as well verified that he and Dempsey had discussed possible opponents and that Jack Sharkey and Jimmy Maloney were both being considered as tune-ups for a rematch with Gene.

While waiting for a big fight to materialize with Dempsey, Tunney or Maloney, Jack was looking to keep busy. In early December he agreed to a rematch with journeyman Homer Smith, a fighter that he had beaten two years prior by decision.

The fight took place on December 15, at the Syracuse Arena and brought in a record gate of $13,000. For Homer it turned out to be a bad night. Sharkey, looking very sharp, put on a masterful display of "scientific" boxing skills and took Homer apart from the opening bell. Halfway through the first round, Smith was sent to the canvas from a vicious right hand

---

54 Ibid.
55 "Dempsey Plans no Hurried Comeback," *Boston Globe,* October 28, 1926, pg.13.

punch. In the second Jack rocked Smith with a right to the jaw that again sent him down for a count of five. From the third through the sixth, Sharkey battered his overmatched opponent from ring post to ring post. Such was the beating that Smith could only fight back a little; instead he was content to hang on and try to take as little punishment as he could.

By the seventh Smith was a gory mess. He was bleeding from a deep cut above his left eye and a badly torn lip. Seeing that Smith was defeated, referee Jack Michaels stepped in and persuaded the beaten fighter to give up the hopeless task of defeating the Bostonian.

Although it was a relatively easy win for Jack, the fight was not without controversy and a little bad luck. In one of the early rounds Sharkey fractured his right hand. The break immediately forced the cancellation of a match Jack had scheduled with James "Sully" Montgomery the following week. The broken hand would also keep Jack out of any further fights for at least a couple of months. To compound matters Smith's manager threatened to file a protest with the New York State Athletic Commission claiming that Jack fouled Smith by hitting him when he was on his knees in round one. And that the referee erred when he let the fight continue. Despite the threats nothing ever came of the foul and eventually the matter was dropped.

Jimmy Maloney climbed into the ring with Harry Persson on December 22, 1926; Harry was being looked at as Sharkey's next opponent (once his hand healed). However, any thoughts of a Persson-Sharkey fight were quickly forgotten after Maloney hammered out a decisive 10-round decision over the Swedish born fighter. After a streak of six wins since his defeat at the hands of Sharkey, Maloney was now in a position to get a match with his old nemesis. But first, Maloney would have to get by Jack Delaney and Sharkey would have to fight ex-light heavyweight king, Mike McTigue.

Michael Francis McTigue was born in Kilnamona, Ireland on November 26, 1892 but moved to the United States when he was 16. Shortly after arriving Mike got a job as a beef handler on New York's West Side. After flattening a drunk that attacked his boss, the teenage boy was encouraged to give boxing a try. He eventually found his way to old time New York boxer, George "Elbows" McFadden. George had gotten his nickname "Elbows" by making sure that if his round-house punches missed his elbows had a chance to land; which they often did. In fact, years after retiring, George openly admitted to using the dirty tactic. "It won me," said an elderly "Elbows" "a lot of fights."[56] New York sportswriter Thomas A.

---

56 Wikipedia, George "Elbows" McFadden.

Dorgan was quoted as saying "McFadden should use four gloves in the ring, one on each fist and one on each elbow."[57]

Despite the questionable tactics that George employed he was without a doubt a great fighter. During a career that spanned from 1894 to 1908 George fought and defeated some of the greatest lightweights of all time. In 1899 "Elbows" fought three of the most prominent lightweight champions of his era: Joe Gans, Frank Ernie, and Kid Lavigne. He knocked out Gans, who had gone eight years without a loss and is considered by some to be pound for pound the greatest fighter to ever live. It should be noted that this was the first meeting between the two. George and Gans fought a total of seven times with Gans winning 3 by decision, 1 by knockout and drawing 2. George then knocked out Lavigne and nearly defeated Frank Ernie. All told "Elbows" retired with a record of 46 wins, 13 defeats and 21 draws, with 26 coming by way of knockout. George also had 16 newspaper decisions: wining 3, losing 7 with 6 draws.

Learning the finer points of boxing from "Elbows" Mike went on to become an outstanding fighter. On March 17, 1923 he won the light heavyweight title by defeating "Battling" Siki. During his title reign McTigue made defenses against such notables as Tommy Loughran, Mickey Walker and Tiger Flowers; all three were outstanding world champions. By defeating such an impressive array of competition Mike had proven that he was a great fighter.

He held the title until Paul Berlenbach defeated him on May 30, 1925. After losing his title to Paul, Mike embarked on a comeback that was called sensational. During his climb he reestablished himself not only by beating light heavyweights but also by making an occasional appearance into the heavyweight division and defeating a few of the big boys. McTigue also displayed a seemingly new-found punch that was powerful enough to knock out legitimate heavyweights such as "King" Solomon. When asked about his new "power punch" Mike said that an operation to remove bone fragments gave him the confidence to throw a hard right hand without fear of pain. After putting together a 12-1-1, (5 by knockout) record since losing his title, "Bold" Mike as he was sometimes called, felt confident enough to challenge Sharkey.

At this point Tex Rickard was staging a heavyweight elimination tournament. Having signed Jack Sharkey and Jimmy Maloney back in December, Tex now had a monopoly on five of the top heavyweight contenders. His list included: Sharkey, Maloney, Dempsey, Paulino Uzqudin, and Swedish contender Harry Persson. Richard's cornering of the heavyweight market caused one of his biggest rivals, Herbert Fugazy to

---

57 Ibid.

proclaim, "Worst thing that could have happened to the fight game in New York."[58]

With his latest heavyweight tournament Tex was looking to find an opponent for Jack Dempsey, and then ultimately an opponent for heavyweight champion Gene Tunney. Maloney and Sharkey in particular because of their popularity and drawing power were being looked at as possible Dempsey opponents. As it stood Sharkey would face Mike McTigue, Jimmy Maloney would square off against Jack Delaney, and Paulino Uzqudin would face Knute Hansen.

On February 18, Maloney defeated Delaney, winning a solid decision. Incidentally, Sharkey picked Delaney to defeat Jimmy saying, "I beat Maloney twice and I admit I can't hit. But that fellow Delaney can punch, and I can't see where Maloney has a chance."[59] Maloney's victory was followed a week later by Paulino wining a decisive 10-round decision over Knute Hanson. Talks quickly turned to a fight between Maloney and Paulino, but Jimmy declined the fight. Instead, feeling that he had fought himself to the top, "Dynamite" Jim demanded a match with either Dempsey or the winner of Sharkey-McTigue. It was now Jack's turn to face Mike McTigue.

With the fight being held at New York's Madison Square Garden on March 3, 1927, Jack once again spent a couple of weeks training at Stillman's Gym. While there the popular Boston fighter was constantly sought out by the press. After one of his workouts Jack sat among a gathering of sports writers and spoke confidently and candidly about his upcoming fight as well as possible future opponents. "Looks like I'm the luckiest guy in the tournament," said a smiling Jack. "McTigue won't last the 15-rounds against me. I've heard all about that knockout punch of his, he can try it on my chin." Responding to a question Jack said, "Maloney? Say, there's an easy one. It would be another Jefferies-Fitzsimmons scrap so far as public interest goes, only this time Sharkey will be the winner."

"What about Dempsey?" asked another reporter.

"I'll take Dempsey, too. If he's in shape he would be tough to handle, but I don't figure he could comeback. Of course I can beat Tunney; he's the man I'm after."[60] Jack finished his final workout on March 1 by going a few rounds on one of Stillman's worn heavy bags. Following his workout, a half a dozen reporters looking to get a final write-up in before the big fight interviewed Jack. Keeping the interview short, Jack said, "I'm going to wipe that Mike McTigue off the map."

---

58 "Rickard's Rival Rises to Object," *Boston Daily Globe*, December 7, 1926, pg.A24.
59 "Jack Sharkey Doesn't Give Maloney a Chance," *Boston Daily Globe*, February 15, 1927, pg.20.
60 "Sharkey Sees Clear Road to Tunney," *Boston Daily Globe*, February 25, 1927, pg.26.

Mike on the other hand was of a mind to give a different version of how the fight would turn out. "I'll make it four KO's in a row when I step into the ring with Jack Sharkey, for I figure he will be as easy as Paul Berlenbach or some of the others I have been laying low. I plan to go right after him from the first bell. It would be foolish to attempt to carry a lad that outweighs me by 25 or 30-pounds. It may take me a round or two to size him up and learn where and when his opening comes, especially if he chooses to box defensively. But I will study them out and when the chance develops I'll shoot in my old haymaker at the spot where it does its best business, and Mr. Sharkey will be no more a contender than is Berlenbach."

Over 15,000 boisterous fans showed up to watch Sharkey battle it out with the former light heavyweight king. At 9:30 Jack entered the ring a 2-1 favorite. A few minutes later Mike and his team followed. Before the pre-fight instructions were given, Joe Walcott, the former welterweight champion was introduced. The well-known Boston favorite stood smiling and waving at his cheering fans. Walcott then went to each fighter's corner and wished both men good luck.

At a solid 189½-pounds Sharkey carried a 19-pound weight advantage over his 170½-pound adversary. Jack also had the added benefit of 3 inches in height and 10-years in age; at the time Jack was 25 and Mike was 35.

Despite a list of disadvantages McTigue put up a tremendous battle and gave as well as he took. Early on, Mike was willing to slug it out with Jack. However, in round two a Sharkey jab broke one of Mike's teeth and in turn ruptured a blood vessel. The injury forced Mike to go from brawler to boxer. From the second through the seventh both fighters were in fine form. They fought on mostly even terms and put on a brilliant display of masterful boxing.

Although noticeably lighter on his feet Mike was not as strong as Jack. Furthermore, Mike's vaunted power punch had little effect on the larger Sharkey. McTigue did, however, manage to cut and swell up the Bostonian's left eye and rip his bottom lip open, but he was never really able to hurt Sharkey even when he landed his famous right hand solidly. In the eighth round Jack suddenly changed his focus to Mike's body; the switch caught Mike off guard and nearly crumpled the Irishman when Jack landed several thudding blows to Mike's stomach. Jack continued to concentrate his attack on Mike's midsection throughout the ninth. By the tenth Jack's body attack had visibly weakened his smaller opponent. By the eleventh Mike looked exhausted and could do little to keep Sharkey off of him. Seeing that Mike was nearly finished Jack poured on the pressure in the twelfth. Bobbing and weaving Jack constantly came forward landing hard jabs, left hooks and solid rights. Spitting blood from his badly cut mouth Mike was a blood-covered mess. As the punishment continued to mount and Mike began to visibly fade the referee finally stepped in and put an end to the fight at the 1:29 mark of round twelve.

Although the stoppage was seen as reasonable due to the punishment he was taking, Mike argued referee McPartland's decision to end the fight. Across the ring a jubilant Sharkey raised his hands, waved to the crowd and celebrated his victory. Minutes later Jack was back in his crowded dressing room. With adrenaline still flowing through his veins, Sharkey shouted his war cry to the assembled press. "Now for Maloney, give me Jimmy Maloney and I'll knock him out! And don't let anyone tell you Mike can't hit. His right hand is a corker. When that landed I saw stars, and I don't mean maybe." When asked about McTigue's fighting abilities Jack was full of praise. "Why he's wonderful. And in the clinches he was mighty hard to hit. But I knew I had him after the fifth round. Game as he was I could feel him weakening. His right lost its sting and after the eighth I hardly bothered to get out of the way. I knew I'd beat him and I did, just as I said I would. I boxed with McTigue, but I'm waiting for Maloney and I'll knock him out."[61]

Beating McTigue was a nice victory, but Jack's critics quickly pointed out that it shouldn't have taken him twelve rounds to do it, especially with all of the advantages he came into the ring with. Two days after the fight Mike was still upset over the stoppage and spoke his mind to the newspapers. "I don't think much of Sharkey as a heavyweight contender. Jack Sharkey reminded me very much of a little boy walking through a graveyard and whistling to keep his courage up. In the third round he whispered to me, 'I can beat you, why don't you lay down before you get hurt?' I answered, why don't you hit me hard enough? I think the crowd that saw the fight will bear witness that I hung around until the twelfth waiting for Sharkey to hit me hard enough to impress people. Sharkey is a good talker inside, he can whisper much better than he can fight. The whispers didn't have any effect on me for until the incident in the twelfth I was fully confident I would win. Many times he tried to bulldoze me with his weight but it didn't work worth a cent. I out fought him. He ought to go into the movies, the faces he made impressed the fans more than the punches he delivered. The marks of battle tell the tale. Today take a look at Sharkey's face and that of the old man. Which one looks like the winner?[62] Mike then called for a rematch, but despite his fine showing against Jack, he was not in team Sharkey's immediate plans. Proceedings were already set in motion for a final and decisive fourth meeting with "Dynamite" Jimmy Maloney.

---

61 "Now For Maloney, Jack Sharkey's Cry," *Boston Daily Globe*, March 4, 1927, pg.23.
62 "Sharkey Can Whisper Better Than He Can Fight, Says Mike," *Boston Daily Globe*, March 5, 1927, pg.19.

CHAPTER 12
SHARKEY-MALONEY IV

Jack and Dorothy left New York at 1:30 in the afternoon on March 6. After a leisurely drive in their comfortable new 1927 Cadillac, which was the first year to feature a radio, they arrived home at around 10:45 p.m. They were greeted by Dorothy's grandparents, Mr. and Mrs. W.H. Pike, who were again on babysitting duty. Anxious to see their children the young couple tiptoed into the room where their daughters were fast asleep and gently kissed each child. After unwinding and visiting for a while, Jack and his wife headed to bed, each looking forward to the first real night's rest since the fight.

A few days later, negotiations began for a Sharkey-Maloney match up. Buckley, along with Jimmy's manager Dan Carroll met up with Tex Rickard to discuss the fight. Tex proposed a May 19 fight to be held at New York's Yankee Stadium. This posed a problem however, since both fighters were already scheduled to fight other opponents around that time. Jimmy was signed to have an April match in Cleveland against Johnny Risko and Sharkey was tentatively scheduled to have a rematch with Pat McCarthy on March 24, in Chicago. Tex assured both managers that he would take care of the situation. Since Sharkey was not "officially" signed to fight McCarthy canceling the fight was easy. On the other hand, it cost Tex $3,500 to buy out and cancel the match between Maloney and Risko.

From the start negotiations were difficult and neither manager wanted to take less money than the other. Both wanted top dollars for their fighter and felt that their man had more drawing power and deserved a bigger piece of the pie. Each demanded a guarantee of $100,000, plus thirty percent of the gate receipts. To make things more complicated, Boston promoter, Tom Goodwin came forward claiming that he held a contract signed by Maloney over a year earlier. Tom alleged that the contract gave him exclusive rights to choose who, and where Jimmy fought. Tom then proposed a summer fight between Jimmy and Jack in Boston at Braves Field. As big as Tom was in Boston he was no match against the might of Tex Rickard. By March 10, Tex had everything wrapped up and the discussions were through.

Rickard announced on March 13 that Sharkey and Maloney had agreed to a 15-round fight. The match would take place on May 19 at Yankee Stadium and the two fighters would split 50 percent of the gate receipts, which would amount to about $100,000 each. Tex also announced that the bout would be the start of a three-fight elimination tournament. Sharkey would fight Jimmy, and Jack Dempsey would take on Paulino Uzqudin. The winners of those fights would then face off to determine who would get a shot at champion Gene Tunney.

Along with the fight announcement Tex also made it clear that both fighters were not allowed to have any other fights or exhibition matches, saying, "I don't want these fellows running around the country taking chances of busting a hand in a bout that doesn't mean anything. It's a business proposition with me, a big one now, and I can't afford to run any unnecessary risks. The Sharkey-Maloney match will be one of the biggest of the year, and I want nothing to interfere with it."[63]

With the signing completed the trash talking began. Team Maloney issued an official statement after hearing that Jack had said that he would "knock Maloney out if they should meet again." The statement read as follows. "Joseph Cucoskey has won two great victories in the past few weeks, one over old Mike McTigue, the other a knockout victory over Jimmy Maloney-in the newspapers. Maloney is no braggart; he does his fighting in the ring. That is where he scores his knockouts and wins his victories. He knows that he will beat Cucoskey, just as he knew he would beat Delaney and he is willing to post from $25,000 to $200,000 with any reputable bank or stake holder in the city of Boston that he will defeat the Pole when they meet. This offer will close at 3 p.m. next Monday. If Cucoskey does not answer before then, our next business with him will be carried on inside the ropes of the ring." In response Buckley said, "I will cover all the money Dan Carroll can raise when Sharkey and Maloney clash, but the coin will have to be placed at ringside odds."[64]

With the fight preparations under way everything was going smoothly, until an issue concerning the Maloney-Risko fight sprang up. Cleveland promoter, Walter Taylor filed an injunction suit in federal court to stop the Sharkey-Maloney fight. The suit was based on the failure of Maloney to box Risko in Cleveland on or before May 1. Paulino Uzqudin and his manager were quick to respond, saying that they would be happy to fill in for Maloney should he be kept from fighting. When word reached Tex, he was angered and assured everyone that he would, "clear the way for the big fight."

Meanwhile, preparations to stage the fight were moving along. 50,000 tickets ranging from $2 to $20 were getting set to go on sale, with another 20,000 being held until the day of the fight.

While Tex ironed out the legal issues concerning the Risko fight, Sharkey and Maloney committed themselves to serious training for their

---

63 "Sharkey-Maloney Barrier Drawn," *Boston Daily Globe,* March 10, 1927, pg.22.
64 "Sharkey's Manager Replies to Carroll," *Boston Daily Globe*, March 10, 1927, pg.22.

grudge match. Both men knew how important this fight was and that a shot at the heavyweight title was nearly within their grasp.

Jimmy and his team set up camp in Long Branch, New Jersey, while Jack headed over to New York with his new trainer, Harry Kelley, to toughen himself up at Stillman's gym. Harry, formerly Maloney's trainer for several fights, had just recently come over to the Sharkey camp. With Harry in his corner Jack would have a huge advantage because of the intimate knowledge that Harry had gained by training Jimmy.

On May 6, Jack went through a short but intense workout at Stillman's and gave his thoughts on the upcoming fight to a group of sportswriters. In front of the press Jack was all confidence and said that he could not see how he could lose. "The fight is a cinch," said Sharkey, "and Maloney is just another fighter that has to be disposed of. I'm in condition to fight Jim tomorrow if necessary. I weigh only 194, about two pounds above my natural fighting weight, so I'm taking things easy. But wait until we get in the ring; I won't be doing anything easy then, I'll hit Jim with everything but the posts."[65]

Over at Team Maloney's camp, everyone was all smiles and Jimmy looked terrific during his training. The 205-pound slugger looked simply vicious as he tore into heavyweight Tim Kirby and left him bleeding from the mouth and wanting no more. After battering Tim, Jim spent three rounds working on his speed with newcomer, and good friend of Sharkey's, 18-year-old Ernie Schaaf. Schaaf had just embarked on his own boxing career two months prior and was scheduled to fight in one of the undercard bouts. After three spirited rounds, Jimmy stood in the ring with perspiration steaming from his head and his face wreathed in the happiest smile he had worn in some time. So happy was his trainer that he planned on reducing Maloney's workout a little as to not over train.

While Sharkey and Maloney were preparing for battle, former heavyweight champion Jack Dempsey was getting himself into shape for his return fight. Dempsey, hidden away at his home in Ojai, California had been training hard. Living off the land, running, hiking and chopping logs had gotten the former champ into great shape; he was now convinced that he could make a run at the title. Jack had been in contact with Tex and had come to an agreement in terms of money and an opponent. Jack was matched with Paulino Uzqudin for a July 9 date at Yankee Stadium; the winner would take on the survivor of the Sharkey-Maloney bout.

With just a week to go before the fight, famed fight manager "Dumb" Dan Morgan spent some time at the Maloney camp. Dan was dubbed "Dumb" by Tad Dorgan, editor of the *New York Journal*, because of his

---

[65] "Sharkey Tells How He Plans To Win," *Boston Daily Globe*, May 6, 1927, pg.30.

excessive talkativeness. Despite the nickname, Dan was anything but dumb. He was in fact, one of boxing's greatest managers and colorful personalities. During his lengthy career, Dan guided hundreds of fighters, including several world champions. After retiring, Dan was hired as a consultant by famed fight managers Jim Norris and Mike Jacobs. After watching Jimmy train, Dan predicted a Maloney victory saying, "Maloney was as strong and as fast today as he was the day he whipped Delaney. He went the equivalent of 12-rounds of boxing with no let up and could have continued at the same speed. The Irishman judges his pace well; he was throwing his right hand accurately. He should punch the gas out of the sailor in three or four rounds."[66]

While Dan was praising Jimmy, writer for the *Boston Globe*, David Egan, reported that Sharkey's speed and wind was remarkable. Retired lightweight champion Benny Leonard, who was working as a columnist for the *Globe* gave his thoughts on Jack after watching the ex-sailor rip into his sparring partners. "He certainly looks great today," Benny noted. He then went on to say that Sharkey looked stronger than when he fought Mike McTigue.

A day later, Benny paid a visit to the Maloney camp and was surprised at how good the Boston slugger looked. Benny reported that Jimmy looked very good against his sparring partners and that he worked fast, hit hard and was surprisingly accurate. Talking with Maloney, Benny said, "Jimmy, you looked like a champion in there today." Jimmy responded with, "Benny, that's now the one great ambition of my life. It didn't used to be so, but now it's in my blood. I never thought I'd be up there fighting for the heavyweight crown. But now I realize I am only a couple of steps away and there's an incentive that will just make me win."[67] After seeing both fighters in training Benny predicted that the cooler headed Jimmy would be victorious over the unpredictable Sharkey, saying, "I've got to face facts in a cold calculating manner and my dope makes Maloney the winner."[68]

On May 15, news broke that Jack had suffered a half-inch long gash below his left eyebrow during a sparring session. Despite the injury, which caused a lot of excitement in the Sharkey camp, Jack assured everyone that the fight was not in jeopardy. Instead of breaking his spirit, the cut only served to motivate him. A cocksure Sharkey remarked, "I'll lick Maloney even if I have only one eye." As a result of the cut, Harry Kelley restricted Jack to gymnastic workouts only. The cut also had an effect on the betting for the fight since it was seen as a handicap; Maloney was sure now to come in as the favorite.

---

66 "Dumb Dan Morgan Picks Jim Maloney," *Boston Daily Globe,* May 14, 1927, pg.7.
67 "Benny Leonard Picks Maloney," *Boston Daily Globe*, May 19, 1927, pg.24.
68 Ibid.

More news surfaced on May 17 that the Dempsey-Paulino bout had been axed. Paulino had been suspended for agreeing to fight Dempsey and refusing to fight Ed Keel. With his suspension, he would not be able to meet Dempsey. After talking with Rickard, Dempsey agreed to instead go directly after the winner of the Sharkey-Maloney fight. Rickard agreed; an announcement to the public followed.

With two days to go before the fight both men were on edge and anxious to get in the ring. Jack finished his final workout on the 17th and declared himself in the best shape of his career, saying that, "I believe my wind is even better than it ever was and I am satisfied with my condition. I was never better for any bout." Jack then added that the cut he had suffered was healed and that his fracture prone hands were stronger than ever. The ex-sailor then confidently predicted he would knockout his hometown rival.

Likewise, Jimmy wrapped up training on the 17th with light calisthenics. Afterwards, he gave his prediction on the fight. "I have his number. I can knock him out and I will. Sharkey may think he can take the fight to me. He won't. I'm going into him punching with both hands. I'll keep punching Jack and sooner or later he will go down."[69] With weeks of intense training over both fighters returned to their respective hotel rooms to await their final confrontation.

At 6:30 on the morning of the fight the sun was shining in all its glory and the sky was a clear blue. Some hours later however, it was pouring rain. As the rain continued its torrential downpour on the city, there was no let up in sight. Rickard, along with the New York Boxing Commission decided to postpone the fight for twenty-four hours. The decision was announced over the local radio stations and telegrams were sent to the all the major newspapers. For the thousands of Bostonians who had come to New York there wasn't much they could do but wait out the storm.

At the famous Astor Hotel, Jack stood in the lobby angered over the postponement and unhappy as he watched the rain pour down violently. In his usual tempestuous manner he called down a curse upon the weather. Disgusted and unable to relax, Sharkey headed over to Stillman's and had a light workout followed by a rubdown. Likewise, Jimmy Maloney was a bundle of nerves and energy as he paced back and forth in his hotel room. To help calm down he planned on donning a raincoat and going for a hike through Central Park. But his manager decided that a relaxing card game would be a better way to spend the dreary afternoon.

Twenty-four hours later the rain had stopped and the skies were clear. By 9:00 o'clock on the evening of May 20, over 60,000 excited fans had piled into Yankee Stadium to see the final climactic battle between two of

---

[69] "Maloney Says He Will Win Tomorrow," *The Boston Daily Globe*, May 18, 1927, pg.17.

Boston's biggest rivals. No longer was this a simple neighborhood rivalry; it was now a big-time show.

Back home in Boston a large crowd, numbering in the hundreds, had gathered outside of the *Boston Globe* headquarters. The excited mob of fight fans came together under the big horns of the *Globe's* public announcing system to listen to the live action broadcast. It was the largest crowd of fight fans to gather on newspaper row since Jack Dempsey took the title from the giant Jess Willard back in 1919.

By 10:00 both fighters were in the ring. To fight off the chill of the evening each wore a long thick robe. In their respective corners both men went over last minute details as referee Lou Magnolia introduced each man and announced their weights. Moments later both teams were called to ring center to receive the referee's instructions. Thick cigarette smoke from thousands of anxious smokers blew across the ring as Lou went over the particulars. Once done, the men returned to their corners to disrobe and await the opening bell.

A moment later a loud gong resonated throughout the excited arena. Both men came out fast jabbing and hooking, but quickly fell into a clinch. In close, Jack landed a short left to Jimmy's jaw just as the referee yelled, "Break!" Separated, Jack fired a fast jab as he came in low bobbing and weaving. In close, they clinched for a moment and then each man landed jolting lefts and rights as they struggled about the ring. Pushing Jack away, Jimmy shot out a long left that missed as Sharkey danced back on his toes. Pressing forward "Dynamite" Jim fired a powerful right followed by a flurry of punches from every angle. Amazingly, Jack dodged all of the blows with skillful head movement. The two then tied up and fought in close throwing short lefts and rights.

During the violent infighting Jack landed a short chopping left that split Jimmy's right eyebrow open; the wound started to pour blood immediately. A moment later the two were separated and circling each other looking for an opening. Jack sent in a jab as Jimmy countered with a big left hook that forced the ex-sailor to give ground. Maloney then pounded in another left to Jack's head just as Jack threw his own left that landed solidly on Jimmy's jaw. The two held momentarily, Jack danced back and then suddenly burst forward with a fast jab and a murderous right hand that barely missed as Maloney ducked and retreated.

Circling each other the rivals traded stiff jabs followed by each throwing a left hook that landed flush. A second later Jimmy shot a jab followed by a series of lefts and rights, most of which Jack avoided by bobbing and weaving. Jack struck back with a quick jab to Jimmy's face. The two then circled each other shooting out range finding jabs. They came in close with Jack landing a right hook to Jimmy's face. In return, Maloney deliberately hammered his left elbow into the right side of Jack's chin. Visibly angered

Sharkey struck back aggressively with a powerful left hook that smashed into Jim's jaw. Fired up after taking the punch Maloney shot in two jabs but neither of them landed on the elusive Sharkey. Jack then threw a jab as Jimmy put together a jab, right hand, left hook combination, but again none of the blows landed clean since Jack rolled with the punches and grabbed hold of his rival.

The two held for a short time until Jimmy pushed Jack back. Circling, each fighter threw light jabs that were short of their mark. Jimmy then rushed in and landed a solid right to Jack's body followed by a left hook that missed and a jab, left, right combo that the ex-sailor easily avoided by ducking low. Striking back, Jack threw two rapid jabs and a looping right that landed squarely on Jimmy's face. Shaken up, Maloney grabbed Jack and the two exchanged some quick uppercuts inside before being separated by the referee.

Once apart, Jack shot out a jab as Jimmy swung a big left hook that would have floored Sharkey had it landed. The momentum of the punch drove both men into the ropes where Jimmy unloaded several mean punches towards Jack's head. Once again Sharkey showed great skill by rolling with and dodging nearly all of Maloney's blows. A second later the bell rang ending the melee.

Both combatants came out jabbing and circling to begin round two. Suddenly, Jack leaped in with a hard right that landed flush on Jimmy's face. "Dynamite" Jim countered quickly with a smashing right to Jack's body. The force of Jack's leaping attack carried the two rivals into the ropes. In an instant the two were the center of a whirlwind of stabbing jabs and smashing hooks. Fighting at close range both fighters opened up with a barrage of hard lefts, rights and uppercuts. A moment later the battle shifted to the center of the ring as each man continued to rain down jolting shots to his enemy's head. Jimmy, being slightly more aggressive, forced Jack across the ring and up against the ropes. From there the two continued to trade short bruising hooks and eventually went into a clinch until pulled apart by the referee.

Jack, obviously aiming for Jimmy's bloodied eye, nailed his rival with a head-snapping jab directly on his cut. The punch sent blood splattering on both fighters as well as some ringside spectators. The action then slowed for a second as each man looked to find a spot to punch for. Seeing an opening, Jack let fly a stiff jab to Jimmy's chin. As Jack came forward bobbing and weaving Jimmy jabbed and threw an uppercut followed by a left hook that Sharkey ducked. Jack, continuing to bob and weave his way inside of Maloney's powerful jab, swung a left that landed with a thud on the side of Maloney's ribs. The two then backed off and reset for a new exchange.

Both fighters jabbed and circled each other, eventually ending up on the ropes in a clinch. Separated by Lou, the Boston slugger threw a jab that Jack deftly slipped. In return, Sharkey countered with a jab that nailed Jimmy and the two then traded a series of snapping jabs. Jimmy having no luck with his jab powered in a right hand that Jack rolled with followed by a left hook that landed on the back of Sharkey's head. Jack answered back with a bruising right hand to the ribs and a left that landed flush on the side of "Dynamite" Jim's temple. Caught up in the heat of battle, Jack violently forced his rival into the ropes with a hail of rights and lefts to the head just as the bell rang loudly.

Through a gray cloud of cigar and cigarette smoke the two rivals came out for round three. A second before the action was to begin Lou called a halt to adjust Jack's shorts, which were pulled up a little too high. A second later the two were jabbing, feinting and circling each other; eventually tying up. As they pushed each other away Jack drove home a short left to Jimmy's temple. In response Maloney jabbed twice at Jack's face. As they once again tied up Jack dug in two lefts to Maloney's ribs. Quickly, Lou stepped in and broke the pair apart. Once they were a few feet away Jimmy shot out a long jab but was unable to hit Jack's ever moving head. Bouncing on his toes, Sharkey danced around and shot out two fast jabs that smacked into Jimmy's face. Coming forward, Maloney struck back and connected with a left to Jack's body followed by a left jab that grazed Sharkey's face and an uppercut that the ex-gob slipped. Continuing to press forward, Jim came in crouching low and swung a left hook that Jack danced away from.

It was obvious at this point of the fight that Jack's greater speed and footwork as well as his bobbing and weaving style were giving "Dynamite" Jim fits. However, Jimmy continued his attack shooting out a nice jab as Jack came weaving toward him. The two then traded stiff jabs to the face and clinched. In close Jack threw an uppercut that landed on Jimmy's heart. Holding Sharkey tightly with his left hand, Maloney hit Jack hard on the back of the head with a hard right. "Break!" yelled the referee. A second later the two fighters backed off while trading jabs.

After quickly resetting, Jimmy rushed in and dug a hard left, right combination to Jack's body. At the same time Sharkey threw a short left hook to the side of Maloney's bloodied face. After a quick clinch, Jimmy shot out four jabs that Jack smartly avoided. Sharkey then bounced back on his toes as both fighters jabbed simultaneously. Jimmy followed his jab with a right hook, left hook, right, but again Jack rolled with the punches and none of them landed cleanly. Maloney then snapped Jack's head back with a strong jab. Angered, Sharkey came roaring back raining down hard lefts and rights to Jimmy's face.

A moment later they circled each other bobbing and weaving. Jimmy sent out two jabs that were short while Jack fired a fast one that snapped

Maloney's head back and sent blood and sweat soaring. Jimmy threw a wicked right that just missed as they came together and exchanged a series of fast blows. The two then jabbed and Sharkey rushed forward with a sweeping left that missed followed by a pulverizing right to the pit of Jimmy's stomach. The blow buckled Maloney's knees as he grimaced in pain and caused ringside observers to cringe when they heard the violent impact. By all accounts it was a fight changing punch. The blow visibly sapped much of Jimmy's strength and he never fully recovered from the damage it inflicted. Hurt, Maloney grabbed hold of Jack, but the two were separated quickly.

Pushed apart by the referee, Jack came forward stalking his rival. As Jimmy back pedaled the two traded jabs. Jack's jab was light but Maloney's landed solid, snapping Sharkey's head back violently. Jimmy followed with another jab as Jack looked to continue his assault on Jim's ribcage. Maloney then jabbed again as Jack jumped forward with a big left that blew by Jimmy's face, missing by just a fraction. The momentum from the punch forced the fighters into the ropes where they traded hard body blows. A second later they were apart, swapping combinations of hard punches in the center of the ring. There was terrific power behind each blow and it was apparent that both fighters were intent on doing maximum damage. After the spirited exchange they clinched momentarily but were pulled apart by the referee. However, at this point both warriors were consumed by the fire of battle and there was nothing that could keep them away from each other. They went right back to trading hard blows with each landing and taking their fair share just as the bell rang.

Round four started with both jabbing nicely, but it quickly turned violent. Jimmy came in low and landed a hard left to Jack's ribs followed by a left hook that found Sharkey's face as the two tied up. Pushing apart the two circled and jabbed. Suddenly, Jack sprang forward driving a left uppercut to Jimmy's belly that landed hard. Jimmy grabbed the back of Jack's head with his left hand and smashed two of his own uppercuts into Jack's chin just as Sharkey crashed a left to Jimmy's face. The force of the melee carried the fighters to a corner where they exchanged a whirlwind of hard shots for a few seconds.

A moment later they were out in the center of the ring throwing stiff jabs. Jack got the better of the jabbing contest as Jimmy was again finding Sharkey a hard target to hit. Suddenly both fighters opened up at the same time and started bombing away with terrific lefts and rights. Jack, on his toes danced back as Jimmy rushed in throwing wild lefts and rights aimed at the body. Jimmy's forward momentum forced Jack up against the ropes where the two held and wrestled until told to break.

On the attack as Jack boxed on his toes, Jimmy pressed forward landing a right, left to Sharkey's body. Grabbing Jimmy with his left, Jack landed a solid right uppercut that snapped Maloney's head back. Pushed apart by Lou, they exchanged fast jabs with Jack again landing the cleaner blows. Unable to out-jab Sharkey, Maloney rushed in landing a left and right to Jack's ribs. Quickly, Jack grabbed his foe to keep him from throwing anymore punches. Coming out of the clinch both men jabbed and opened up with clubbing lefts and rights to the head. Moving back, Jack bobbed and weaved as Jimmy threw several punches that missed. Seeing an opening Sharkey snapped out a fast jab that smacked into Jimmy's face. The two then exchanged several jabs; Jimmy's missed but Jack's landed clean.

Maloney, perhaps frustrated at being out jabbed, rushed in throwing a combination of blows. But again he found it difficult to land on Sharkey who was constantly bobbing and weaving and rolling with punches. Forced in close by Jimmy's attack, Sharkey smashed Maloney with two short lefts and pushed him up against the ropes where they tied up. After being yanked apart by the referee they circled and jabbed. Jimmy suddenly rushed in with a left and right aimed at Jack's head but missed both blows. Jack quickly returned fire and caught Jimmy with a punishing right to the chin followed by a perfectly timed left hook that dropped Jim to the canvas. Despite being put down hard the Boston slugger jumped right back up. A second later the bell rang ending the round. Maloney, bleeding from his nose, mouth and eye was a bloody mess as he headed to his corner. Jack, sensing that Jimmy was fading fast, strode confidently back to his corner.

Knowing he had Jimmy on the way out, Jack came out jabbing to start round five. Maloney returned with two jabs of his own and as they went into a clinch Jack nailed Maloney with a right uppercut to the body and a short chopping left hook to the jaw. As they came apart Jimmy shot out a jab. Avoiding the punch, Jack leaped in with a powerful left hook that caught Maloney clean on the side of the face, staggering the Boston fighter. In response, Maloney jabbed twice while Jack rushed in with a terrific right hand that connected with Jimmy's chin and drove him into the ropes. With Maloney pinned against the ropes, Jack unloaded a barrage of lefts and rights to his rival's head and body.

Stunned, Jimmy retreated away from his opponent while throwing out two jabs. Coming on aggressively, Jack came over the top with a sweeping right hook. The blow landed on the back of Maloney's head once again knocking him to the canvas. As Jack turned and headed towards a neutral corner, Jimmy sprang to his feet. Although hurt "Dynamite" Jim went on the attack. He grabbed Sharkey around the neck with his left and unloaded five right hands to Jack's body and face. Pried apart by the referee, Jimmy came forward, backing Sharkey up with a jab. Patiently, Jack relented, waiting for his moment to strike. Just as Jimmy came in Jack swung a terrific overhand right that crashed against Jimmy's temple. He followed the blow with a crushing left to the jaw and a looping right to Maloney's face that had all of his power and body weight behind it. Staggered, Jimmy fell to the canvas, his head coming to rest on the lowest rope. Incredibly, he turned over and managed to struggle to his knees but fell back down. Again, Maloney forced himself to rise. But as he gained his footing he was unsteady and could not balance himself. He fell back down and out at .52 seconds of the fifth round. Moments later he was lifted by the referee and his corner men and dragged back to his corner. Jack, exuberant over his win, walked around the ring with his hands raised, smiling.

Back in his dressing room no happier pair of men could be found than Jack and Buckley. Although ecstatic over the victory both were happy the fight was over. When asked by a reporter what he was going to do first, Jack replied, "I am going back to the hotel to see my wife, who has been in a room there for three hours. She wanted no company, and I am going right over to her. I am feeling fit. I will take a hot salt-water bath and go to bed, get up in the morning and drive home to see my two kiddies as soon as I can. Yes, it was a greater strain on my wife than me, and by her side I will stay."[70] Continuing after a barrage of questions that came faster than Maloney's punches, Jack had this to say about Jimmy. "I felt that if one man was made to order for me it was Maloney. That is one of the reasons that I was so cock-sure of victory. I planned my battle under the care of trainer Harry Kelley. There was not one thing I did not do. I kept popping my left, made Maloney miss and when I felt I had him at my mercy I let go everything I had and my right hand did the trick."[71]

"Now there's no one who knew it but I went into the fight with my spine strapped up. I had adhesive plaster placed on my back by Dr. Fraelich. I was squirming around in pain on the floor earlier in the day, but I was determined I would go into the fight and win as I said I would, by a knockout. I trained 29 days for the bout and am delighted that it is over." When asked if he was ever hurt Jack responded with, "Oh yes, Maloney is a good hitter but he only really hurt me once and I shook that off." After a dozen more questions Jack bid farewell to the press saying, "Bring the next man on. I will be ready after I take a rest."[72]

Rest is what Jack would need. His next opponent would be Jack Dempsey, "The Manassas Mauler," one of the most fearsome fighters that ever lived. And the fight would be one of the most controversial of all time.

---

70 "Victory Makes Sharkey logical Title Contender," *Boston Daily Globe,* May 21, 1927, pg.10.
71 Ibid.
72 Ibid.

CHAPTER 13
SHARKEY DEMPSEY, THE BUILD UP

Sharkey was a fighter who ran both hot and cold and gave erratic performances throughout his career. Nevertheless, his dismantling of Jimmy Maloney was Sharkey at his finest and indeed Jack was now at the peak of his physical powers. The win showed Jack's incredible boxing skills and underrated punching power. In addition, his victory showed just how good he could be when motivated. Over 60-years later, Jack would say, "I needed a cause to fight for." He had found that cause in Jimmy. With his knockout over his great rival, Sharkey had proven that he was the best of the contenders and the next logical challenger for Gene Tunney's title.

It was shortly after defeating Maloney that Jack gained his most famous nickname, "The Boston Gob." The name fit right alongside with "The Weeping Warrior" and "The Garrulous Gob." It's unclear as to who dubbed Jack with the moniker, but the earliest usage was found in newspapers in June of 1927, during the buildup to his fight with Jack Dempsey.

Two days after the fight with Maloney, Jack and Buckley visited Tex at his Madison Square Garden office. While there, Jack received a check (the first of two) in the amount of $49,288.16 and discussed the possibility of a match with either Tunney or Dempsey. Rickard made it clear that if Jack didn't get a fight with Dempsey he would get one with Tunney.

Arriving home from New York at 11:20 p.m. on May 22, Jack and Dorothy were surprised as they pulled up the long driveway. The outside of their house was adorned with red, white and blue decorations and there were about thirty friends and fans gathered on the large front porch. Under the direction of J. Edward Bulger of Cambridge and Jerry Buckley (brother of Jack's manager) the group of Sharkey admirers had worked all day to get the house ready for Jack's triumphant return. Once out of the car Jack shook hands all around and modestly thanked everyone for the warm reception and congratulations. The young couple then ran quietly upstairs, kissed their sleeping daughters and spent a few moments catching up with Mr. and Mrs. Pike, who had once again volunteered for babysitting duty.

For the next two hours Jack visited with his friends, talking about the fight, fishing and future bouts. Finally, at about 2:00 a.m. he wearily trudged upstairs and into his warm bed.

In South Boston just a few hours before Jack arrived home, Jimmy Maloney stepped off a train. Much to his surprise he found that over two thousand adoring fans had shown up to show their support and welcome him home. Overcome with emotion, Jimmy shook hands all around and was given encouraging hugs. "Gee, I never expected this," said a smiling Maloney. Finally, after sometime he made his way to his car. Standing on the running boards just before leaving, Maloney waved to his fans and said, "Boys, I thank you." Equally excited to have Jim home was his wife who said she was glad that the fight was over.

Following his battle with Sharkey, Jimmy continued to fight for another seven years. When he retired in 1934 "Dynamite" Jim had amassed a record of 50-18-2 with 22 knockouts and had defeated some of the finest fighters of his time. After retirement Maloney remained active in boxing as an instructor and referee. Although he never became heavyweight champion, Jimmy was always proud of his boxing accomplishments.

Jack and Buckley wasted no time trying to secure a fight with Tunney. In fact, even Gene seemed willing. On May 23, Tunney, who was at the Sharkey-Maloney fight, was interviewed and had nothing but good things to say about his challenger. "Jack Sharkey is a good a fighter. Sharkey is fast, clever and a hitter. He's just the type you can't lay back against, because he'll out point you. If you try to out point him he's liable to knock you out. I consider him the outstanding challenger for my title."[73]

Although Jack was looking to get into the ring with Gene, there was a lot of buzz circulating about a Sharkey-Dempsey fight. Rickard wanted to match the two fighters in a final elimination bout, with the winner getting a shot at Gene's title. On June 4, Dempsey sent a telegram to Rickard saying that he expected to finish up his training in the California mountains within ten days. He would then test himself with some intense sparring and if he feels that he can unleash the speed and power that brought him the title, he would then be more than willing to face Sharkey.

In mid June, Buckley was in Los Angeles with one of his fighters, Johnny Vacca. Vacca was taking on Newsboy Brown at the Olympic Auditorium. While in California, Johnny met up with Jack Dempsey to discuss a possible fight. The following telegram was sent by Johnny and printed in the Boston papers. "Talked with Dempsey, he has signed nothing with Rickard as yet, but he is ready to fight about August 1. I am waiting to hear from Rickard. Dempsey looks great."[74] The very next day, Tex announced officially that Sharkey and Dempsey would fight on July 21, 1927 at Yankee Stadium.

The announcement was followed by a statement from the former champ and released in the *Boston Globe* on June 16. "I'm glad the suspense is over," said Dempsey in regards to the ongoing negotiations through which he hoped to get a chance to regain the crown he'd lost to Gene. "I started my

---

73 "Tunney Selects Sharkey As Outstanding Contender." *Boston Globe*, May 24, 1927, pg.15.
74 "Dempsey to be Fit to Fight by August 1," *Boston Globe*, June 14, 1927, pg.22.

comeback training ten weeks ago and the daily progress more than satisfied my most skeptical friends. When I first started work it was for a return fight with Tunney. Since that time, Sharkey, through his decisive defeat of Jim Maloney, has earned the right to be considered a logical challenger for the heavyweight crown. Make no mistake, I am not underestimating Sharkey. Jack is a tough boy, vastly more dangerous that Tunney, but he is going to meet a tougher boy. I'm not boasting I'm simply stating facts. I'm in the best shape of my career."[75] The announcement of the fight caused so much excitement that just a day later there were already over a thousand requests for seat reservations. With such an early demand for tickets, Tex boldly predicted that the gate would climb past the $1,250,000 mark.

Dempsey arrived in New York on June 22 with his wife, actress Estelle Taylor. Their arrival was kept a secret and the couple was brought to their room through the hotel's kitchen to throw off the crowd of reporters that awaited the ex-champ's arrival. The next day Dempsey met with Rickard and quickly agreed to the terms that were offered. It was decided that Jack would receive thirty percent of the gate. And if he beat Sharkey he would get a guaranteed fight with Tunney. Following Dempsey's meeting with Tex, Sharkey and Buckley were next. Tex initially offered Sharkey twenty percent of the gate receipts; however, Buckley refused the offer saying that Jack deserved at least twenty five percent. Buckley and Tex eventually came to an agreement after two days of negotiations; Jack would receive twenty-two and a half percent.

On June 24, Sharkey arrived at Rickard's Madison Square Garden office. Knowing that he was going to meet Dempsey for the first time there, Jack had mentally prepared himself during the drive. By the time Sharkey stepped into Rickard's office he had his best tough guy face on and was ready to confront his enemy. A few moments later Dempsey came walking in. Much to Sharkey's surprise Dempsey greeted him warmly, with a handshake and a smile. Dempsey's demeanor completely upset Sharkey's plans to give his opponent "the stare down." Jack then complimented Sharkey on his recent victories and asked how his family was doing; Sharkey's tough guy glare quickly faded. A few minutes later the two were talking like old pals and signing the contracts for their big fight. Before a battery of bright, flashing cameras the contracts were signed and each fighter posted a $2,500 appearance forfeit.

With the signing out of the way, Sharkey headed out on a weeklong fishing trip to Spencer, Massachusetts before committing himself to the grind of getting ready to face "The Manassas Mauler." Dempsey on the other hand headed over to his training camp at Saratoga Lake. The White

---

75 "Dempsey Claims His Old Punch Is There," *Boston Globe* June 16, 1927, pg.13.

Sulfur Springs Hotel where he was staying was throwing a huge birthday party. His wife, along with dozens of friends was anxiously awaiting Dempsey so they could celebrate his 32nd birthday.

Before Mike Tyson, there was Jack Dempsey. Born William Harris Dempsey in Manassas, Colorado on June 24, 1895, Jack was one of the most ferocious fighters to ever lace on a pair of boxing gloves. He was famous for his ultra aggressive, bobbing and weaving fighting style and exceptional knockout punch. His ring wars are now the stuff of legend.

Jack began fighting as a teenager shortly after he left home around the age of 16. Known as "Kid Blackie," Jack fought in no holds barred fights in small mining towns and saloons around Colorado. From 1911 to 1916 the boy traveled and lived as a hobo, often riding underneath freight trains only inches from death. By 1919 Dempsey had battled his way to the top of the heavyweight mountain with wins over top contenders, Fred Fulton, Billy Miske, Carl Morris and "Battling" Levinsky. His reward was a shot at the world's heavyweight title held by the giant cowboy, Jess Willard. On a blisteringly hot July 4 day in Toledo, Ohio, Jack, who stood 6'1" and weighed in at 187-pounds met the 6'6½", 260-pound champion. Willard, despite being 37-years-old and not having fought in three years, thought he would easily beat his much smaller opponent; in fact, he was worried that he might kill Jack.

When the bell rang to start the fight the Pottawatomie Giant was woefully unprepared for Jack's vicious onslaught. Dempsey tore into the giant and dealt him one of the most severe beatings ever administered to a fighter. In round one, Jess was knocked down for the first time in his career and another six times before the round was over. Dempsey's savage attack continued throughout rounds two and three. When the bell rang to start round four Willard was a bruised and bloody mess, unable to continue the battle. The beating that Jess received was said to be tremendous. Some reports claimed that Jess had a cracked skull, a jaw fractured in thirteen places, a fractured eye socket, two broken ribs, eight missing teeth, a broken nose and multiple facial cuts. There is no doubt that the whipping Jack handed to Jess was severe; however, the reports concerning the damage may have been greatly exaggerated. A more conservative report has Jess with a cut and swollen left eye, a swollen left cheek, a split lip and some bruised ribs.

Thus began the rise of Jack Dempsey. He would go on to become one of the most famous and beloved sports icons the world has ever known as well as one of the all time greatest fighters.

Sharkey returned from his fishing trip on July 1. For the next five days he trained at Kelly and Haye's gym going through some punishing rounds with heavyweight Rocky Stone. On the last day of training before leaving for New York, Jack gave a quick interview saying, "I'll knock Dempsey out.

For the first three rounds I'll fight his heart out. And then he can worry about the last twelve, because I won't have to." Originally, Jack planned on training at Stillmans, which had become his regular hangout, because he felt the place lucky. However, Rickard offered Jack the use of the ultra modern gymnasium at Madison Square Garden. Despite his feelings about Stillmans, Jack accepted the offer. And then tragedy struck that threatened to cause the fight's cancellation.

On July 2, news surfaced that Dempsey's older brother, John Dempsey had shot himself to death after killing his wife. According to reports John, who suffered from mental depression and drug addiction, had been arguing with his wife, Edna. At some point the argument turned violent and ended with the shooting. The news brought an instant halt to Dempsey's training. Distraught over the tragedy, Jack and his advisor Leo Flynn drove over to Schenectady, New York with the terrible task of having to identify the bodies. With tears of grief streaming down his face Dempsey confirmed the identity of his brother and sister in-law. "It's terrible," said Jack. "But that's life isn't it."

Heartbroken over the death of his brother, Jack began the process of funeral arrangements. It looked for a time that the grief stricken ex-champion would have to call off the fight; however Dempsey insisted that he would return to training after the funeral.

Even though Dempsey remained adamant that he would not cancel the fight because of his brother's death, rumors persisted that the fight might be called off. And some people in Dempsey's camp felt that because of the interruption in his training he would not have enough time to prepare properly. To put all doubts to rest Dempsey conducted a closed door workout even though he had said that he would not return to training until after his brother's funeral. The workout came as a complete surprise to both the newspapermen and Dempsey's handlers and put to rest any uncertainty about whether or not the ex-champ wanted to fight. Although the workout was supposed to be private, a few reporters were able to gain a view of the sparring from the building's upper windows. What they saw was Dempsey mercilessly batter his sparring partners. One reporter said, "Jack swept around the ring in a fury and battered badly each man that faced him. All the pain and mental agony of the past two days seemed to well up in the ex-title holder as he faced his sparring partners and for five rounds the viciousness of the Manassas man killer ruled the tiny canvas battleground."[76]

---

[76] "Boxing in Savage Style Dempsey Tries to Shake Off Memory of Brother's Tragic End," *The Boston Globe*, July 4, 1927, pg.5.

Two days later it was reported that Dempsey was torturing sparring partners again. This time he sent the rugged New York middleweight Eddie McMullin flying through the ropes and into the laps of surprised reporters with a terrific left hook to the chin. The punch, said to have traveled no more than a foot, was so powerful that Eddie was left unconscious and had to be carried to his dressing room where he remained out cold for several minutes. After regaining consciousness Eddie decided to call it a day.

After a nine-hour drive from Boston, Sharkey and his wife arrived in New York on July 7. The challenger for the heavyweight title looked perfectly fit as he stepped out of his car and spoke with a group of newspapermen that had been awaiting "The Boston Gob's" arrival. "I feel fit and ready to fight now," said Sharkey. "I've put in quite a spell of training in Kelly's Gym in Boston, so I haven't been idle. I weigh 195-pounds. I won't weight much under that when I face Dempsey in the ring. And of course I'll win," added the Boston fighter with a laugh. With that, Jack and Dorothy hurried to their room to get settled in and await the arrival of Buckley and Jack's trainers, Harry Kelly and Tony Polazzolo.

The next day Jack, Harry and Tony headed to the gym and had a light workout. They also spent some time doing interviews. Sports writer Grantland Rice reported that Jack looked to be in great shape saying that, "In his bobbing, ducking, weaving, and side stepping Sharkey again showed the natural speed resources he has in feet, hands and body. He is one of the fastest of all of the big men, and his quickness of action goes up and down the length of his frame."[77]

Over at the Dempsey camp the ex-champ was working hard to recapture the form that won him the heavyweight title. Benny Leonard reported that he was surprised at how good Dempsey looked when sparring, saying that Jack still had his old punch and was hitting hard. However, he was not impressed with Dempsey's defense, which he was trying to improve.

Just a few days later Benny came out with another opinion of Jack's condition, saying that Jack didn't look sharp, was in need of real work and could not afford anymore lay-offs. "It looked to me, come to think of it, as if Jack wasn't seeing all of the openings left by his sparring partners. If he did he wasn't taking advantage of them and I know that Jack never saves a sparring partner."[78] Tex, who was among the spectators at Dempsey's workout, had a different opinion. He was impressed with Jack's fine physical condition as he tore into his sparring partners saying that,

---

77 "Sharkey Looks Good in Brief Workout," *The Boston Globe*, July 9, 1927, pg.5.
78 "Dempsey Sadly in Need of Real Work," *The Boston Globe*, July 9, 1927, pg.A20.

"Dempsey certainly looks better that he did at Atlantic City while training for the losing fight with Gene Tunney last fall."[79]

As if the drama of his brother death was not enough, news surfaced that Jack "Doc" Kearns, Dempsey's former manager was on his way to New York to pursue a lawsuit and collect money that Dempsey allegedly owed him. The news of Kearns' pending arrival gave some worry to the Dempsey camp. Dempsey's attorney Richard Mackey felt that Kearns might try and put a stop to the fight. In preparation for Kearns' arrival Mackey filed an injunction which put a stop to Kearns prosecuting any of the four suits he had against Dempsey, at least for the time being.

With just 10 days to go before the fight, news came out that Sharkey had been knocked down while sparring with Leo Gates. The report brought a grin to the ex-champion's swarthy face. "Gates put Sharkey down?"[80] asked Dempsey's advisor, Leo Flynn. "Well Dempsey will put him down and keep him there."[81] While Jack was happy about Sharkey being floored, Benny Leonard was a little concerned with Dempsey's preparation. He wrote about his concerns in his daily newspaper column saying that Dempsey looked to be in great condition. However, Benny thought that Jack's choice of sparring partners were a poor lot. "His sparring partners are all afraid of him," said Leonard. Benny then went on to say that he believed that Jack was not getting the type of sparring that he really needed to sharpen his timing and punch. Furthermore, he was still concerned that Dempsey was taking too many days off to play golf and rest.

Having heard that Sharkey's knockdown pleased the Dempsey camp, Buckley laughed the matter aside and said, 'We're glad that the Dempsey crowd is pleased about it. That's great news. Maybe it will give Dempsey a little more courage and he will put up a better fight than we expect. And that's what we want. The hotter the scrap the better it will be for Sharkey." Sharkey however was not happy with being dumped on the seat of his pants, even if it was just a trip. During the next day's workout Jack said there would be no more funny business. He then proceeded to tear into Leo Gates, the Mohawk sporting Indian, giving him a solid whipping for three merciless rounds. Sharkey then hammered Johnny Urban, eventually causing him to give up before the first session was over. Sharkey continued his rampage with a shellacking of Rocky Stone and a spirited session with Marcus Polo.

---

[79] "Rickard Impressed With Showing of Dempsey," *The Boston Daily Globe*, July 9, 1927, pg.A20.
[80] "Dempsey's Real Condition Has Experts Guessing," *The Boston Globe*, July 11, 1927, pg.7.
[81] Ibid.

Six days out Sharkey and his team felt supremely confident in terms of condition, so much so that the team decided to take a day off to rest and keep from going stale.

Many of the reports concerning Dempsey were not as positive. Several were saying that although Jack appeared to be hitting hard and looked to be in terrific shape, the ex-champ also looked slow and felt that he had gone stale. In fact, it was reported that light heavyweight Leo Gains had been let go after out boxing Jack and drawing blood from his nose. Middleweight Jack Herman was also let go; allegedly he was too fast and nearly knocked Dempsey out. Because of the negative press Jack decided to keep the remainder of his workouts private and stop training two days before the fight. In an interview just days before the match, Dempsey said, "I'll get him in the second. I'm ready for the bell and I wish I were going to the ring tonight."[82] He then predicted an early victory, saying his left hook would do it.

With the fight two days away, several predictions made their way into print. Jimmy Maloney's manager Dan Carroll picked Sharkey, saying, "I pick Sharkey to beat Dempsey in six rounds. It was my business to watch him when Jimmy and Jack were preparing to settle their differences. And I think Jack looks better mentally and physically than he has since he started his boxing career."[83] Former heavyweight champion and all time great James J. Jefferies also picked Sharkey. "I'd like to see Dempsey win against Sharkey but I can't figure it. Sharkey has speed, punch, and boxing cleverness. He has everything Dempsey ever had and something Dempsey hasn't got now, youth. Sharkey should win."[84] Top rated contender Paulino Uzcudun likewise went with Sharkey saying that Dempsey will tire and Jack will out box him. Rickard considered the fight a "toss up" and could not decide. A poll conducted that consisted of fighters, trainers, newspapermen and gym owners showed that 23 out of 38 picked Sharkey to win. Benny Leonard after having studied both fighters on numerous occasions finally picked Sharkey to win.

Both fighters ended their training on July 19, and the next day each gave interviews. Sharkey having previously said he would out box Dempsey, expressed a ton of confidence when he said that he would stretch Dempsey out on the canvas. "I'll knock Jack Dempsey out," boasted "The Boston Gob," "and I may even make a quick job of it. I know a lot of folks will say something about the bragging sailor doing his stuff again. However, some of the newspaper boys put the thing up to me and there's my answer."[85]

---

82 "Dempsey Promises to Win in the Second," *Boston Daily Globe*, July 17, 1927, pg.A1.
83 "All Sharkey Predicts Maloney's Manager," *Boston Daily Globe*, July 19, 1927, pg.10.
84 "Jefferies Sees Only Defeat For Dempsey," *The Boston Daily Globe*, July 19, 1927, pg.11.
85 "Sharkey Now Talks of Quick Knockout," *The Boston Daily Globe*, July 19, 1927, pg.1.

Likewise, Dempsey predicted that he would knockout Sharkey, saying, "I'll knock Sharkey out in two rounds. But if I don't, have no fear that my strength will not carry over the long rout. I'm in the finest shape of my career and I can bowl Sharkey over in the fifteenth as easily as the first."[86]

With the fight just hours away a series radio messages that were supposed to be confidential arrived to friends of Jack "Doc" Kearns. Kearns announced that the fight would positively not take place Thursday night. Kearns also wired the Dempsey camp. The message read, "Am arriving Wednesday morning and am assured of obtaining injunctions which will prevent the fight being held."[87] "Good lord, is the Doc going to start that all over again?" groaned Dempsey when he heard the news. As promised, Kearns arrived in New York but was unable to do much in terms of stopping the fight. In fact, he said he didn't want to stop the fight. All he wanted was to collect the $600,000 he felt Dempsey and Rickard owed him. When asked by sports writers who he thought would win the fight Kearns replied, "Jack is through. I pick Sharkey to win easily."[88]

At noon on the day of the fight Sharkey arrived for the official weigh in at Madison Square Garden. As blustery and confident as ever, Jack strode in and looked around. "Where's the big boy," he asked, refereeing to his opponent. Unknown to Sharkey, Dempsey had already weighed in and departed. "Is he afraid to meet me?" exclaimed Sharkey with a half sneer. Stepping on the scale Jack tipped the beams at 196-pounds. Dempsey had weighed 194½. With the weigh in done Sharkey returned to his hotel room to spend a little time with his wife and await the call to battle.

---

86 "Dempsey Asserts He Can Win as Easily in the 15th as the First," *Boston Daily Globe*, July 20, 1927, pg.12.
87 "Jack Kearns Wires Will Stop Fight," *The Boston Daily Globe*, July 19, 1927, pg.12.
88 "Dempsey Through, Say Kearns." *The Boston Daily Globe,* July 21, 1927, pg.12.

Jack in the Navy, Coddington Point, New Port Rhode Island, 1924. Courtesy of Jack Sharkey III.

Jack Sr, Jack Jr., Marilyn, Dorothy, daughter Dorothy.
Back Row: Dorothy's grandparents Mr. and Mrs. W.H. Pike. Below,
Dorothy, Jack, Mr. and Mrs. Pike, Jack Jr. Courtesy of Jack Sharkey III.

Jack, Dorothy and Ernie Schaff.
Courtesy of Jack Sharkey III.

Five miles away from Max Schmeling's camp, Mr. and Mrs. Ben Zukarskas of Binghamton, N. Y., admire photo of their son, Jack Sharkey.

Jack's parents admiring a photo of their boy. Below: Jack, Dorothy, Jack Jr. Courtesy of Jack Sharkey III.

Jack and his wife Dorothy.
Courtesy of Jack Sharkey III.

Jack and Dorothy.
Courtesy of Jack Sharkey III.

A dapper looking Sharkey.
Courtesy of Jack Sharkey III.

Jack Sharkey Jr.
Courtesy of Jack Sharkey III.

Jack with his good friend Ernie Schaaf and Jack Jr. Courtesy of Jack Sharkey III.

Ernie Schaff, Dorothy, Jack Jr., Marilyn and Jack. Courtesy of Jack Sharkey III.

Jack and his manager Johnny Buckley.
Courtesy of Jack Sharkey III.

Jack Dempsey and Jack Sharkey. Courtesy of Jack Sharkey III.

Signing to fight Primo Carnera May 12, 1933. Left to right front row: Jack Sharkey, Jimmy Johnston, Primo Carnera. Left to right back row: Johnny Buckley, Billy Duffy, Luigi Soresi (Duffy and Soresi were Carnera's handlers).

From left to right: Ernie Schaaf, Johnny Buckley, Jack Sharkey and Al Lacey in front of Toland's gym. September 5, 1931. Courtesy of Jack Sharkey III.

Jack taking a break with his trainer Tony Polazzolo.
Courtesy of Jack Sharkey III.

Jack while training.
Courtesy of Tony Triem.

Chuggin water after the Louis fight.
Courtesy Tony Triem.

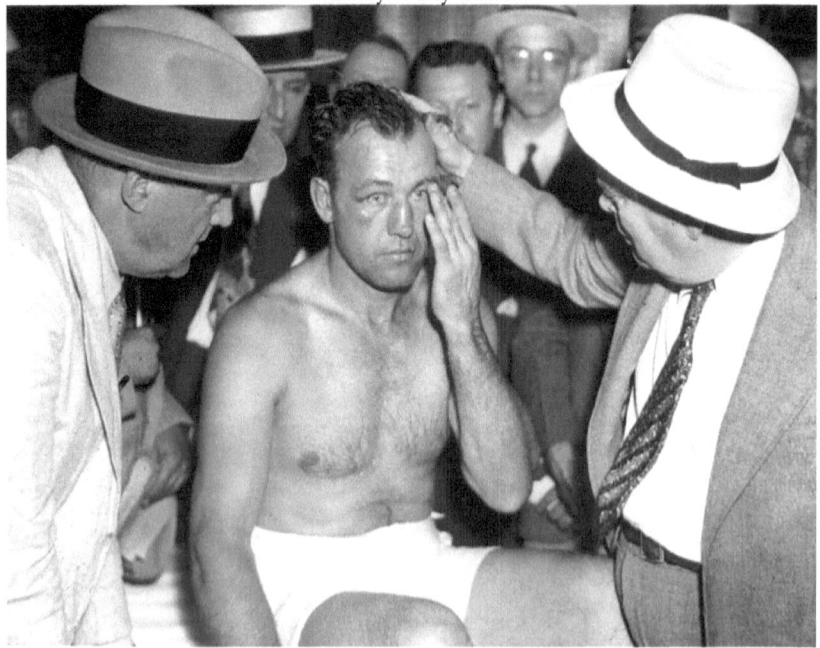

The aftermath of his fight with Joe Louis.
Courtesy of Tony Triem.

Jack while training.
Courtesy of Tony Triem.

Jack in battle gear prepairing for Schmeling. Courtesy of Jack Sharkey III.

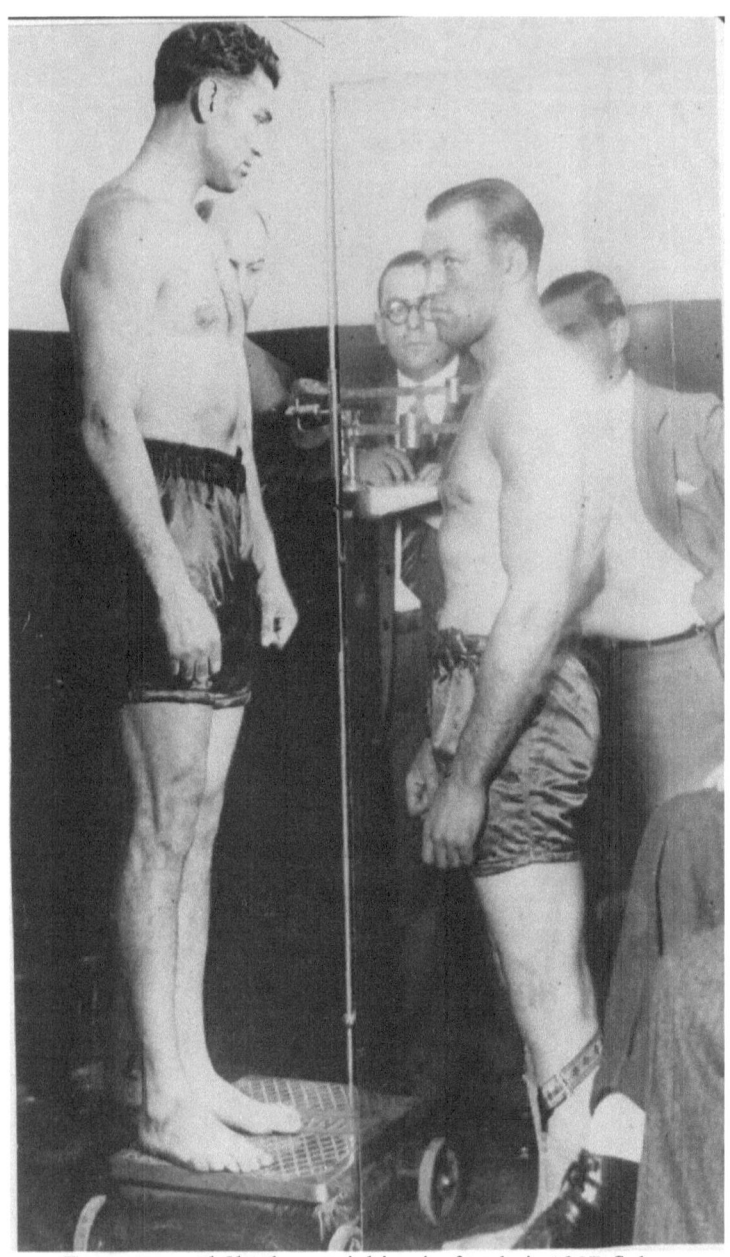

Dempsey and Sharkey weighing in for their 1927 fight.
Back row, unknown. Author's collection.

Jack's great rival, "Dynamite" Jimmy Maloney.
Courtesy of David Roak.

Tom Heeney.
Courtesy of John Gay.

Mickey Walker "The Toy Bull Dog."
Courtesy of John Gay.

"The Black Panther" Harry Wills.
Courtesy of John Gay.

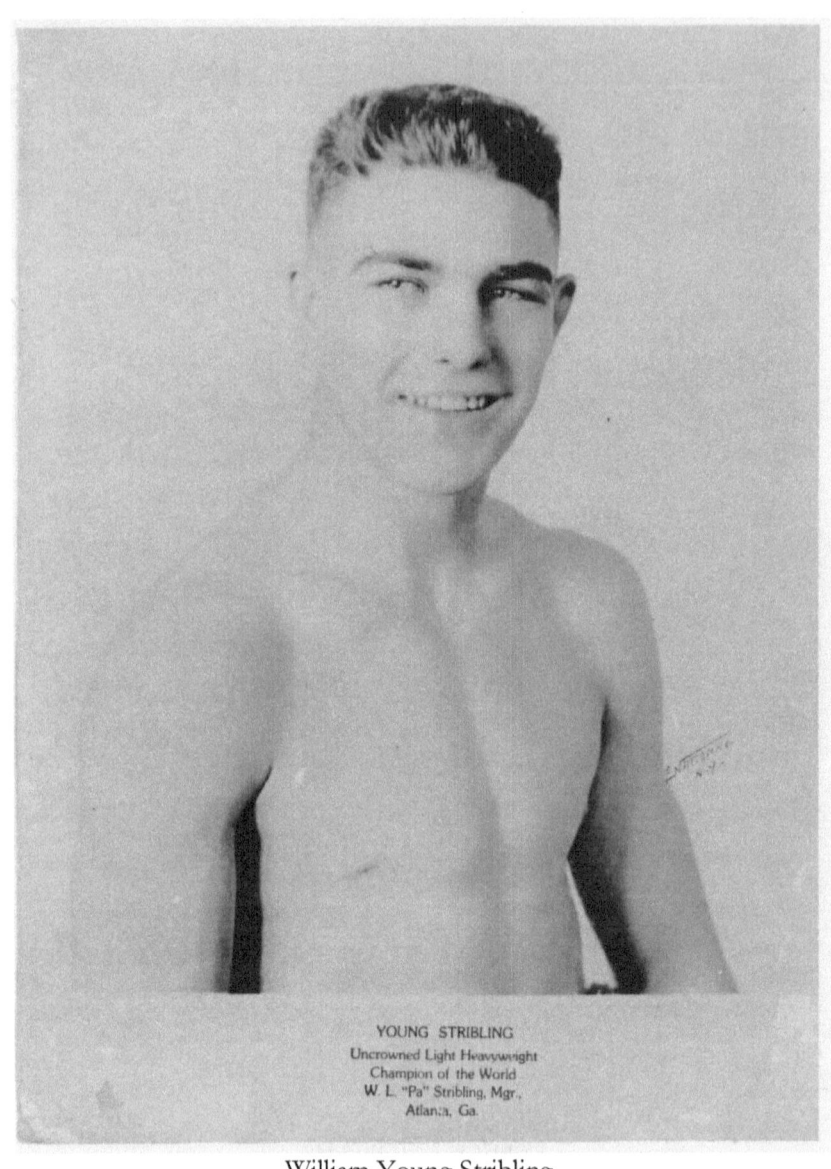

William Young Stribling.
Courtesy of John Gay.

Max Schmeling. Author's collection

Jack moments after wining the title. June 21, 1932.
Author's collection.

Jack and Max Schmeling shake hands moments before their first fight. June 21, 1932. To Jack's left, Tony Polazzolo, Al Lacy and Johnny Buckley. Author's collection.

Primo lands a left hook in his first bout with Jack Sharkey at Ebbets Field on October 12, 1931. Courtesy of Joe Page.

Referee Arthur Donavan counts Sharkey out in the sixth round of his title fight with Primo Carnera. June 29, 1933. Courtesy of Joe Page.

Jack Fly fishing, 1967.
Author's collection.

Ted Williams and Jack Sharkey Fly fishing at a sportman show. Below, good friends Ted and Jack. Courtesy of Jack Sharkey III.

Ted and Jack looking over some flies at a Boston sportman show, 1963. Author's collection.

Jack in the good old days.
Courtesy of Jack Sharkey III.

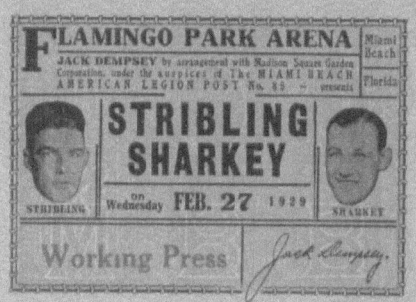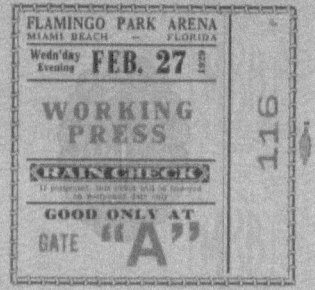

Tickets courtesy of John Gay.

Jack enjoying some hunting.
Courtesy of Jack Sharkey III.

Jack with the infamous gangster Al "Scarface" Capone.
Author's collection.

Jack with a record catch.
Courtesy of Jack Sharkey III.

Back row: actor Frank Morgan (the wizard in the Wizard of Oz) Jack Sharkey, Boston police Supt. Mike Crowley, Fred Astair, center unknown. Below: Jack Sharkey, unknown, Florence Chadwick, Micky Mantle, unknown. Courtesy of Jack Sharkey III.

Four generations: Jack Sharkey Sr., Jack Sharkey III, Jack Sharkey IV and Jack Sharkey Jr. Courtesy of Jack Sharkey III.

Jack Sharkey III at Jack and Dorothy's grave site.
Courtesy of Jack Sharkey III.

Jack and Dorothy's headstone.
Courtesy of Jack Sharkey III.

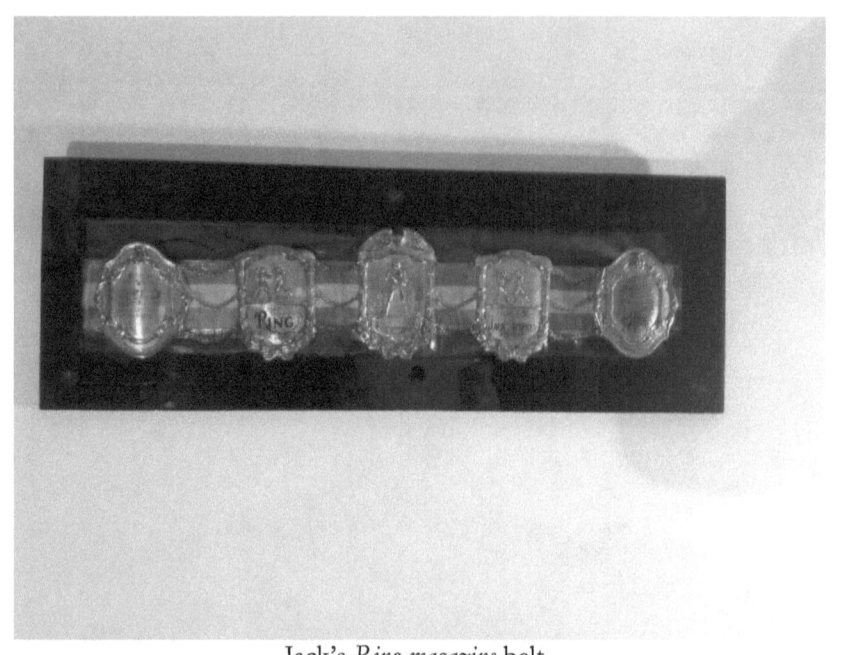

Jack's *Ring magazine* belt.
Courtesy of Jack Sharkey III.

Jack in 1987 at his home in Epping, NH.
Author's collection.

CHAPTER 14
SHARKEY-DEMPSEY, THE FIGHT

By 8:30, over 80,000 fanatic fans, caught up in what promised to be a great fight, had filled the bleachers at Yankee Stadium to overflowing. Collectively, they had paid over $1,100,000, making the gate the largest ever for a non-title fight. So big was the fight that the National Broadcasting Company announced that the radio hookup was the greatest on record with 51 stations connecting in a coast to coast and border to Gulf network. In addition, several foreign countries were expected to tune in as well. The hookup of 51 stations surpassed the previous record of 50 for the welcome home to Col. Charles A. Lindbergh.

With the preliminary fights out of the way Dempsey entered the ring first at about 10:00 o'clock. With a sweater draped across his shoulders to help fight off the chill of the evening, he walked across the ring waving; his admirers roared a hearty welcome. Minutes later Sharkey, wearing a long dark robe ducked under the ropes followed by his handlers; likewise Jack received loud cheers from his supporters. The two men met in the center of the ring in a show of sportsmanship and shook hands.

As both men stood in their corners going over last minute instructions, ring announcer Joe Humphries introduced heavyweight champion Gene Tunney. Before exiting the ring, Tunney went to Sharkey's corner, shook his hand and wished him luck. At Dempsey's corner Gene shook the ex-champion's hand and said, "Knock him out, knock him out."[89]

Following a quick meeting at ring center to go over referee Jack O'Sullivan's instructions the two teams returned to their respective corners; shortly thereafter the bell rang to start the action.

Both men came out fast and met in the center of the ring in a whirlwind of punches. There was no feeling out process, no circling and jabbing cautiously. Dempsey was an offensive fighter and Sharkey, when he set his mind to it, could play that game as well. To start things off, Sharkey threw a powerful sweeping left uppercut that missed. The two then came face to face and fell into a clinch followed by a furious exchange of punches. Dempsey got the better of the action by hammering in five short rights to Sharkey's body.

Pushed apart by O'Sullivan they went right back to fighting at close quarters. Dempsey dug in several hard smashes to Sharkey's ribs as the ex-gob returned fire with two left hooks that landed on Dempsey's chin. After

---

[89] "Tactics of Sharkey Fatal, says Leonard," *The Boston Daily Globe*, July 22, 1927, pg.11.

a quick clinch, Sharkey landed a sizzling left, right, left, combination to the head. Dempsey, bobbing and weaving bore in taking two more hard Sharkey lefts to the face. Once inside, Dempsey unloaded a half dozen thudding body shots followed by a left hook that snapped Sharkey's head back. Sharkey grabbed Jack but instead of trying to smother Dempsey's punches he threw two uppercuts that found Dempsey's jaw. The blows shook the ex-champion for a moment. Dazed, Dempsey wove about the ring under attack from Sharkey's right hands that were landing hard. Missing a long right, the bell rang a second later as Sharkey threw a right hand aimed at Dempsey's face. It had been an exciting, fast paced round that saw Sharkey out slugging the famed "Manassas Mauler."

Between rounds Dempsey's seconds worked on their fighter, while Sharkey lay back talking with Buckley, calm and confident.

The two warriors came out a little slower for round two. However, things quickly picked up right where they ended in round one. Sharkey rushed Dempsey with his fists flailing away. A solid right to the jaw drove the ex-champion into the ropes. Fiercely, Dempsey fought back landing a couple of hard blows to Sharkey's stomach. The two then held for a moment and wrestled about the ring. In close, they swapped body shots and Dempsey missed a wild left hook. Sharkey threw a left to Dempsey's head and forced him back into the ropes with a short right to the jaw. With Dempsey up against the ropes, Sharkey landed solid lefts and rights to Dempsey's face that staggered him. Dempsey fought back gamely with two left hooks to Sharkey's jaw. The blows forced "The Boston Gob" back out to the center of the ring where the two slugged it out in a violent exchange of leather. Looking a little tired after the heated exchanges, Dempsey managed to get in two solid left hooks to Sharkey's face just before the bell rang.

Just moments after round three began Sharkey opened a cut under Dempsey's left eye with a slashing jab. Feeling the blood run down his cheek, Dempsey responded with a left to Sharkey's stomach but took a left hook, right uppercut as he came weaving in. In close, Dempsey missed a short left but nailed Sharkey with two jolting rights to the jaw. Locked in a clinch Dempsey landed some bruising body shots. Pushed apart by the referee, Dempsey threw a fast uppercut as he came weaving in. Sharkey skillfully avoided the blow and caught the Manassa Mauler with a solid right to the chin. Pressing forward, Dempsey crowded Sharkey and wailed away at "The Boston Gob's" body. Sharkey, showing his willingness to mix it up pounded Dempsey's body with two lefts of his own that caused Dempsey to back up a little. Coming in to reengage, Sharkey suddenly slipped and fell to the canvas. The fall was ruled a slip as no blow was landed. A second later the bell rang ending the third.

Sharkey missed a wide right to start round four. Dempsey bobbed out of the way of Sharkey's follow up jabs and then rushed in. Back and forth the two struggled across the ring locked in a savage, fistic battle. First Dempsey would force Sharkey back with hard body shots only to be pushed back himself by Sharkey's ripping uppercuts. Coming out of a clinch Dempsey caught Sharkey with a left to the chin followed by a right to the ribs. In response, Sharkey shot out three stinging jabs to Dempsey's face, each one aimed at Jack's bloody eye. He then followed with a left hook, right hand combo that sent blood and sweat flying across the ring. With blood streaming down his face, Dempsey came in low and landed a short right to the body followed by a right uppercut that lifted Sharkey's head. Sharkey missed an uppercut of his own and took two left hooks from the ex-champ. Dempsey followed with a hard left that landed flush on Sharkey's jaw. The blow drove the ex-sailor into the ropes where the two pounded away in an intense exchange of body blows until the bell sounded.

The two combatants shuffled out to begin round five. Bobbing and weaving, they wearily circled each other. Dempsey skimmed Sharkey's chin with a left. Sharkey countered with stabbing jabs and caught Dempsey with a left hook to the nose. Stepping back, Sharkey spit out a mouthful of blood as Dempsey came rushing back in firing shots aimed at Sharkey's midsection. Sharkey met Dempsey's rush with a quick counter right uppercut. At close range, Dempsey landed two lefts to the ribs just as Sharkey landed a right to Jack's face that opened up a cut on his left cheek. The two fell into a clinch and wrestled for a few seconds until separated by the referee.

A split second later they went right back at it with Dempsey throwing rights to the body and Sharkey landing four fast lefts to the face. Pulling back, Dempsey hooked a hard left to Sharkey's face that wobbled the ex-sailor. Another left forced Sharkey to give ground, but he came roaring back in, slugging Dempsey hard just as the bell sounded.

Sharkey appeared to be the fresher fighter when round six began. At this point of the fight Dempsey was being busted up. His left eye was cut and nearly swollen shut, his right was cut and starting to swell as well. Nevertheless, at the start of the round he rushed in and missed a long left aimed at Sharkey's face. Sharkey fired back quickly, missing a left but connecting with a right hand solidly on Dempsey's jaw. Dempsey returned with a left that missed but nailed Sharkey with some hard body blows that forced Sharkey to use his arms to try and block the painful punches. To counteract Dempsey's blows Sharkey caught Jack with a counter right to the chin. A second later, the two were bobbing, weaving and circling each other looking for an opening. Seeing an opportunity, Sharkey threw a powerful uppercut that landed hard on Dempsey's jaw and lifted his head straight up. The punch shook Jack and was the hardest and cleanest blow of the fight so far. Despite being stunned, Dempsey came on. He pushed

Sharkey into the ropes and landed three punches to Sharkey's head a second before the bell rang.

Between rounds six and seven Dempsey was in bad shape. The tired ex-champion gulped water while his corner worked quickly to clean him up and administered smelling salt to revive their fighter.

Coming out for the seventh, both fighters were tired from the whirlwind pace of the previous rounds. But, despite their fatigue they met in the center of the ring and immediately began slugging. Dempsey, coming forward forced Jack up against the ropes as the two traded blistering punches. Sharkey fought his way off the ropes pushing Dempsey back out to the center of the ring. Mercilessly, Dempsey kept punching with ripping uppercuts and fierce body blows. While doing so, he drove in two blows, both landing well below Sharkey's belt line. Sharkey, usually the most vocal of fighters when it came to complaining had said nothing up to this point about being hit low repeatedly throughout the fight. Now, finally fed up with Dempsey's dirty tactics Sharkey turned to the referee to voice his complaint. At that moment, with his guard down, Dempsey struck with the instinct of a man who had been fighting since he was 16-years-old. He threw a short, powerful left hook that caught "The Boston Gob" flush on the jaw. The blow had all of "The Manassas Mauler's" famed power behind it and lifted Sharkey clean off his feet. Jack crashed to the canvas clutching his groin in agony as the referee counted him out.

Instantly, thousands in the crowd rose together. Overcome with joy over Dempsey's victory they threw their hats into the air and cheered loudly. Dozens of cameras flashed and smoked as the moments were forever caught on celluloid. As thousands of hats came down like rain over the ring, thousands more sat in stunned silence wondering why O'Sullivan had not called foul when Dempsey had clearly landed two low blows.

Buckley was first into the ring followed by Harry Kelly. Together they lifted their man and dragged him to his corner while Dempsey paraded around the ring with his arm raised in victory.

Cries of foul and controversy quickly followed the fight and were splattered all over every newspaper for weeks. Sports columnist Grantland Rice, who was ringside, wrote, "There must have been five or six punches delivered below the belt before the seventh round came on." Speaking of the punches that ended the fight, Rice said, "As the seventh opened, Dempsey who had been hitting low all night circled Sharkey and as a left flashed out they crashed together. They started slugging away and then Dempsey drove a left hook at least eight inches below Sharkey's belt line. It was one of the most palpable fouls any crowd ever looked upon. As Dempsey drove in his low left he followed with another, at least ten inches below the belt line, more clearly foul than the first punch. As the second foul blow landed, Sharkey bent over and half backed away to claim foul. As he turned his head slightly Dempsey in a flash struck Sharkey on the point of the jaw with a short left hook and the sailor fell flat upon his face, extended at full range"[90]

Giving his own thoughts on the fight, Sharkey, playing the part of newspaper writer, wrote about his feelings in the *Boston Daily Globe*. "All that I have to say is I'll have my day. Jack Dempsey won, and let him have all the credit in the world, but I don't think he is entitled to think that he is the better man if tonight's work is the best he can do. If ever a man was deliberately fouled then I was by the ex-champion and though I hate to say it, I think he struck me low in the seventh to save himself. I know I had him in bad shape and that his blows didn't mean a thing to me until he had me weakened by a lifting right to the groin. But the pain from this blow was so fierce that I doubled up and as I turned to the referee, thinking he would step in and disqualify Dempsey, Jack stepped in and swung a left to my jaw with everything he had left. It was not the shot to the jaw that kept me down, however, but the pain of the right below the belt line that had me so weakened my legs wouldn't straighten out."[91]

Benny Leonard, who also sat ringside, gave his observation of the controversial ending. "The seventh round had gone about 30 seconds when Dempsey reached out with a straight right and hit Sharkey low. Sharkey bent forward a bit with agony in his face, dropped his guard and made a motion of complaint to referee O'Sullivan. There was no question about the blow being low. From where I was sitting Sharkey was facing me and I could see the blow struck."[92]

The day after the fight Dempsey quietly slipped out of New York. The reason for his secret departure was due in large part because of a warrant for his arrest held by Pennsylvania officials. Apparently, Dempsey was charged with striking a woman during a melee at ringside after his fight with Tunney. As Jack hustled into his automobile he was a little indignant about the claims of a low blow, and said to the group of reporters, "I never struck a fairer blow in my life. I could feel my right bury into Sharkey's body just under his ribs and I knew he was gone. He just slumped and a left hook to the jaw finished him."[93]

Three days after the fight the controversy over the low blows raged on. To try and put matters to rest a meeting was called. The group included John Buckley, Tex Rickard, referee Jack O'Sullivan and one of the two

---

[90] "Finish Queerest in all History of Fing," *The Boston Daily Globe*.
[91] "Cry of Foul Raised by Beaten Fighter," by Jack Sharkey, *The Boston Daily Globe*, July 22, 1927, pg.1.
[92] "Tactics of Sharkey Fatal, Says Leonard," by Benny Leonard, *The Boston Daily Globe*, July 22, 1927, pg.11.
[93] "Dempsey Scurries Away in Secret," *The Boston Daily Globe*, July 23, 1927, pg.8.

official fight judges, Charles F. Matheson as well as James A. Farley, chairman of the New York State Athletic Commission.

As the film played (in slow motion) Rickard said, "There goes the right. It lands on the pit of the stomach. The blow as I see it is fair. Now the left goes to the jaw. That's the knockout. All very plain."[94] A few feet away Buckley declared, "There it goes, foul! Dempsey fouls Sharkey twice as plain as day."[95] He went on to add that Jack had been in severe pain after the fight and throughout the night. In addition, Buckley added that Sharkey had some swelling and had to apply an ice pack to his groin. Despite his best efforts to get the outcome of the fight overturned the ruling was not going to be changed. "Whatever the merits of the controversy, the decision stands," said Chairman James Farley. He then added that referee O'Sullivan made the decision, "as he saw it." James then pointed out that the Commission had never overturned a decision and that O'Sullivan is one of the most competent and efficient referees that the Commission employs.

In defense of himself O'Sullivan said that throughout the fight both fighters were guilty of throwing low blows and that he warned both of them. However, O'Sullivan did admit that Dempsey landed a low punch on Sharkey's thigh/leg just before he landed a punch to the solar plexus, followed by the left hook that dropped Sharkey. O'Sullivan added that he did not consider the punch damaging, nevertheless he quickly warned Dempsey saying, 'Watch your punch, Jack." Realizing that there were two Jacks, he added, "I'm talking to you, Dempsey."[96]

60-years later, Sharkey, reminiscing about the fight, said, "He broke every rule of the prize ring. He'd do everything to keep you on the floor. Kick you even…why, he hit me in the nuts all night long." A moment later a thin smile played across Sharkey's face as he relived the moment. When asked if he was bitter, Jack said, "Nah, he saw an opening and he took it. Besides, when people talk about that fight they still think of Jack Sharkey."

To this day the debate over the fight is still a subject of intense controversy.

---

94 "Word War Over Knockout Blow Rages Unabated," *The Boston Daily Globe*, July 23, 1927, pg.8.
95 Ibid.
96 "Dempsey Warned to Stop Hitting Low," *The Boston Daily Globe*, July 23, 1927, pg.8.

CHAPTER 15
A CONTENDER NO MORE

A week after his fight with Dempsey, rumors were flying all over New England that Jack Sharkey was dead. *Boston Globe* telephone operators were kept busy answering phone calls from concerned fans and denying the rumors. The gossip of Jack's death started when he visited St. Elizabeth's hospital. After being examined by Dr. Martin Spellman it was found that Jack was suffering from intestinal hemorrhages. Furthermore, Martin stated that, "Sharkey has several severe bruises on the right groin. He has had discharges of several ounces of blood and will be under treatment for 10 days more."[97] In response to questions Dr. Spellman said that it would be impossible for body punches to have caused such a reaction and he attributed it solely to foul punches delivered by Dempsey.

Resting at home after his examination, Jack agreed to a phone interview. He refused to say much about the injuries, except that he was feeling well. "What's the use of saying anything? The story is two days old, it all happened Sunday and everything is all right now, except for a few treatments in the hospital later in the week. If I said anything everybody would think I was squawking."[98] During the incident Jack was besieged with calls which pleased him far more than any of the victories he had won in the ring. "It certainly is nice to get all these calls. What a great feeling to know you have all these friends."[99]

Following the Dempsey fight Buckley had Jack set up to fight Paulino Uzcudun. Unfortunately, Paulino lost to Jack Delaney in August of 1927 and the fight was canned. Buckley quickly rebounded and by October had a November 18 match lined up with New Zealand fighter Tom Heeney, aka "The Hard Rock from Down Under." But, during training for the fight Jack broke his left hand when he hit the top of his sparring partner's head. The injured hand forced a cancellation of the match, and sidelined Jack for weeks. The injury also cost him an estimated $80,000 in purse money. In all, "The Boston Gob" would go nearly six months without a fight. This was a long time for a fighter who typically fought one to two times a month.

During his time off the big event in boxing was the much-anticipated rematch between Gene Tunney and Jack Dempsey. Like everyone else Sharkey was caught up in the excitement of the big fight; there were even rumors that Sharkey was helping Gene. However, Sharkey denied these

---

97 "Sharkey Death Rumors False," *The Boston Globe*, July 27, 1927, pg.1.
98 Ibid.
99 Ibid.

rumors saying, "After I had talked to Gene at the Cedar Crest Country Club all sorts of rumors began to float around that I had been giving the champion some hot dope on Dempsey's style of fighting. That's all bunk. Gene and I just had a pleasant little chat and Dempsey's name wasn't mentioned once. My position on the fight is absolutely neutral."[100] Jack's position on the fight may have been neutral, but after spending time at both fighters' camps and observing each man train he picked Dempsey to win.

On September 22, 1927 Jack Dempsey attempted to regain his crown from Gene Tunney. The fight unfolded before a massive crowd of 104,943 people who paid a staggering $2,658,660. For the first seven rounds the bout was a replay of the first match. Tunney boxed brilliantly, while Dempsey, always coming forward, pursued his elusive foe looking to trap him in a corner or along the ropes where he could unleash his power shots. In the seventh Jack got his opportunity. Forcing Gene back with a combination of punches, Gene's backward motion was stopped for a second when he backed into the ropes. A second was all "The Manassas Mauler" needed. Jack unloaded a barrage of fast punches that landed on Gene's chin and the ex-marine went down. The referee instantly pushed Dempsey away and motioned him to a neutral corner. Dempsey however, did not go directly to a neutral corner. Instead he stood in the corner near Gene. This prompted the referee to again motion Dempsey to go to a neutral corner. Finally, realizing what the referee wanted him to do, Dempsey complied. By then several seconds had already elapsed, seconds that were helping the dazed Tunney recover.

After corralling Dempsey, referee Dave Barry turned to Gene and started his count. He was supposed to start it to match the timekeeper's count, which was at four or five, instead he started at one. When he reached nine Gene rose, however Tunney had actually been down for fourteen or fifteen seconds. Once up, Gene had recovered enough of his wits to get on his bicycle and stay away from the rampaging Dempsey. Boxing smartly, Gene lasted out the remaining three rounds and was awarded a unanimous decision. The fight, famously known as, "The battle of the long count," would go down in history as one of the most controversial of all time. The question as to whether or not Gene could have beaten the count is argued to this day.

By late December Jack's hand had healed and he was cleared by the New York State Boxing Commission to meet Tom Heeney. The new date for the fight was January 13, 1928 at the famed Madison Square Garden. During the build up for the fight it was reported by Tex Rickard that the

---

100 "Sharkey Denies Helping Tunney, by Jack Sharkey," *The Boston Globe*, September 18, 1927, pg. A20.

winner would likely get a shot at Tunney. This news had a big impact on both fighters and each was expected to throw everything they had into the fight.

Before a crowd of 16,948 people Sharkey entered the ring an overwhelming favorite at 3-to-1 to defeat Tom. According to all reports, Sharkey possessed far more boxing skill than Heeney who was described as a plodding, short armed slugger, although very durable. Being the more skillful fighter it was expected that Jack would beat Tom. But, as he had shown in the past, Sharkey could look spectacular in one fight and average in the next.

The fight started off with some excitement when in the first minute Tom caught Sharkey with a big right to the jaw that turned Jack's legs to rubber for a few moments. After recovering, Jack boxed well and edged out the round with the use of his jab. Sharkey then went on to take round two and at one point had Heeney in trouble when he landed a smashing overhand right, however his momentum ended there.

Heeney came back to take the third handily as Jack inexplicably let off the gas. Tom hurt Jack with a big right cross halfway through the round and just before the bell clanged he nailed Sharkey with a succession of lefts and rights that had the ex-sailor covering up. Tom kept up the pressure in the fourth and ripped a cut under Jack's left eye after landing a right cross. He then concentrated his attack on Jack's body and won the round easily.

The fifth saw Heeney hurt Jack with a big left hook followed by a terrific right cross that was described as the best punch of the fight. The blows staggered Jack and sent him into the ropes, nearly putting him on the canvas. Tom followed up with a right but Jack took the blow and survived the remainder of the round.

Heeney was again on top in the sixth and had Jack on the defensive by crowding the ex-sailor and hooking lefts and rights to the body. After one particularly hard body blow, Jack's legs buckled under him and he staggered into the ropes. Not wanting to be pinned to the ropes Sharkey fought back savagely. He hammered several punches to Tom's face and head, but "The Hard Rock from Down Under" seemed impervious to the punishing blows.

The seventh and eighth were about even with neither fighter doing much but clinching and missing with big right hand punches. Jack gained some momentum near the end of the eighth and scored well with a blinding assortment of rights and lefts to Tom's head just as the bell rang. His momentum continued in round nine and he scored several times with solid body shots that appeared to weaken Tom. In the tenth Sharkey continued to improve; his vaunted foot works, jab and left hooks working in perfect unison. However, despite his fine display of coordination, Sharkey fell flat on his face and nearly out of the ring when he missed a wild right hand swing.

In the eleventh both men clinched a lot and fired short punches during mostly boring infighting. Heeney finished the round with a rally and had the crowd screaming when he caught Jack with a blistering volley of punches. The blows sent "The Boston Gob" staggering around the ring on the defensive. The twelfth was a continuation or the eleventh. Again the two clinched and spent most of the round hammering away with their free hands. The referee tried several times to separate the two but they would invariably return to holding. Once again, near the end of the round, Tom suddenly opened up landing three head-snapping uppercuts. Staggered, Sharkey again went on the defensive as Heeney tore after him with a fierce barrage of short-armed punches. Luckily for Jack the bell rang a few seconds later, ending the fight.

When the fight was declared a draw the crowd roared their disapproval. Most of the fans in attendance thought that Tom clearly deserved the win. The next day the *Boston Globe* reported, "It was a close fight from start to finish, and a shock to the critics who had installed Sharkey as a heavy favorite, as well as a disappointment to those expecting the bout to develop an outstanding contender for Gene Tunney's crown."

Sharkey's draw with Heeney was a disappointment to Tex; in fact, he was disappointed with both fighters. Tex was hoping to get a dominant win from one of the two so he could build excitement for a Tunney fight. With the draw he was now back at square one. His plan now was to put together a do or die elimination tournament. But first, Tex wanted a third fight between Tunney and Dempsey, in spite of Dempsey insisting on retiring. His master plan was to have Tunney and Dempsey square off in June or July. The winner would then meet Sharkey, in a fall match, if Sharkey could rebound with a win in his next fight. If Sharkey were to lose his next fight, plan B would be to match the Dempsey-Tunney winner against one of the other top contenders for a fall match. However, even the best thought-out plans have a way of getting messed up.

As it turned out Tex's do or die elimination tournament pitted Jack Delaney against Tom Heeney and Sharkey against Johnny Risko. Delaney and Heeney met at Madison Square Garden on March 1. After what was described as a slow 15-round battle Tom out pointed Delaney and was awarded a popular decision.

Sharkey and Risko followed eleven days later on March 12, at the same venue. Having already defeated Risko back in 1925, Jack came into the fight a favorite. And having trained at Stillmans, Jack's lucky gym, Sharkey was confident of a victory. However, 15-rounds later he was handed a loss.

The next day the morning papers read, "Boston Jack Sharkey's champion hopes went glimmering out in Madison Square Garden tonight when he was out-pointed and outfought by Johnny Risko of Cleveland. For 15-rounds he boxed with the mid-western scrapper, now and then throwing in hard, sharp, clean-cut blows and when his defense was forced by the aggressive Johnny, hammering away at the body. But Risko forced the fight constantly boring in with wild rushes and throwing punches to the body with abandon. Risko recklessly invited blows that have rocked bigger and stronger men, yet they were not able to hammer down the iron, desperate resolution that finally brought him victory."[101] The papers went on to claim that Jack was through as a contender. And that his loss settled two hotly disputed points to the satisfaction of most experts. "(1) That Jack could no longer "take it" lending color to the view that the Boston sailor could be put down as another victim of Jack Dempsey's vicious body punches. (2) That if there had been any undiscovered schemes to boost Sharkey into a title fight with Gene those plans had now fallen completely apart."[102]

Sharkey's loss to Risko essentially eliminated him as a challenger for Tunney's title. And because Dempsey decided to retire for good, Tex was unable to get a third Tunney-Dempsey match. Still in need of an opponent for Tunney, Tom Heeney got the call and negotiations began. As for Sharkey, he would prove that he was far from through. "The Boston Gob" would bounce back with a vengeance and go on a seven fight win streak. His impressive victories would earn him a shot at the heavyweight title, a fight that would end in typical Sharkey fashion with massive controversy.

---

101 "Risko Winner by Safe Margin, by Roger Batchelder," *Daily Boston Globe*, March 13, 1928, pg.1.
102 "Sharkey All Done, New York verdict," *Daily Boston Globe*, March 14, 1928, pg.26.

CHAPTER 16
DELANEY

Sharkey's rise to the title began when he signed to fight ex-light heavyweight champion Jack Delaney on April 30, 1928 at Madison Square Garden. Like Sharkey, Delaney was hoping a victory would earn him a shot at Tunney. Although no more than 175-pounds, Delaney carried one punch knockout power in his right hand. Furthermore, he was a master boxer and an artist in the ring.

On July 16, 1927, Delaney won the light heavyweight championship of the world by defeating Paul Berlenbach. From there he went on to defend his title two times. He then decided to relinquish his crown and jump into the heavyweight division; with the goal of getting bigger paydays and capturing the title. As a heavyweight Delaney was relatively successful. However, his lack of ruggedness against the big boys kept him from becoming a serious threat to the title. By the time he met Sharkey, Delaney had a record of 6-3 as a heavyweight.

On April 17 Sharkey left for New York to complete his training at Gus Wilson's training camp, without a trainer. Just a few days prior word leaked out that Jack and his trainer Harry Kelly had parted ways. Kelly, typically regarded as one of the best trainers and handlers of boxers had been in charge of Jack's conditioning since before his third fight with Maloney back in 1925. The break between the two could be traced back to the Dempsey fight when Sharkey tossed aside Kelly's carefully arranged plans and went out to fight Dempsey. Kelly criticized Jack in no uncertain terms after the fight, and his criticism so angered Jack that the separation from Kelly was almost a certainty. So it was decided after Jack's loss to Risko that Kelly's services would no longer be needed. Nevertheless, Kelly said that he and Jack were parting on the best of terms. And in large measure Jack had always been his own trainer and had regularly refused to follow instructions.

Jack also had another reason for wanting to split with Kelly. He felt that over the course of his last couple of fights he had become too much of a stand up fighter. And that he wanted to recapture the bobbing and weaving style of fighting that made him famous. Jack believed that much of his success in the ring was due to his unorthodox style of fighting taught to him by the featherweight fighter Abe Friedman. "I'm going to roll and weave and bob. I'll throw overhand rights and do as I please. I'll get myself into condition and see what the effect is."[103]

While Jack was preparing to meet Delaney, Tex Rickard officially announced that New York would host the heavyweight clash between Gene Tunney and Tom Heeney. The fight would be at Yankee Stadium on July 26, 1928.

Just a few days out from the fight Sharkey was looking fit and expressed a lot of confidence saying, "I am in fine shape. I am not bragging when I say that I am supremely confident that my showing against Delaney Monday night will prove a revelation."

"It will not be 'just one of those things'," chimed in Johnny Buckley. "Anyone who saw this afternoon's workout would be convinced that a new Jack is about to enter the ring."[104]

As was usual for Delaney he was hidden away in Bridgeport, Connecticut in a place described as "stuffy" by famous fight trainer Jimmy De Forest. The reason for the seclusion was because of Delaney's drinking problem. By training away from the big cities, there were fewer temptations. Furthermore, while training Team Delaney had a strict no liquor allowed rule. In spite of the rule, Delaney had at previous times, while training, disappeared for a day or two on a drinking bender. If alcohol was an issue during his training for Sharkey, De Forest did not report it. In fact, he said that Delaney looked lively in his sparring sessions. After spending time at both camps, De Forest gave his prediction, picking Sharkey by a knockout. "Yes sir Sharkey ought to win. But then, the big Gob should have won certain other fights, but he didn't."

The day before the fight Jack was in high spirits. He expressed his thoughts in a special dispatch to the *Boston Globe* that he wrote. It read, "Not since the time that I fought Wills have I trained in the open and I am beginning to think that my indoor training for the later fights had a great deal to do with my slowing up once I got into the ring. While I have been confident and often over confident, I am judging my present status by my physical condition days before my fight with Jimmy Maloney last May. I have never felt better and the open air has been responsible. There is one important thing that you can say and that is that I am going to fight my own fight on Monday night. I am down to 191 and I think that I will enter the

---

103 "Jack Sharkey Parts With Kelly, Will Train Himself," by David F. Egan, *The Boston Globe*, April 18, 1928, pg.6.
104 "Sharkey Putting on Finishing Touches," by Roger Batchelder, *The Boston Globe*, April 28, 1928, pg.8.

ring at that weight. This is going to be my own fight and I can promise you that I will knockout Delaney, I've got to."[105]

This fight was looked at as do or die for both men. The winner would go out to the Sun, while the loser would go at once into the ranks of the second raters. Coming into the fight Jack was the bettering favorite. At 192-pounds he held a 14-pound weight advantage over the 178-pound Delaney, along with a height and reach advantage. Entering the ring Jack was met by a mixed reception of cheers and boos. The handsome Delaney, on the other hand, was met by an enthusiastic ovation from his fans, especially his female fan base known as "Delaney's screaming mammies."

In 73 seconds it was over. From the moment the bell rang to the fight's decisive ending it was action that had everyone holding their collective breath as the drama unfolded. The moment the opening bell clanged, Sharkey sprang from his corner with a mad rush. Delaney, caught off guard, could do nothing but try and ward off Jack's dynamic attack. Sharkey missed a murderous left by an inch and a right cross by a foot. Jabbing, Delaney retreated before Jack's furious two fisted attack. Sharkey landed a long straight left that pushed the ex-light heavyweight champ back into the ropes. A follow up roundhouse right nearly floored Delaney.

Shaking off the effect of the punch Delaney tried to get a moment of reprieve by clinching, but Sharkey refused to be held. Pushing his opponent away, Jack drove in a powerful short left that caught Delaney on the side of his face followed by a clubbing right to the jaw that sent the desperate Delaney to the canvas. A look of pain came to Delaney's face as he rose to his feet. Cleared to continue by the referee, Delaney lashed out with an ineffective jab. Sharkey easily slipped the punch and threw a right uppercut that started from the floor and finished on the point of Delaney's chin. The powerful blow sent Delaney to the canvas groping in the resin dust. Lou began the count. By nine Delaney had incredibly staggered to his feet. Jack, who had been pacing like a caged beast while the seconds were being counted off, charged back into battle. The first uppercut lifted Delaney's head and split his bottom lip wide open sending a spray of blood splattering across the ring. The second, delivered with all of Sharkey's considerable power lifted Delaney clean off his feet and sent him crashing to the canvas.

Face down and bleeding from his mouth and ear Delaney could not get up. Quickly, Lou stepped in and put an end to the one sided slaughter. Jack, unable to control his feelings had tears of pent up emotions rolling down his face as the crowd went berserk roaring their acclaim of him.

---

105 "Sharkey Expects to Get Knockout," by Jack Sharkey, *The Boston Daily Globe*, April 29, 1928, pg.A20.

Moments later back in his dressing room Sharkey said somewhat bitterly, "I showed them. Now I'm going to fight and keep on fighting without a break or an upset. I am sure that the bad luck has run out and that the future will be surprising. Don't think that this wasn't a fight because it ended so quickly. I caught a fast one on the ear that I can still feel, and you'll figure out that this red mark on my left shoulder did not come from playing tag. I went right in tonight with all my determination to show the public what I could do. I think that after this I will be more popularly received."[106]

As he had predicted Sharkey had come back and scored the promised knockout. However, his victory was not without the typical controversy following one of his fights. Two days after the bout reports surfaced that the fight was not on the level. And that Delaney had not trained seriously. Rumors spread like wildfire that Delaney had trained on beer and women and had spent little time actually getting into shape. Other reports said that Delaney had actually gone into the ring bloated and drunk. The New York Athletic Commission promised a full investigation.

Jack, who had arrived home on May 2, was surprised to hear the news. "As soon as I do something they start investigating," said an angry Sharkey. "Why didn't they investigate the referee after my bout with Dempsey to see if that was in the bag? Why didn't they investigate the judges and referee after my draw with Heeney and my defeat by Risko? They refused to do anything in those bouts although two members of the commissions said I should have received the decision against Risko and Heeney, and every reputable newspaper man in the country said Dempsey had fouled me time after time. I'm not a squawker," continued Sharkey. "But why should they pick on me? I knew I'd knock Delaney out. A fellow as big as I am can knock out any light heavyweight in the world and that includes Tommy Loughran, the champion. Those fellows aren't big enough; that's all. Besides, I was in the best shape of my life Monday night and I think I'd have knocked out Heeney or Risko too.

"As far as the investigation is concerned I'll welcome it. I don't know anything about Delaney's physical condition, but I don't think he could have gotten up twice if he hadn't been in pretty good shape. Every fight I won in New York I won and a lot of them I won I didn't get. I'd like to suggest to the commission that they investigate every one of my fights especially the Dempsey, Heeney and Risko and Delaney ones. And I'd also like to suggest that it isn't too late for them to look into that Maloney-Heeney fight that was held here."[107]

---

106 "I showed them," Sharkey's Comment, *The Boston Globe*, May 1, 1928, pg.23.
107 "New York to Probe Reports Fight Was Not on the Level," by David F. Egan, *the Boston Globe*, May 2, 1928, pg.15.

When news reached Delaney that his performance was going to be investigated he got red in the face and angrily denied that the fight was a set up. "I have never thrown a bout in my life. Every time I get licked I have trouble with people calling me crooked; I took a beating from Sharkey, but I took it on the level."[108] He then demanded that those who had watched him train state that they had viewed his workouts and that he had tried to place himself in proper physical condition. Nevertheless, the rumors persisted that he had finished his training for the Sharkey battle with a cigar and a bottle of beer.

---

108 "Report Delaney Finished Up With a Bottle of Beer," *Boston Globe,* May 3, 1928, pg. 13.

CHAPTER 17
DEKUH, TEX, AND CHRISTNER

A week after the Delaney fiasco things had returned to normal. In terms of an investigation nothing ever became of it and talks eventually died down. On May 8 Jack was a guest at a luncheon given in honor of ex-heavyweight king "Gentleman" James Corbett. Corbett was in Boston for a week's engagement at Loews theatre to perform his Vaudeville act. While at the luncheon Corbett spoke about eternal youth and gave Jack some advice on beating Tunney, should he find himself in a fight with the champion. "Youth," said Corbett, "is nothing but happiness and contentment. Do a little good each day and it will keep you young and happy."[109] Speaking of Tunney, Corbett said he did not rate Gene with the great fighters in history. "I never saw him block a blow or duck a blow in my life. He has a stiff, straight left hand and he follows it with a right cross to the head. He is the only heavyweight with a straight left that hurts, and that is why he wins fights."[110] Leaning over at the podium Corbett then directed his words toward Sharkey. "Jack. If you should ever fight Tunney, cross-counter with your right when Tunney throws his right hand. Probably Jack Dempsey doesn't know it, but that is what he did in the seventh round in Chicago. Tunney stands up straight with his head high after he throws his right hand, and you shouldn't have any trouble cross-countering."[111]

On May 24, Boston promoter Tom Goodwin passed away. Goodwin was an important part of Jack's early career and was often accused of having a financial interest in "The Boston Gob," as well as several other fighters. The boxing game is a selfish one and those who played a part could not understand how a prominent promoter could sacrifice his own time and money to help develop young fighters. "Tom Goodwin did exactly that, he developed Jack Sharkey so that Sharkey could step into the big money in New York. He started the big sailor and he ran at least half a dozen main bouts in which Sharkey figured and only once did he make even a dollar." Tom was laid to rest on May 28. Those in attendance included many notable boxers such as Jack Sharkey, Jimmy Maloney, Al Mello and Dick "Honey Boy" Finnegan. All rivalries were stripped away as boxers, managers and promoters paid their last respects to a man who had done much for them and a sport that he loved.

---

109 "Corbett Tells Jack Sharkey How to Defeat Gene Tunney," by David F. Egan, *The Boston Globe*, May 8, 1928, pg.1.
110 Ibid.
111 Ibid.

A few days after Goodwin's funeral, Tex announced that Sharkey would be fighting Native American Leo Gates at the Battery Arena on June 18, 1928 in St. Louis, Missouri. Before leaving for Missouri, Jack spent several weeks at Stillmans getting into fighting trim. He arrived in St. Louis with his wife and team on Saturday the 16th expecting to fight on the 18th. However, the fight was postponed twice and didn't take place until the 21st.

The fight was another great showing from Sharkey. From the start Jack was the aggressor and had his opponent on the defensive. Leo spent rounds one and two mostly clinching and running. The end came shortly after round three began when Sharkey rushed from his corner and with a swift volley of hooks followed by a left jab to the stomach sent Gates down for the count.

A month after his win over Gates, Sharkey sat ringside and watched Gene Tunney successfully defend his title with an 11th round technical knockout over Tom Heeney. One can imagine after his close fight with Heeney, Jack probably felt that it should have been him fighting Gene.

Following his win over Heeney, there were rumors that Gene would retire. His response was that the retirement talks were premature. Rumors were also flying around that Sharkey would be Gene's next opponent, if the champion decided to continue fighting. On July 31, Gene ended the suspense and announced his retirement from boxing. Immediately talks turned to Dempsey and Sharkey fighting for the vacated title. The rumors grew in strength when Dempsey arrived in Boston on his way to New York. Stepping off the train Dempsey was greeted by over 5,000 screaming fans. The smiling "Manassas Mauler" waved and shook hands as he pushed his way through the large crowd. Later that evening Sharkey and Dempsey were seen at the Ernie Schaaf-Harold Mays fight. Anxious to get the latest news, reporters hounded both fighters as to a possible match. If exciting news was what they were looking for they were disappointed. Sharkey was too busy working Ernie Schaaf's corner to say much and Dempsey reiterated that he had no plans on returning to the ring.

Gene's retirement left the heavyweight division wide open and several of the leading contenders were scrambling for matches. Rickard's job now was to find a new heavyweight champion. His strategy was to hold a series of elimination fights with the goal of having two outstanding contenders left to fight for the vacant crown. He was also holding out hope that he could get Dempsey back into the mix. "Just now there are only about six outstanding contenders in the country. I will set them to work in September in the first of a series of eliminations. I have no idea yet who will start the show, although I may pair Jack Sharkey with Paulino Uzcudun for a match in September. Johnny Risko must be considered along with Tom Heeney, Knute Henson and Phil Scott."[112]

With the scramble on to get a shot at the heavyweight title Jack wasn't waiting around for the elimination tournament. Buckley had a fight signed with "Big Boy" Peterson for August 23. But while training at Stillmans, Sharkey severely injured his left knee during the last round of the last day of his sparring session with Andy Wallace. Just as the round came to an end Jack was bobbing and weaving away from Andy's punches. Straightening up he started for his corner to take a drink of water from trainer Tony Polazzolo when his left leg suddenly collapsed. When he injured the knee he could not say. Only that it gave out when he took his first step to his corner. Jack was immediately taken to the hospital where famous bone specialist Dr. William Fralich took x-rays. The doctor found that a ligament was injured and that an upper bone in the knee was out of line with the lower bone. Jack's leg was then put in a splint and he was given crutches. The injury would put him out of action for six weeks and caused a cancellation of at least two fights that Sharkey had planned for the next few weeks. Following his doctor's visit Jack and Buckley boarded the midnight train and headed for Boston to meet with the boxing commission.

In response to Jack's injury, "Big Boy's" manager, Mike Collins sent out statements to all parts of the country that Jack was afraid of Peterson and had run out of the match because of Peterson's impressive showing during sparring with "Big" Bill Hartwell at Toland's gym.

With Jack unable to fight there was a scramble to find an opponent for Peterson. Jack's good friend, Ernie Schaaf agreed to step in for Sharkey. However, the fight quickly ran into some problems. Schaaf and Peterson had fought before with Peterson winning a close decision after having to pick himself up from the floor. Peterson's manager saw no point in a second fight and figured there was nothing to gain and everything to lose by fighting the dangerous Schaaf. Finally, after hours of much bickering between matchmaker Bob McKirdy, and the managers of the two fighters, Phil Schlossberg and Mike Collins, it was finally agreed that Ernie could step in. On the day of the fight ticket sales were nearly nonexistent. After a few hours behind the counter, Bob McKirdy discovered that the fans wanted to see Sharkey-Peterson and only Sharkey-Peterson. After some thought he decided to cancel the fight and offer a full refund for any tickets that were purchased.

Returning to Boston on crutches, Jack appeared before the boxing commission. The next day he was looked at by Dr. Isaac Klein. After a lengthy examination, Isaac gave his opinion that Jack's injury was serious

---

112 "Rickard's Job to Find New Champion," *The Boston Globe*, July 21, 1928, pg.1.

and that he would be out of the ring for at least two months and up to six months. Finished with his hearing, Jack motored back to New York for further examinations by Dr. Fralich. Fralich was concerned that the injury would affect Jack's footwork and speed and could very well impact the rest of his career. He was confident though, that Jack would make a full recovery. Being injured and out of the ring actually had its advantages for Jack at this time. His wife Dorothy was pregnant and being unable to fight allowed Jack to stay home and take care of her. On August 18, 1928 she gave birth to their only son, Jack Sharkey Jr.

By mid September it was being reported that Sharkey was going to have his cast removed. In place of a cast he would be wearing adhesive tape and would undergo physical therapy. With his leg on the mend, Jack was looking forward to getting back to the gym and resuming his training. After all the trash talk that Peterson's manager had done Sharkey was anxious to get into the ring with "Big Boy." However, after weeks of trying to put together another fight with Peterson, negotiations eventually fizzled out. Instead of Peterson the resourceful Buckley managed to secure a fight with Italian fighter Arthur DeKuh for a December 10 showdown.

After seven months out of the ring it seemed as though Jack had gained in popularity and the Boston fans had missed "The Garrulous Gob." When Jack climbed into the ring at the Boston Arena he received a huge roar from most of the 13,000 in attendance. This brought a smile to Sharkey's face as he danced around the ring waving.

Facing his opponent while receiving Johnny Brassil's instruction the 6', 196-pound Sharkey was noticeably smaller than the 6'3", 204-pound DeKuh. Arthur's size advantage, though, helped him little. In what turned out to be another great showing, Jack boxed a keen and careful fight against his hard hitting opponent, winning every round decisively. In the sixth Jack threw caution to the wind and opened with a barrage of punches and caught Arthur with a right to the jaw that wobbled the big Italian. With the unerring instinct of the fighting man, Sharkey jumped on his opponent and opened up with a blistering series of punches to the body and head. Whipping over a hard left to the jaw followed by an uppercut DeKuh dropped to the mat. Immediately, Brassil started his count, but when he reached five he stopped. Apparently, Jack had gone to the wrong neutral corner, so Brassil ordered Jack to go to the correct one. Brassil then resumed his count. The interruption, however gave Arthur about five extra seconds to clear his head and recover from the knockdown. As a result the "long count" caused a small controversy as many felt that Arthur would not have beaten the count. After regaining his feet DeKuh managed to weather Sharkey's attack and last out the round. For the remainder of the fight Arthur took a shellacking and was lucky to finish on his feet.

With his victory over DeKuh, Sharkey was feeling great and his future was bright. Following the fight Jack returned to the "affluent" Chestnut Hill area where the final touches were being completed on his new custom built home.

Sitting on several acres of land, surrounded by a beautifully landscaped yard, the house, of early English and Norman design has walls of handmade brick, whitewashed and broken here and there with bits of solid oak timber work. Upon entering one steps into a vestibule flanked by two doors, one directly in front leading to an entrance hall, while a portal on the right admits to a covered terrace. To the right of the entrance hall is the spacious living room with rough plastered walls and hewn oaken ceiling beams. Beyond the living room is a sun room with doors admitting to the front and rear patio. The rear patio is ornamented with a wall fountain of handmade tiles. To the left of the entrance hall is a cozy library, with built in bookcases and vaulted ceilings. The library as well as the dining room is furnished with early American antique furniture collected by Mrs. Sharkey; a hobby of hers. Beyond the library there is a spacious pantry, breakfast room and kitchen. A short hallway next to the kitchen admits into the garage and rear porch.

Stepping from the entrance hall into the large living room one sees a curved staircase with a black wrought iron balustrade leading to the second story where four bedrooms and three baths are located. The owner's suite, finished in pale green features a dressing room, bath and two spacious walk-in closets beside a cedar closet, with a window, for furs. Above the garage are the servant quarters, two rooms and a bath. Below the house is a large basement and receiving room finished in English tavern style with a large open fireplace made of old brick and timber. The house was designed and built under the supervision of Vincent E. Squires. The architect was the renowned and famous Royal Barry Wills.

With the completion of Sharkey's new home, Tex Rickard announced that Jack and outstanding light heavyweight, William Young Stribling had agreed to meet in an elimination bout to be held in Miami, Florida on February 27, 1929. Jack's fight with Stribling would kick off a series of elimination matches that Tex planned on promoting. Rickard's goal was to find the two outstanding contenders and have them fight for Tunney's vacated title, thus crowning a new champion. Tex was also holding out hope that Dempsey would return to the ring, and wanted Jack to fight the winner of the Stribling-Sharkey bout. Dempsey initially refused to say much about fighting and said the only way he would get back into the ring was as a referee. Nevertheless, rumors persisted that Dempsey was contemplating a return. He was reported to be doing some road work just to see how his body reacted to the training.

Just over a week after announcing that Sharkey and Stribling would be fighting, the boxing world was devastated to hear that Tex Rickard had unexpectedly died on January 6, 1929. The king of the fight promoters was in Florida preparing for the upcoming bout when he became ill. At the hospital he was diagnosed with acute appendicitis; an immediate operation was performed. At first everything seemed fine and Rickard was pronounced to be on the road to recovery. However, a few days later Tex relapsed and an infection developed. Showing the toughness of the fighters he promoted, Tex told Dempsey, who was at his bedside, "Jack, I'm going to win this fight."[113] Throughout the evening Dempsey and Rickard's wife kept a vigil. By 9:30 the next morning Tex had passed away at the age of 59, thus ended the life of one of the greatest fight promoters of all time.

With the passing of Tex there was some concern that Sharkey's battle with Stribling would have to be called off. However, Jack Dempsey along with longtime friend of Tex, Walter Field came forward and announced that the fight would go on as planned and he would be stepping in as promoter. In a formal statement Dempsey said, "I've lost the best pal I ever had. The world has lost a fair and square man, one who thought things and accomplished them. He has left his affairs in such order that Walter Field and I can carry on where he left off. We will run the Stribling-Sharkey fight as Tex planned and we will do just the things he would want us to do."[114]

With the Stribling bout still a go, Jack decided to stay busy with a tune-up match against "K.O." Christner. Known as Meyers Wilson Christner to his family and "K.O." to his fans, Christner didn't start boxing pro until the advanced age of 30. The story goes that while working for Firestone tires in Akron, Ohio Christner got into an argument with a co-worker. Eventually punches were thrown and with one devastating right hand Christner left his opponent unconscious on the tire factory's floor with a broken jaw. Word of Christner's prowess reached a local promoter of amateur fights and eventually Christner was talked into boxing. Having been a semi-pro baseball and football player Christner was a good athlete and took to boxing easily. Over the next few months "K.O." honed his craft. His amateur career peaked when he won the heavyweight championship of Ohio after working all day and driving 50 miles to the bout. Shortly thereafter Christner jumped into the punch for pay ranks and became a professional fighter.

Coming into the fight the 26-year-old Sharkey was almost 10-years younger than Christner but had a lot more ring experience. By all reports Jack was a far more technically refined fighter and was a huge betting

---

113 "Tex Rickard Dies At Miami Beach," *Boston Daily Globe*, January 7, 1929, pg.1.
114 "I lost the Best Pal I Ever Had," declares Jack Dempsey, *Boston Daily Globe*, January 7, 1929, pg.10.

favorite. Christner who was described as a powerful, yet awkward brawler had only two years of ring experience and 19 fights, three of those being newspaper decisions. Jack was by far the best fighter "K.O." had ever faced.

The fight turned out to be a furiously entertaining battle. For the first five rounds the two slugged it out at an intense pace. Christner had some success during the early rounds landing several big bombs, but Jack stayed calm and took the punches well. In the sixth, Jack's superior skills began to show against Christner's awkward style. He beat Christner from stem to stern and back again with cracking punches that had the slugger on the defensive for the first time. The whipping continued throughout rounds seven, eight and nine. By the tenth Jack had broken Christner's spirit and only grim tenacity held "K.O." up long enough to hear the final bell.

At the end of the fight a grinning Jack grabbed Christner's head in his hands, told him what a glorious showing he had made and slapped him three times on the back. To Jack went the glory of the win. To Christner, went the credit for his display of fighting heart and being a magnificent loser. With his win over "K.O.," Jack began preparations to meet one of the greatest knockout artists of all time, William Stribling "The King of the Canebrakes."

CHAPTER 18
STRIBLING AND THE PHANTOM OF PHILLY

William Lawrence Stribling, Jr. was born October 3, 1904 in Bainbridge, Georgia. During much of his childhood William traveled with his family as part of a vaudeville show that featured gymnastics and balancing acts. At the end of the performance he and his younger brother Herbert would box a few rounds much to the delight of the crowd. The wholesome, family oriented show was so popular that the Stribling's traveled for years throughout the United States and more than 30 foreign countries.

The Stribling family eventually put down roots in Macon, Georgia, shortly before the outbreak of World War One. In high school, Lawrence or "Strib" as he was called by his friends excelled at basketball and was one of the best players in the country. During his senior year William and his team went to the national interscholastic tournament in Chicago, but Lawrence was ruled ineligible to play because he had started boxing professionally. While in high school "Strib" boxed 75 professional bouts, being managed and trained by Pa and Ma Stribling.

Just a few years out of high school the young fighter caught national attention when he fought to a draw with world light heavyweight champion Mike McTigue in 1923. Initially, Stribling was declared the winner, but an hour later referee Harry Ertle apparently changed his decision and controversy quickly ensued. In a signed statement, Ertle said he originally ruled the bout a draw and did not change his decision. He blamed the mess on John Jones, head of the American Legion, for grabbing Stribling's hand and announcing him the winner before all the verdicts were known.

With such a fine showing against McTigue, "Strib" was besieged with offers to fight all over the United States, Europe, South America and Africa; everyone wanted to see the young prodigy. Already accustomed to a life of travel the Stribling family purchased a bus and began a tour of America. William fought anywhere they could pitch a tent and took on all comers. During the family's travel Lawrence fought in as many as 38-bouts in one year. By the time he agreed to fight Sharkey he had fought nearly 200 matches all across the country and had scored more knockouts up to that point than any fighter in history.

Jack and Buckley along with their wives arrived in Miami on February 2. Stepping off the train they were given an enthusiastic welcome by a large crowd of fans anxiously awaiting the arrival of "The Boston Gob." From the train station they were driven to the Miami Beach Kennel Club to watch the Greyhounds run and then over to the Heise-Ranger fight. It was here that Sharkey and Stribling along with Jack Dempsey exchanged pleasantries and sat together watching the evening's bouts. When asked by roving reporters how the fight was coming along and how he liked being a promoter, Dempsey admitted to being a little nervous but had breathed a sigh of relief now that both fighters had arrived safely in town.

The next morning Sharkey was up early inspecting his workout site that his trainers, Polazzolo and Al Lacey had set up for him at the Kennel Club. Satisfied with the ring and his equipment, Jack began intense training the following day. Stribling, who had arrived a few days before Jack, had already set up his training camp and was working hard. When not getting in shape for the fight, Stribling, a licensed pilot was giving Dempsey fits. The young daredevil was spending most of his free time flying his airplane and riding his motorcycle. Dempsey, worried that William would get hurt, ordered the young fighter to stay grounded and off of his bike until after the fight. Reluctantly, "Strib" gave in saying, "I was going to get a lot of recreation out of my plane before the fight, but it looks like I'll have to use an automobile or shank horses if I want to feel the breeze in my face."[115]

With both fighters deep in training a new 40,000 seat stadium was set to begin construction at the old Flamingo Golf Course. On February 3, at a ceremony to kick off the construction, Jack Dempsey with a hammer and a smile drove in the first nail before dozens of flashing cameras.

While everyone was preparing for the big fight, events were unfolding in other parts of the boxing world. Max Schmeling, the rising German contender became a serious threat when he defeated Johnny Risko on February 1, 1929. Following his victory he called out any and all top contenders. Likewise, light heavyweight champion Tommy Loughran issued a formal challenge to the winner of the Sharkey-Stribling match-up. Even Jack's old rival, Jimmy Maloney was making some noise. Jimmy had put together an impressive record or 15 wins, 2 losses and 2 draws since losing to Jack and wanted nothing more than to get another crack at his old foe and the vacated title.

As the fight drew near, sports writer Grantland Rice, who was in town for the big event gave his thoughts after seeing both men train. "They look as closely matched as any heavyweights I have been around. They are swinging down the home stretch evenly matched, well conditioned and physically ready to go. Just how keen they will be to tear one another limb from limb and ear from ear is another matter to be decided next week."[116]

Training ended for both men on February 26. The next day at 2:30 the official weigh-in was held. With both fighters and their teams present, things got a little heated when Sharkey, noticing that Stribling's team looked

---

115 "Stribling Hates to Stay on the Ground," *Daily Boston Globe*, February 6, 1929, pg.15.
116 "Sharkey in Fine Shape for Miami Beach Bout," *The Boston Daily Globe*, by Grantland Rice, February 19, 1929, pg.25.

a bit nervous, thought to poke some fun at William. "What are you excited and nervous about?" asked Sharkey.

"Nobody would get excited about you," snapped Stribling. "You won't be in there with any Delaney, who will do a flop for you. You'll be fighting Stribling."

Sharkey's eyes flashed with anger and Stribling glared back, but for the moment the peace was kept. Once the doctor finished his examinations the hostilities flared back up when Tony Polazzolo said to Stribling, "I'll bet you $10,000 that Jack knocks you out." The comment had little effect on Stribling; his father however, took it more seriously. Jumping up, Pa Stribling rushed across the room and threw a right aimed at Tony's face. Suddenly, the room was chaos and everybody was pushing, shoving and yelling. Eventually, the two men were separated and order was restored. With the weigh in completed Stribling returned to his hotel room and Jack headed out to get some lunch.

Eight hours later the stands were crowded with over 35,000 noisy fans. The evening began with a Battle Royale of six black fighters. Blindfolded, they were brought into the ring and fought a bare knuckle free-for-all until only one was left standing. A half-hour later Stribling, followed by his Ma and Pa entered the ring. Jack made his entrance a few minutes later.

Jack was confident when he climbed into the ring. At 192-pounds he was at his perfect fighting weight and held a 10-pound advantage over his rival. The king of the Canebrakes, though, held a tremendous edge in experience. Despite being 25-years-old, two years younger than Sharkey, "Strib" had fought over a 100 more fights than Jack, who had up to this point fought 38 bouts.

When the bell rang it didn't take long for everyone to see that Jack looked very sharp. In fact, his performance was said to be one of the best of his career. The next day Referee Lou Magnolia wrote about his unique perspective on the fight exclusively for the *Boston Globe*, saying, "I gave the decision to Jack Sharkey in his 10-round fight with W.L Stribling tonight because of the cleaner and harder hitting. The blows that were most damaging were terrific rights and lefts to the body that caused W.L to jump into the air. My check of the rounds gave six to Sharkey, three to Stribling and one even. Throughout the fight Sharkey showed greater general aggressiveness and better boxing ability. Also he was much the stronger, and at the finish he was able to go the long distance yet. Jack did not have a mark on him, while the Southerner was smeared with blood from nose and mouth.

"There is no doubt that Stribling hits hard. He showed that twice by shaking the sailor with his right and had he fought a better planned fight Jack might have gone. Sharkey it seems to me fought an excellent fight. He boxed well, and switched his attack from head to body with good judgment.

At no time did he really hurt the Southerner with any single punch, but all his punches were, certainly he showed enormous improvement over his bouts with Tom Heeney and "K.O." Christner. Anyone that questions Jack ability to take it must have formed a different opinion. The wallop that Stribling landed in the fourth and other almost as hard later in the fight would have would have dazed most men. Those punches did shake the sailor for an instant, but he recovered so quickly that W.L had no chance to take advantage of them. In my opinion there was no question concerning the justice of the verdict, Sharkey was getting stronger with every passing round, and Stribling was palpably slowing up."[117] Despite Sharkey's solid performance, Ma Stribling believed that her son was robbed and Pa Stribling blamed the loss on a case of neuritis.

Following the fight, "The Squire of Chestnut Hill," (a nickname that newspaperman David F. Egan gave to Jack) returned to his newly built home in Chestnut Hill to spend time with his family and do a little fishing.

While Jack enjoyed time away from boxing, Buckley was busy arranging Sharkey's next fight. Two possible opponents, Jack Dempsey and Max Schmelling topped the list. Rumors still persisted that Dempsey would return to the ring and Buckley was anxious to make the fight. Dempsey however, insisted that he was through and would stick to promoting. Talks seemed a little more serious about a match with Max Schmeling. Schmeling's recent victory over Johnny Risko had elevated the German's popularity and everyone wanted to see him fight. William F. Carey, the man who took over when Tex Rickard died, proposed a match with Sharkey, with the winner being recognized as heavyweight champion of the world. After weeks of debating by the New York State boxing commission and Madison Square Garden, over contracts, managers, fight locations and if the winner should be recognized as champion, the fight eventually fell through.

Talks at Madison Square Garden then turned to a tournament with Jimmy Maloney taking on Max Schmelling, and Sharkey taking on Paulino Uzcudun, with the two winners meeting for the right to fight for the heavyweight championship. This plan did not go over well with Buckley, who responded, "Jack Sharkey is not signed to box Paulino, Sharkey can whip the Spaniard without a great deal of trouble, but I want him to box Schmeling in June at Yankee Stadium. He and Sharkey would bring in $800,000 in New York, and Sharkey will box Schmeling or nobody."[118] Not wanting Sharkey to get rusty, Buckley decided to take Tommy Loughran up on his challenge. The fight was put together for September 26, 1929 at

---

117 "Cleaner Hitting of Sharkey Decisive," by Referee Lou Magnolia, The *Boston Globe* February 28, 1929, pg.1.
118 "Buckley Punctures Sharkey Program," by David F. Egan, *The Boston Daily Globe*, March 13, 1929, pg.12.

Yankee Stadium. The winner would be officially recognized as, "The American Heavyweight Champion."

Thomas Patrick Loughran was born in Philadelphia on November 29, 1902. He began his boxing career in 1919 and is considered one of the most skilled fighters of all time. Between 1927 and 1929 he was the undefeated world light heavyweight champion. Although he lacked a knockout punch, Tommy had great footwork, a sound defense and was a master counter puncher. Like many of the light heavyweights from Tommy's era, Loughran frequently crossed paths with heavyweights. During his career he defeated such notable big men as Max Bear, Johnny Risko and Paulino Uzcudun. At light heavyweight he bested, James J. Braddock, the famous "Cinderella man," Mike McTigue and Young Stribling. Arguably his most impressive win may have been a 10-round decision over the phenomenal Harry Greb, possibly the greatest fighter that ever lived and certainly top five pound-for-pound. On March 1, 1934 Tommy challenged the giant Primo Carnera for the heavyweight title. Eight inches shorter and 85-pounds lighter than the massive Carnera, Tommy still managed to last the 15-round distance, but lost the decision.

During the signing of the fight, Loughran was confident of victory and felt that he would defeat "The Boston Gob," saying, "My greater experience will defeat Jack Sharkey when we meet in Yankee stadium next Thursday night. He has been fighting for about five years, and I have been fighting twice as long. I think I know too much boxing for him. There is nothing Sharkey can do that I can't do, and anything he can do I can do a whole lot better. I am confident that I will win handily."

Sharkey, as expected predicted a different outcome to the fight. "I'll knockout Tommy Loughran when we fight at Yankee Stadium. I'm too big and strong for him and hit too hard. Another thing Loughran's boosters seem to forget is that old Jack Sharkey can do a little bit of boxing himself. I can sock in the old wallop and I don't think Loughran can hurt me with his punches. If anybody will fight with me I'll fight back, I've proven that. If Loughran tries to make a runaway fight of it I'll catch him and slow him down with body punches. Aw, I'll knock him out and that's all there is to it."[119]

Continuing his march towards the heavyweight title, Jack put together another great performance; quite possibly the best of his career.

The first round started well for "The Phantom of Philadelphia." The two fighters came out circling and jabbing. Jack, looking to mix it up went on the attack early, ramming hard lefts and rights into Tommy's belly.

---

119 "Sharkey, Loughran Tell How Each is Going to Win," *The Boston Globe*, September 21, 1929, pg.10.

Remaining calm, Tommy used a rappid fire, precision jab to keep Jack off balance and his amazing defense to avoid the big left hooks that Sharkey looked to land. Jack was able to close the round by landing a number of hard body blows on his elusive opponent, but overall it was Tommy's round.

The two came out for round two circling and looking for openings. Seeing a spot, Jack leaped in with a rapid fire combination of lefts and rights to Tommy's body. Tommy, not wanting to mix it up tried to box smartly and keep a distance between himself and Jack, but throughout the round Sharkey continued to rush in aggressively with big left hooks, right hand leads and hard body blows. Tommy was able to smother some of Sharkey's rushes and big punches by grabbing "The Boston Gob," but couldn't avoid all of them. Jack was able to catch Loughran with more than one hard shot to the jaw and midsection. As the round neared its end Sharkey feinted with his left and drove in a powerful right to Tommy's jaw that shook "The Phantom of Philly" to the soles of his feet.

Round three started with Jack throwing a leaping left hook and Tommy back peddling quickly. Following his retreating opponent, Jack came forward bobbing and weaving and threw a right hand that landed like a sledgehammer flush on Tommy's jaw. The blow flattened Tommy to the mat; the momentum of the punch carried Jack ricocheting into the ropes and bouncing off. A second later referee Lou Magnolia began his count. Tommy, using the bottom rope for support, staggered to his feet as Lou reached 8. Realizing that Tommy was in no shape to continue, Lou waved the fight over, .27 seconds after the round had began. Jack, seeing Tommy rise, ran across the ring like a blood mad gladiator with the intent of finishing off his enemy. Seeing that Sharkey intended to continue the fight, Lou grabbed Jack and ordered him to a neutral corner.

Disoriented, Tommy said to Magnolia as he was helped to his corner, "Leave me sit down a moment."[120] Other reports have Tommy saying, "Let me sit down till I see where I'm at."[121] In his corner, Tommy's corner men tended to their beaten fighter and Sharkey had his hand raised in victory. It was Tommy's first loss in over four years and the first time in 114 fights that he had ever been knocked out. For Jack it was one of his most impressive victories and would pave the way for a title fight with Max Schmeling, to determine the championship of the world.

---

120 "Jack Sharkey Out to Beat Loughran," *Boston Globe*, September 25, 1929, pg.7.
121 "Jack Sharkey Wins Over Loughran," *Burlington Daily Times*, September 27, 1929, pg.13.

CHAPTER 19
PHIL SCOTT

A month after Jack's victory over Loughran the stock market crashed. The day, infamous as "Black Tuesday" occurred on October 29, 1929 and plunged the United States along with most of the civilized world into a decade-long economic decline known as "The Great Depression." While disastrous for the economy, boxing suffered little. Although unemployment and poverty rose to a record high following the crash, people used sports like boxing and baseball as a form of escapism from the daily nightmare of the Depression. And even though most were broke they were still willing to spend what little money they had to see a good fight.

Following his outstanding performance over Tommy, there were talks of Sharkey fighting Tuffy Griffiths and even his good friend Ernie Schaaf. Jack was opposed to a fight with Ernie because of their friendship and didn't want to fight Tuffy, saying, "If I fought Griffiths, people would get the idea I was asking for setups. I don't want another fight like the one here last year. Stribling was a good fighter but his style made me fight to poor advantage and consequently we offered a poor go. I don't want another one like that anymore than the fans do."[122]

As it worked out, Jack didn't have to fight Schaaf or Tuffy. On January 7, 1930 it was announced that Jack would meet British Empire heavyweight champion Phil Scott at the second annual "Battle of the Palms" in Miami, Florida on February 27, 1930. Again Jack would be fighting at Flamingo Park stadium, where he fought Stribling, and training at the Kennel Club.

With the signing of the fight completed, Jack and Buckley, along with Tony Polazzolo and assistant trainer Al Lacy left for Florida on January 10. A week later, Jack was joined by Dorothy and his children, who quickly found that the sunny beaches of Florida were a lot more fun than watching Jack train.

Throughout training for the fight there was a lot of talk about Max Schmeling taking on the winner. In fact, Schmeling's manager, Joe Jacobs cancelled a proposed fight in Atlantic City on August 29, saying that Max would instead meet the winner of Sharkey-Scott. Furthermore, Jacobs expected the fight to be for the world's heavyweight title.

Hearing the news Sharkey was elated, saying, "Best news I've heard since coming down here. I felt right along the bout would never take place

---

[122] "Sharkey Willing to Fight in Miami, But Not With Griffiths," *Boston Globe*, January 6, 1930, pg.11.

because I figured Schmeling would be foolish to take chances when a championship bout was in his reach. Now that Schmeling has made his decision I'll have greater incentive than ever to win my fight with Scott. I'll work hard to land a knockout in the shortest possible time."[123]

Over at the Oasis club where tea and strumpets were being served Phil was training hard. He was taking the fight seriously but despite his best efforts the lanky Englishman was viewed as little more than an opponent. It also didn't help that Phil had a bad reputation for wining fights by claiming foul; he had, in fact won seven because his opponents had been disqualified. The disqualification wins had earned Phil the nickname "Fainting Phil." Even Phil's manager, Jimmy Johnston, gave Scott little chance saying, "Scott is here to be knocked out." Which, according to sports writer David Egan, was what everyone believed was going to happen. Going into the fight the odds were 5-1 and nobody was putting any money on Phil.

Even though Scott was "just an opponent" the fight turned out to be an entertaining battle while it lasted, and not without the typical share of controversy following a Sharkey fight.

Round one started with Jack bolting from his corner and throwing a big right hand. Phil, at 6'3"½ was surprisingly nimble on his feet and bounced out of the way of the rampaging Sharkey. Using his 82" reach the Englishman sent out his long jab as the two circled. Jack, bobbing and weaving rushed in with a volley of rapid punches. Quickly, Phil tied up the ex-gob and they wrestled into the ropes and out to the center of the ring where Jack connected with an elbow to Phil's jaw. The Englishman answered back with a hard uppercut that snapped Sharkey's head back. Separated by referee Lou Magnolia, Jack came back in with a powerful left hook that Phil blocked with his long arms. The two then circled and exchanged a series of hard blows, each finding a spot on the other's face to land some punches. Next they clinched quickly with Jack landing a short, powerful left to Phil's belly but they then let go of each other and backed off.

Bobbing up and down, Jack stormed back in after his retreating opponent with a left hook to the head. Both men then opened up with a couple of punches before clinching. Parted by Magnolia, Phil came at Jack with a flurry of blows and then tied Sharkey up. Separated again by the referee, Jack rushed into Phil with blistering punches backing up his adversary before being held. Pushed apart, Jack came forward throwing left hooks that forced Phil into the ropes. A moment later they were back out in the center of the ring. Jack jabbed his way in and followed with ripping left

---

123 "Sharkey Expects to Fight Schmeling," *Boston Globe*, January 23, 1930, pg.25.

hooks and elbows to Phil's head. Shaken, Phil grabbed hold of Jack. Again separated by the referee the two traded jabs and Jack came in low with a hard left to Phil's face. Jack then rushed Phil throwing a hard right hand at the retreating Englishman. The two then exchanged long lefts and opened up with lefts and rights; an elbow from Sharkey landed on Phil's jaw as they went into a clinch. Pushed apart yet again, Phil threw a long left right combination at his weaving opponent, but missed. Jack charged in with a hard right that Phil avoided and the two exchanged punches just as the bell rang ending an even round.

The second round began with both fighters circling. Sharkey suddenly came forward with a chopping right and a leaping left hook. Phil backed up and jabbed trying to keep the charging Sharkey away. Bobbing and weaving Jack followed his back pedaling opponent. Suddenly, Sharkey surged in with two powerful lefts that caught Phil flush on his face sending him to the canvas. While falling, Phil grabbed Jack and nearly pulled him down, but Sharkey yanked himself free and headed to a neutral corner. The crowd, excited over the knockdown, roared in unison and were on their feet as Magnolia began the count. By six Scott was up. Jack raced back in with a volley of lefts and elbows trying to finish his lanky foe. Scott, just trying to survive, grabbed Jack and held on. Finally yanked apart by Lou, Jack stormed after Scott with hard jabs backing the big man up. Scott, in full defensive mode used his long jab while Sharkey came on with the intention of finishing Phil on the spot. Despite Jack's best efforts, Scott managed to survive the remainder of the round by jabbing, running and holding on anytime Jack came in close.

The third turned out to be one of the most riotous rounds ever seen in ring history. It began with the fighters circling and jabbing. Pressing forward, Sharkey sprang in with a straight right to the jaw and Phil quickly tied him up, spun him around and pushed him into the ropes. The two then traded a number of jabs. Jack, bouncing on his toes got around Phil's long left and smashed in a solid left to the body. They exchanged jabs and then Phil sent in a one two as Jack drove in another powerful right to the body that forced Phil to clinch. Pushed apart by the referee, Jack came right back with a left that caught Phil on the side of his face. Shaken a bit, Scott went on the defensive and backed off. A second later both men opened up with lefts and rights in a wild exchange of leather. Stopping for an instant Jack reset and came back with a left elbow and a left hook followed by two lefts to the body and a grazing left to the head that sent Scott to the canvas.

Up at seven, Phil steadied himself as Jack rushed in. Putting all his power behind each blow, Jack landed a hard left to the body and missed a looping left to the head as Phil grabbed hold. Told to break by Magnolia both men backed off. Sharkey reset and went right back on the attack with a left to the body and a left to the head. Scott again grabbed to smother

Jack's attack. Pulled apart by the referee, Sharkey again sprang in, landing a left to Phil's midsection and again Phil grabbed the rampaging Sharkey.

Fighting in close, Jack pounded in another crushing left to the ribs followed by a left to the head that missed. Overcome with pain from Sharkey's vicious body punching, Phil went down clutching his right hip. Magnolia started his count and Scott was up at seven. Jack came in aggressively firing another murderous left to the body that sent Phil back to the canvas clutching his hip. In obvious pain Phil managed to make it halfway to his feet as Lou counted, but then collapsed, rolling over in agony.

Seeing their fighter in distress Phil's corner men jumped into the ring yelling and screaming that Jack's blows were low. After a brief argument, the referee agreed to give Phil some time to recover. With the aid of his corner men Phil limped back to his stool for a rest period.

Over in the Sharkey corner Jack was confused and his temper was about to erupt. He didn't know if the fight had been stopped, or if "Fainting Phil" was trying to live up to his nickname and win by claiming foul.

After about a 30 second rest Phil was ready to continue and the fight resumed. Jack, fired up at this point, roared across the ring back into battle throwing looping left hooks while Phil tried desperately to cling to his enraged opponent. Wrenched apart by Lou, Jack tore in with wild lefts and rights. Phil threw a few feeble punches and used his flailing arm to block some of Jack's wild swings, but Jack, infuriated beyond reason continued to swing as if possessed. One final time Sharkey rushed at Phil with a left to the body and a left to the head that sent the Englishman sagging into the ropes. Seeing that Phil was a beaten man, the referee stepped in, pushed Jack away and ended the fight.

Unable to hold himself up Scott grabbed Magnolia and the ropes for support. Heading back to his corner Sharkey's anger boiled over. Thinking that Phil was trying to claim foul, Jack was yelling and screaming. He then turned around and headed back to Phil, screaming at him at the top of his lungs. Pulled away by Polazzolo, Jack returned to his corner. Absolutely irate, Jack was jumping up and down in rage. A moment later, he turned back and once again stood before Phil screaming in anger while Scott's seconds rushed into the ring. Phil, unable to move, clutched the ropes for support as one of his corner men brought him a stool. Again the maddened Sharkey was pulled to his corner by Polazzolo where he continued to aggressively display his anger. The ring quickly filled with boxing officials and policemen. Thinking it was better to get Jack out of the ring before a riot ensued, Buckley grabbed his man and led him to his dressing room.

During an interview from his dressing room Phil was quoted as saying, "It was a rotten wicked decision. I know I was fouled at least half a dozen times, I counted them. I have never seen anything like it in my life."[124]

The next day Jack wrote of the fight for the *Boston Globe* saying, "He quit cold. That's all I have to say about the fight. I was about to start a left to the body. He saw it coming; he was almost on the ropes at the time and was in a panic 'Oh you hurt me!' he yelled. Now that's a fine thing for a heavyweight to say. I didn't even strike that left hook before he quit. I was surprised, in fact, dumbfounded when he told me that I was hurting him. What did he think it was, a cream-puff party?"[125]

The battle of words continued to rage a few days after the fight when Scott's manager Johnson claimed that Sharkey blinded Phil in the second by stealthily placing acid on his gloves that got into Phil's eyes. And that Magnolia had at first disqualified Sharkey and then later reversed his decision saying that, "Scott couldn't win and we knew it." Sharkey, disgusted with the whole thing refused to even comment. Referee Magnolia however was not so inclined to keep his mouth closed. "Scott has claimed foul ever since he landed in this country. I expected him to claim foul when I was giving instructions."[126]

Eventually the war of words died down and on March 15, Phil climbed aboard the ocean liner RMS *Majestic* to return home, promising to return, but still feeling that he had received a raw deal.

For Jack, he had other things to think about. A title fight with Max Schmeling was next.

---

124 "Wicked Decision, Verdict of Scott," *Boston Globe*, February 28, 1930, pg.27.
125 "Scott Quit Cold, Declares Sharkey," by Jack Sharkey, *Boston Globe*, February 28, 1930, pg.27.
126 "Acid on Sharkey's Gloves Latest Charge," by David Egan, *Boston Globe*, March 1, 1930, pg.11.

CHAPTER 20
SHARKEY-SCHMELING I

On April 2, 1930 the New York Athletic Commission announced that they had agreed to sanction a 15-round title fight between Jack Sharkey and Max Schmeling, billed as "The Battle of the Continents." Scheduled for June 12, at Yankee Stadium the winner would be recognized as the new heavyweight champion. Finally, after six years of ups and downs, the Squire of Chestnut Hill was getting his shot at the crown.

Jack's opponent, Maximillian Adolph Otto Siegfried Schmeling was born in Klein Luckow, Mecklenburg-Vorpommern, Germany on September 28, 1905. As a boy Max's father took him to watch a film of the heavyweight fight between Jack Dempsey and George Carpentier, and from that moment Max was hooked on boxing. He began as an amateur and by 1924 had won Germany's national amateur light heavyweight title; shortly thereafter he turned professional. Although a great admirer of Dempsey's aggressive bob and weave fighting style, Max developed into a careful, methodical counter puncher with a powerful right hand.

By 1928, Max was Germany's heavyweight champion. Having acheived all he could in his own country, Max knew if he wanted to be heavyweight champion of the world he would have to conquer America. At the time America dominated when it came to the heavyweight champion. Being heavyweight champion was looked at as an American birthright and the title's lineage could be traced back to the first champion, John L. Sullivan in 1852.

Max arrived in New York for the first time in November of 1928. Considered by many as just another stiff European fighter who had never fought anyone, he was hardly noticed and had little opportunity. It wasn't until Max met fight manager, Joe Jacobs a.k.a. "Yussel the muscle" (Yussel being the Yiddish name for Joseph) that his career started to move in the right direction. After five victories in America, two of which were over top contenders, Johnny Risko and Paulino Uzcudun, fight fans began to take notice. With his powerful right hand, dark haired good looks and a striking resemblance to Jack Dempsey, Max's popularity soared and fans wanted to see more of the German.

Schmeling arrived in New York on May 4, 1930 for his fight with Sharkey. The next day he and Jacobs stood before the New York State Athletic Commission to apply for reinstatement. A year before Max had been suspended from fighting in America for refusing to fight Phil Scott. The reinstatement was however a mere formality inasmuch as the fight had already been approved by the New York Commission.

Both fighters began training on May 12, Sharkey at Gus Wilson's camp in Orangeburg, New York and Schmeling at the Enjoie health club in Endicott, New York.

Right from the start reports were coming out that both men looked in fine form. Former lightweight champion Benny Leonard visited Jack's camp saying, "the big boy looks good, mighty good." While there the former champ found out firsthand just how good. At only 5'5" and 163-pounds Leonard climbed into the ring with Jack, who was seven inches taller and 30-pounds heavier and sparred a few rounds. Although Leonard was several years removed from his prime, he still possessed much of his old skill and speed, but wound up with a reddened nose. Jack, knowing that Benny was a master boxer with a lot of knowledge asked the former lightweight king to stick around. Leonard agreed to hang around for a week and work with Jack.

On the day of the fight both fighters and their managers gave their predictions. Max, speaking with a thick German accent said, "I am fit. I am confident I hope for the best. I know I will not disgrace my country and my race. I present my compliments to Jack Sharkey; extend him the hand of good sportsmanship, hope for a fair, square, stand-up match in which both loser and winner will acquit themselves manfully and may the best man win."

Jacobs was a little more animated with his prediction. "Max Schmeling will knockout Jack Sharkey inside of ten rounds. I make no conditions. I have no ifs' or butts.' My fighter is 100 percent better than he was a year ago when he knocked out Johnny Risko, who defeated Sharkey and hammered to near helplessness Paulino Uzcudun, whom Sharkey refused to meet."

Sharkey, not to be undone, unlimbered his proclamations to the American boxing public saying, "This is the greatest fight of my life. I feel that the responsibility of retaining a title that has become traditional to America is placed on my shoulders and I promise I will do my utmost to win. Max will find a true American facing him. He will find a man determined of victory and one who will not admit defeat until every ounce of energy is exhausted in him."

Johnny Buckley, the sailor's manager was sweet and to the point. "We'll knock him out in five rounds. You can go to sleep on it."[127]

Unfortunately, the predictions were not fulfilled on either side. Instead the fight turned out to be one of the most controversial heavyweight title fights the ring has ever seen.

---

127 "What the Fighters Say of Chances," *Boston Globe*, June 12, 1930, pg.30.

Both fighters showed up in tremendous condition, Jack at 197-pounds and Schmeling at 188. There were, however some reports that Schmeling had hurt his ankle in training and had not been able to train properly.

Yankee Stadium attendance topped 85,000 and the fans were geared up for a great fight. Max entered the ring first and was introduced as "the fighting son of the fatherland." A few minutes later, Jack, a 2-1 favorite, made his entrance wearing an American flag draped over his shoulders. This brought a mixed reaction from the crowd with some booing and others cheering. The ring announcer then proclaimed Jack as, "the man on whom every American pins his faith."

Moments later the fans were treated to the best of Jack Sharkey. And for three and a half rounds "The Boson Gob" fought one of the best fights of his career. Stronger and faster, Jack won the first round by staying poised and popping Max with stinging jabs and crisp left hooks to the face and body. But, it was Max who drew first blood when he landed a hard left hook to Jack's mouth that had Sharkey spitting blood.

The second was again another good round for Jack. Boxing smartly, he caught Max with hard right crosses, ripping uppercuts and quick flurries of left, right, left combinations whenever Schmeling came in close. Max was able to catch Jack with a couple of hard right hands but the blows had little effect on Sharkey.

Jack continued his lacing of Schmeling in the third. Early in the round he had the crowd on its feet when he landed a stiff jab and a punishing right that clearly shook the German. Again, Max was able to occasionally land with his right hand, but Jack absorbed the blows with little effect. The ex-gob continued to hammer Max for the remainder of the round with crisp jabs, hard right crosses and head snapping uppercuts that left the German groggy. Near the end of the third Sharkey caught Schmeling with a terrific left hook to the belly that hurt Max. Going back to his corner Max was a bit unsteady. As he sat down his corner man tried to administer smelling salt, but Max refused it.

Jack opened the fourth with a jab and a flurry of punches to Max's head. Max kept boring in, but Jack boxed smartly behind his jab catching Schmeling with several clean right crosses. And then, out of nowhere as Max was coming forward throwing a left hook, Sharkey threw a left uppercut aimed at the belly. The blow appeared to land low and Schmeling went down as if he had been shot. Jack instantly ran to a neutral corner as Max grimaced in pain clutching his groin.

What followed was absolute confusion as the ring filled with people and everyone tried to figure out if the punch was fair or foul. Jacobs was one of the first to jump into the ring screaming "foul!" Max's corner men rushed over and picked Schmeling up and carried him to his stool. Referee Jim Crowley went over and asked the judges if they had seen a low blow, and both said no. Then things got interesting. Arthur Brisbane, a highly respected journalist was sitting behind Judge Harold Barnes. As legend has it, Brisbane shouted, "That was a foul below the belt, and unless Schmeling is given the decision it will kill boxing in New York."[128] "When judge Barnes heard that, he recanted and told Crowley he had seen a foul. "So I had to concur," said Crowley. Barnes later denied being influenced by Brisbane's comment or that Brisbane even commented until after the decision was announced. Barnes said he gave Crowley the foul sign three times. "Brisbane was sitting next to me," said Barnes, "but he did not open his mouth until the decision was rendered. Then he turned to me. 'Sonny,' he said 'you just saved boxing.'"

With the judges and referee trying to figure out what happened, Sharkey went over to Schmeling's corner. He tried to get a word in to Max but was unable to get through the crowd that surrounded the German. Frustrated, Jack jumped up and down and headed back to his corner. Several tense moments followed and finally the fight was awarded to Schmeling on a foul, making Max the first to win the title in such a fashion. No champion had ever won the title sitting down, and because the rules were quickly changed due to the outrage over the fight, no one ever would again.

Sometime later a crestfallen Sharkey sat in his dressing room surrounded by a horde of newspaper men. Jack smacked one hand into the other, glowered about the assembly and said softly. "I would have rather lost every other fight I ever fought than this one tonight."[129] Jack then stared blankly about the room, went to his locker, sat down on a bench before it and held his head in his hands. His eyes filled with tears and he shook his head. More questions followed from the press. "What do you think of Max as a fighter?" asked one of them. "Well," Jack said quietly, "I don't think much of Schmeling's ability as a fighter. I was playing along with him and I was positive I could have knocked him out anytime I wanted to. It was just like a game of tag and he was it."[130] Jack then turned to Buckley, and said mildly, "Couldn't you have done something?" Buckley answered somewhat angrily. "Jack, I done everything I could do, that there was to do."[131]

As to the question of a low blow, most who were at the fight agreed that the blow was low, but absolutely unintentional. Benny Leonard, who was at ringside, gave his observation in his sports column saying, "The fight was all Sharkey. All of a sudden, near the end of the round, I saw Jack start a left

---

[128] "Jack Sharkey The Least Remembered Heavyweight," by Roger Mooney, *Ring Magazine*, 1994, pg.60.
[129] "Sharkey in Gloom in Dressing Room," *Boston Globe*, June 13, 1930, pg.30.
[130] Ibid.
[131] Ibid.

hook and as it got around to Schmeling I never saw it land, as Max's body was in front of me. However, foul or no foul it was accidental, for Sharkey was way out in front and looked a sure winner when the final blow landed. I ran over to the other side of the ring and talked to Patsy Haley, a referee. I asked Patsy if he saw the blow, he said, 'Yes, Benny, the blow was low alright, it was all an accident, for Schmeling hopped up a bit as Jack let the blow fly.'"[132]

Gene Tunney, having watched the fight at ringside gave his thoughts. "It was a foul. It was unfortunate, very unfortunate, for clearly the foul was absolutely unintentional, but it was obviously a foul. It was a blow that will cause excruciating pain and there is no doubt in my mind that Schmeling was incapacitated."[133]

Two days after the fight Jack was interviewed at his home in Chestnut Hill by sports writer John Hallahan. While relaxing on the front lawn and playing with his three children Jack spoke of the alleged foul blow. "I never dealt a fairer body blow than that which I struck Max Schmeling in the fourth round. It was a right to the navel. To be declared the loser on a foul with victory in my grasp, I could not be anything but keenly disappointed." When asked what he thought about Max as a fighter Jack responded with, "I never thought Schmeling was so easy to hit. He had little to offer. I would like to get another chance at him, although I doubt he will give me the opportunity he is reported to have promised." When asked if he thought the judges were swayed, Jack answered, "I do believe that Judge Barnes, who decided the contest was swayed by the German newspapermen who sat close to him. They were the first to yell, so I've been told. They were standing up when Crowley went over to talk to Barnes."[134]

Likewise, Max was interviewed a day after the fight by New York sports writer Paul Gallico and had this to say. "I did not want to win that way. I want to be heavyweight champion of the world, but not on a foul. And I would have been. My head was clear. Sharkey had done his worst. Did I go down? I wouldn't even take smelling salt in my own corner. When I didn't go down in that third round and came out for the fourth, I felt that Sharkey is not the same anymore. I could see it in his eyes. I hit him a good left hook in the mouth. I knew that I could come on then. I think he is not so much anymore. You notice that I am a little more careless, eh? Oh, I am disgusted. Yes, I am heavyweight champion of the world, but I want to prove it. I promise you I would have proven it. And when Sharkey fights

---

132 "Foul Accidental, Leonard's Belief," by Benny Leonard, *Boston Globe*, June 13, 1930, pg.30.
133 "Tunney Believes Foul Unintentional," *Boston Globe*, June 13, 1930, pg.30.
134 "Sharkey Insists Blow Ending Fight Was Fair," by John Hallahan, *Boston Globe*, June 14, 1930, pg.10.

me again I do prove it." When asked about the low blow Max answered with, "I am up against the ropes, Sharkey throws a right. I duck under, and in comes a left hook. It is low. You see it. I do not have to tell you. It is terrible pain, I cannot move, I am nearly mad. What must I do? No one knows whether the referee says I am fouled. Sharkey is over in my corner for a minute then I hear that I am heavyweight champion of the world. And there is no lift in my heart. It was not the right way. I did not want it so."

With such a disappointing end to a fight that was expected to reestablish a new heavyweight king, there was an immediate outcry for a return match. Fran Bruen, general manager for Madison Square Garden met with Max's German manager Arthur Buelow to discuss a rematch. Right from the start negotiations were fraught with difficulties. Although Max wanted to fight he refused to do so until at least October, which was when his contract with Buelow ran out. Joe Jacobs, Max's American manager and the manager that Max wanted to go with, insisted that he be reinstated; Jacobs was on the New York State Athletics Committee's black list and had been suspended when Max refused to fight Phil Scott over a year before. Jacobs had only been granted a temporary license as a second for the Sharkey fight. Then there was a tangled mess concerning the splitting of the receipts and who got what. Everyone had a claim to part of the $750,000 gate and was putting "plasters" or attachments on moneys. Jacobs put a plaster on Buelow's share of Max's purse.

Jack, desperate for a rematch by September and hearing that there were problems with negotiation came up with his own plan. First, Sharkey offered Max 37½ percent of the receipts and agreed to take the short end of 12½ percent. Sharkey then offered to pay the 20 percent to Arthur Buelow that he was entitled to under his contract to Max, from his 12½, which amounted to about $50,000. Furthermore, Jack offered a unique solution to any controversy that might arise from a foul. He suggested a rain check arrangement and another fight free of charge to the customers the following night if the return fight ended in another foul. He also agreed to not allow himself to be declared the winner on a foul and all but promised to go and jump in a lake if he dropped one low again. And even went as far as to say he would fight for free if necessary.

Initially, Buelow agreed to the offer Sharkey made and Schmeling agreed to a September fight, provided that he was given a release from the managerial contract which Buelow held. Buelow, however, refused to cut Schmeling loose from his contract, and negotiations stalled. Unable to come to an agreement the fight slipped away; it would be two years before Jack and Max would again meet in a ring.

In the end it was really a tragedy for both fighters. Jack had done nothing wrong deliberately and was handily wining the fight. It was simply bad luck. Max as well did nothing wrong, but because of the way he won his victory was tarnished. Although at first Max was happy with his win, reality quickly set in. Back in Germany there was some celebrating over Schmeling's victory but the overwhelming reaction was embarrassment. When the fight film was shown in German theatres audiences laughed raucously and Max became the butt of many a joke. He was even given nicknames like "The low blow champ."

60-years later when Jack recalled the fight, he said somewhat bitterly, "I never hit'em low." He would however, get another crack at Schmeling, but he would have to fight a toy bulldog and a giant to do it.

CHAPTER 21
THE TOY BULL DOG

With the hopes of an immediate Schmeling rematch dashed, Buckley wasted little time trying to finding another fight. Team Sharkey met with Frank Bruen in August of 1930. Bruen suggested a match with Victorio Campolo, but talks came to a halt when Bruen refused to guarantee Sharkey $100,000, saying, "Jack seems to have forgotten that he lost the Schmeling bout."[135]

A few days later negotiations turned to a Sharkey-Stribling rematch. Stribling had just beaten Phil Scott and was considered a logical opponent. The plan was for the winner to get a shot at Schmeling. But again negotiations stalled when Sharkey demanded a promised guarantee of $100,000 plus a percentage of the gates receipts.

Discussions then turned to a possible fight with the giant Italian, Primo Carnera and again negotiations ended after only a few meetings. Team Sharkey then went back into talks with Stribling, but by this time Stribling had his eye on Schmeling and had lost interest in "The Boston Gob."

By December 1930 the New York Athletic Commission was fed up with negotiations and Schmeling's six month grace period to defend his title was past due. Chairman James A. Farley wired Max in Germany demanding that he accept the challenge that was formerly issued by Sharkey months earlier or face the possibility of having his title stripped. Max, however, wouldn't budge and responded with a cable that said, "Gentleman Joe, he knows what to do. Jacobs is now my manager and I have just cabled him to go before your body and handle this matter." Unfortunately, the commission did not recognize Jacobs as Schmeling manager and required that Max speak for himself, so talks and threats of taking away the German's title continued.

Sharkey, perturbed with the mess, met with the New York Commission. They were in full support of Jack and felt that he should get a rematch with Max, but unfortunately Jack lacked the support of a big promoter. In fact, most promoters and critics insisted that a Sharkey-Schmeling rematch would be a financial failure. Instead all eyes were now on Stribling, who had stolen Sharkey's spotlight.

By January 4, 1931 Schmeling and Stribling had agreed to a summer fight and Jack was out of luck. Discussions went back to a fight with Primo

---

[135] "Sharkey Demands to Much for Bruen," by Walter Trumbull, *Boston Globe*, July 22, 1930, pg.15.

Carnera and everything was going well until a dispute over a contract sprang up. An injunction was filed and the fight was off as quickly as it had begun.

It was then that the most unlikely of opponents stepped up and offered to meet Sharkey, former middleweight champion, turned heavyweight contender, Mickey "The Toy Bulldog" Walker.

Finally, a year after his match with Schmeling, Jack had a fight. On July 6, 1931 Sharkey signed to fight Mickey Walker. It was said that Jack had a bemused look on his face as he eyed the much smaller man and affixed his name to the contract.

Despite the fact that Mickey started his career as a welterweight and stood only 5'7" he was not one to be taken lightly; he is in fact, considered one of the greatest fighters of all time.

Born Edward Patrick Walker in Elizabeth, New Jersey on July 13, 1901 (some sources say 1903) Mickey began his career as a welterweight in 1919. His debut fight was against a fellow named Dominic Orsini, for which he was paid ten dollars. With no amateur experience or formal training Mickey was crude from the start, but had power in both hands and used his aggressiveness to overwhelm opponents. He was also inhumanly tough and his ability to absorb punishment earned him the nickname "The Toy Bulldog."

In the first two years of his career, Walker lost just twice in 40 contests. This was good enough to get him a non-title match with Jack Britton, the reigning welterweight champion. On July 18, 1921 Mickey took the champion the full 12-rounds. Officially the bout was a "no decision" or newspaper decision bout with neither fighter being declared winner or loser. The general consensus in the next day's newspapers was that the champion appeared to get the better of Mickey.

With his impressive showing against Britton, Mickey was now a legitimate contender. He went on to beat Dave Shade and Artie Bird which secured him a second try at champion Britton.

On November 1, 1922 at the tender age of 21, Walker took the title from Britton with a hard fought 15-round decision. Shortly thereafter Walker began campaigning as a middleweight, occasionally dropping back down and defending his welterweight title. While fighting as a middleweight Walker attracted the attention of Jack "Doc Kearns" former manager of heavyweight champion Jack Dempsey. Walker and Kearns became great friends and rumors of their escapades of carousing, whorehouses and bar hopping became the talk of boxing.

As a middleweight Mickey took on light heavyweight champion Mike McTigue. Although Mickey was outweighed he was in control of the fight, but unable to knock McTigue out. Because the fight went the full 12-rounds there was officially a "no-decision" which allowed McTigue to keep his title. On July 2, 1925 Mickey faced the reigning middleweight champion Harry Greb. Greb, known as "The Human Windmill" is to this day considered by most to be the single greatest middleweight of all time.

In front of 60,000 spectators Greb and Walker fought one of the most savage and bloody battles of the century. Although Walker took some of the early rounds it was Greb who came on strong giving Mickey a terrible beating and winning the decision. "The Toy Bulldog," however, managed to finish the fight on his feet even, according to sportswriter Damon Runyon, out fighting Greb in the 15th and final round.

As legend has it the two fighters ran into each other later that evening at a bar. Following some trash talk the two agreed to meet in the back alley. As the story goes, Walker emerging victorious from the fight after sucker punching Greb while he was taking off his coat.

Following his loss to Greb, Walker made two defenses of his welterweight title before losing it to Pete Latzo on May 20, 1926. Mickey then won three in a row at middleweight and secured a fight with middleweight champion Tiger Flowers, who had taken the title from Greb. In what turned out to be an exciting battle, Tiger took the early rounds with his superior boxing skills and had Mickey bleeding badly by the fourth. As tough as his name suggested, Walker hung in there and applied constant pressure. In the ninth Walker dropped the champion and in the last few rounds Mickey's constant bombardment of punches had Tiger shaken on a number of occasions. Despite dropping the champion and taking the last few rounds the crowd booed loudly when the decision was given to Walker.

Mickey defended his middleweight title twice but by this time he was making forays in to the light heavyweight division and earning bigger purses. In a 1927 rematch he defeated Mike McTigue by first round knockout and then battered former light heavyweight champion Paul Berlenbach three weeks later. Mickey then stepped it up and took on light heavyweight king Tommy Loughran. Unable to cope with Tommy's speed and skill, Mickey lost a 10-round decision. By the end of 1929 Mickey abandoned his middleweight title, stating his intention to move up to heavyweight and go after the biggest prize in all sports: the heavyweight championship of the world.

Mickey made his heavyweight debut by beating a tough but aging Johnny Risko. Following another win over Johnny Risko and an impressive win over Bearcat Wright, who stood six inches taller and outweighed Mickey by 42-pounds, Walker challenged Sharkey.

On July 3 Sharkey spent the day golfing and fishing with Babe Ruth at Bow Lake. Later that evening Jack sat next to his radio and listened to Schmeling defeat Stribling, stopping the Georgian in the 15th round with only 14 seconds to go.

Nineteen days later, Jack and Mickey met in the ring at Ebbet's Field on July 22, 1931. 35,000 curious fans showed up to watch what many thought was a gross mismatch. Jack came in at 198½ to Mickey's 169½. What they saw was Sharkey and Walker fight to an indecisive 15-round draw. Jack's performance was described by David Egan who said, "He just lazed along in a don't-care-a-whoop manner, scoring when he pleased with left jabs to Mickey's shaggy head, but in general giving the opinion that he didn't wish to knockout or seriously harm Walker."[136] Jack's lack of aggression may lend some truth to the rumors that legendary gangster Al "Scarface" Capone had summoned Sharkey to a meeting and suggested that Jack allow Mickey to go the distance. This is in no way to say that Walker had an easy time or did not bring the battle to Jack. He did, in fact, fight one of the best fights of his career.

Egan wrote that Mickey fought "a willing stand-up battle against a man who out weighted him by 30-pounds and there was nothing but high glee on the part of the pew holders when he received a draw." When it was over the judges were in disagreement as to who won. Two of them had it for Mickey, one had it a draw. Several experts at ringside felt that Jack should have gotten the nod with a few believing that he had won at least 9 or 10 rounds.

Sports writer Grantland Rice felt that the decision was a good one saying, "Mickey Walker, "The Toy Bulldog," held Jack Sharkey to a draw after 15-grueling rounds. The decision was exactly right. In my count I gave Walker eight rounds and Sharkey seven, but Sharkey did far greater damage through his superior punching. Walker fought one of the most surprising fights in the history of the ring. Outweighed by 30-pounds and six inches shorter, with a short reach, he tore into the big sailor from the first gong and never quit a game tireless, hard-charging attack. Sharkey threw lefts and rights with vicious intent, but they seldom landed as the fast bobbing Walker ducked and sidestepped, or blocked them with his lifted shoulders. Sharkey fought only in spurts. When he came in with a rush he had Walker in trouble, only to ease up again and let Mickey take the play away. Mickey might have won the decision if Sharkey had not cut open his left eye, which near the finish left him fighting with one eye."[137]

Well respected Walter Trumbull, writer for the *New York Sun* gave his opinion saying, "Mickey Walker fought his usual courageous in his bout with Jack Sharkey here tonight, but it seemed to most of us that he got a lucky break. In my opinion it was a very bad decision. According to my

---

136 "Sharkey, Walker Fight to Draw," by David F. Egan, *Boston Globe*, July 23, 1931, pg.1.
137 "Results of Preliminary Bout," by Grantland Rice, *Boston Globe*, July 23, 1931, pg.1.

score, Sharkey took nine rounds, Walker took four and two were about even."[138]

Back in his dressing room Jack was questioned by the press. "I was a better fighter," he said as he pulled on his clothes, his face unmarked except for a slight redness under the eyes. "Four or five years ago when I was fighting 14 times a year, more than I am now, I laid off too long and it hurt me. But I'm not going to try and take any credit from Mickey. He's a great little fighter and don't let anyone tell you he can't hurt. I thought I won, but it will go down in the record books as a draw for Walker and that's what counts."[139] 60-years later when Jack recalled the fight he said, "I took it easy on him cuz I thought I was a big shot."[140]

Across the hall a happy Walker was interviewed. "It was a good fair fight all the way and I could fight 15 more rounds like it right now," said a jubilant Walker. "Sharkey never did hurt me, but heck I cut easily and I bleed a lot, and I suppose that looked bad and counted against me. I thought I won all right, but that don't matter."[141]

Following his fight with Jack, Walker continued to campaign as a heavyweight, beating such notables as King Levinsky and Paulino Uzcudun. In 1932 he would lose to Max Schmeling. After a few more fights Mickey took on light heavyweight champion Maxie Rosenbloom in a bid for the title. Despite physical disadvantages and fighting one of the finest light heavyweight champions of all time the fight was extremely close. At the end of 15-rounds Maxie was given the decision, however there were many who felt that Mickey had won the fight, including the referee who had it for Walker. Following the Rosenbloom fight Walker fought on for another two years, then retired in 1935. After retiring, "The Toy Bulldog" would go down in history as one of the greatest welterweight and middleweight champions of all time.

The draw with Mickey was actually a loss for Jack, it cost him an immediate return fight with Schmeling. Instead, Jack would have to fight the man mountain, Primo Carnera, before his second try at Max and the heavyweight title.

---

138 "Trumbull Thinks Sharkey Won Fight," by Walter Trumbull, *Boston Globe*, July 23, 1931, pg.10.
139 "Sharkey Starts for Home in Fast Car," *Boston Globe*, July 23, 1931, pg.1.
140 "The Story of Jack Sharkey, Boxing's Tragic Figure," by Jim Brady, *Boxing illustrated*, pg.82.
141 Ibid.

CHAPTER 22
SHARKEY-CARNERA I

Jack's lackluster performance against Walker cost him a much wanted return match with Schmeling. After the Walker fight, Schmeling's manager Jacobs said, "So far as Max Schmeling and I are concerned, Jack Sharkey is out of the picture. We'll take Walker next summer and draw plenty of money. I thought Walker should have been given the decision. I gave Walker seven rounds, Sharkey six, and called two even."[142]

As if a draw with a middleweight wasn't bad enough Jack was crucified by some of his enemies in the newspaper profession who were writing that "The Boston Gob" was washed up as a fighter. But despite the draw, Jack was still considered "The American heavyweight champion" and ranked number one right behind Schmeling. Furthermore, he had every intention of carrying on and getting another chance at Schmeling and the title.

By September 1931 the match that had been talked about for months was finalized. Sharkey and the giant Primo Carnera had agreed to meet October 12, 1931. Jack knew that a win over Carnera would put him right back in line for a shot at Schmeling. He also knew that a loss would be devastating to his career.

Primo Carnera was born in Sequals, a village to the northeast of Italy on October 26, 1906. At 17-years-old while working as a brick layer in France the huge teen was talked into boxing by Amilcare Piana. Primo agreed to try boxing and began working out at the Le Mans Sporting Association. Although massively strong, Primo was slow and cumbersome in the ring, but early on he displayed a good jab and learned to use it effectively. Over time his speed and footwork improved and he would become surprisingly light on his feet for a man of his size.

Primo trained at Le Mans until 1926, when he was spotted by a traveling circus owner. At 6' 7" and nearly 300-pounds Primo was a perfect fit as the circus strong man and wrestler. Tired of being a bricklayer and making little money, Primo jumped at the opportunity.

Billed as "Juan the Invincible" or "Juan the Guadalajara Terror," Primo lifted weights, and also boxed or wrestled all comers as part of his show. Although he would say later in life that he didn't like the job, it did pay better than a bricklayer and he wasn't hungry.

---

142 "Manager of Schmeling Says Sharkey Out as Challenger," *Boston Globe*, July 23, 1931, pg.10.

Primo's boxing career was conceived on March 15, 1928 when his circus stopped in the French seaside town of Arcachon. While in town Primo took on a tough challenger and disposed of him in two rounds with a left to the jaw. More importantly Primo attracted the attention of Paul Journee, a former French heavyweight fighter who happened to be in attendance. Journee was George Carpentier's main sparring partner when George was preparing to battle Jack Dempsey. After a meeting with Journee, Primo agreed to give professional boxing a try. In time Journee introduced Primo to Leon See, the man who would become his manager. From there Primo would go on to have one of the most controversial and interesting boxing careers of all time. A career that involved mobsters, accusations of fixed fights, and shady back room deals.

Primo arrived in America on December 31, 1929. His first fight was against Clayton "Big Boy" Peterson in front of a packed house at Madison Square Garden. Over 17,000 fans showed up to get a look at the much talked about gigantic Italian. But, if they were hoping to get a good look at Primo and his abilities they were disappointed. The fight ended at 1:10 of the first round after Primo dropped "Big Boy" four times.

Following his debut Carnera won 23 in a row before losing to former Sharkey opponent Jimmy Maloney. After the Maloney defeat, Primo won nine in a row including a rematch with Maloney and top contender Paulino Uzcudun. With his impressive wins Primo secured a shot at Jack.

The two met at Ebbet's Field in New York on October 12, 1931. A large crowd of over 30,000 were on hand to witness Sharkey at his best. Despite daunting physical disadvantages, Sharkey at 6' and 201½-pounds and Primo at 6' 7" and 261-pounds, "The Boston Gob" easily out boxed his larger foe and put on one of the best performances of his career. Primo to his credit fought well through the first three and a half rounds showing good footwork, speed and a nice jab that kept Jack off balance. But in the fourth Jack caught Primo with a vicious left hook and the giant hit the deck hard and controversy quickly followed.

Sportswriter John Kieran recalled that when Primo went down, "The ring platform quaked and quivered under the terrific impact of that gross tonnage."[143] Using the ropes for support, Primo struggled to his feet as referee Ed "Gunboat" Smith counted. By six, Primo was up, however his corner had been yelling for him to stay down until the count of nine. Seeing Sharkey coming and finally hearing his corner's instruction he dropped back down to his knee. Instantly, Sharkey started to yell and protest to "Gunboat." "He went down without being hit, he's disqualified. Count him

---

143 John Kieran, Sports of the Times, *New York Times*, October 14, 1931.

out!"[144] yelled Sharkey. Ignoring Jack, Ed continued his count and Primo rose at nine. At that point Sharkey's volatile temper erupted. Irate, he made to leave the ring believing the fight was over and he was the winner on a disqualification. Buckley, seeing what Jack was about to do, grabbed Sharkey and pushed him back into the ring. A moment later the fight was back on. By the time the action resumed Primo had over 20 seconds to recover; the rest, however, did him little good.

After the devastating knockdown Primo was not the same fighter and with the exception of round 13 Jack dominated the action and gave the giant a thorough shellacking. In round 15 he battered the Italian mercilessly, with hard lefts and rights that nearly sent Carnera back to the canvas. When it was over there was no argument as to who won; Sharkey's arm was raised in victory.

The win shot Sharkey right back to the forefront of the heavyweight division. As for Carnera the loss answered several questions about the giant. Primo proved that he was more than a circus freak. He showed that he was fast, and possessed a fairly good defense. The fight also showed that he had courage, strength and stamina. However, the fight confirmed that despite his 260-plus pounds Primo was not a devastating hitter.

With his impressive performance against Carnera, Sharkey would get his rematch with Schmeling and another try at the championship.

---

144 Herbert W. Barker, *Nashville Banner*, October 13, 1931.

CHAPTER 23
SHARKEY-SCHMELING II, WINNING THE TITLE

By January 1932 Max Schmeling was back in America after spending nearly a year in Germany following his fight with Young Stribling. Trying to capitalize on his championship, Max was on a 40 city exhibition tour as well as looking for his next fight. On January 12 the champion made a stop at the Boston arena to box three rounds. Amid a roar of hostile boos Max was introduced. A moment later Sharkey entered the ring and received a much more cordial welcome from his fans. Jack addressed Max asking in German how he was doing. Max replied in English, "fine." "You have a nice house here tonight," said Jack. "Yes, it's nice," replied a smiling Schmeling, "but not as good as when you and I box." "Well what's the matter with you? Let's get together on this."[145] The two were unable to talk further because a moment later Max was rushed to the center of the ring to receive instructions and Sharkey was ordered to clear out.

Max's exhibition tour turned out to be poorly received so he cut it short. Team Schmeling then went into negotiations for a fight with Mickey Walker but found that the big time promoters wanted nothing to do with it. Realizing that there was only one fistic foe that could spark interest and draw big money, Team Schmeling and Team Sharkey were soon negotiating.

On February 3, 1932 Jack and Max made it official by signing contracts and each handing over $25,000 for an appearance forfeit.

Opinions as to who would win were divided more so this time than during the buildup to their last fight. Benny Leonard picked Sharkey to win the first fight but now picked Schmeling, saying, "When they met before I picked Sharkey. I knew that Jack was the better boxer and I also knew that Schmeling was not in the best of shape. You remember that Schmeling hurt his ankle and couldn't train properly. But now, conditions have changed, Schmeling is a lot better than he was and he has the added confidence and cockiness which always is the asset of a man who holds the title."[146]

The two met on June 21, 1932 at Yankee Stadium almost exactly two years to the day after their last encounter. Sharkey, now at 30-years-old entered the ring at 205-pounds. Max, at 27, came in at 188. A massive crowd of 75,000 fans had that had the bleachers groaning witnessed a close,

---

[145] "let's Get Together, Whispers Jack to Max at Meeting in Arena," *Boston Globe*, June 12, 1932, pg.21.
[146] "Schmeling Picked by Benny Leonard," by Walter Trumbull, *Boston Globe*, June 8, 1932, pg.24.

tame, methodical fight; not at all like the first. When it was over the crowd was divided as to who won, but the edge seemed to belong to Max. The judges were split two to one, with Referee "Gunboat" Smith and George F. Kelly electing Sharkey and Judge Charles Matison voting for Schmeling.

Moments after the final bell, both corners waited anxiously for the decision. "The Winnah," said Joe Humphries, "and new champ" and before he could complete his announcement Sharkey's corner exploded in exhilaration. Caught up in the exciting moment Tony Polazzolo and Al Lacy swept Sharkey up and carried him to the center of the ring. And controversy followed. Max, in a show of good sportsmanship walked over and congratulated Jack as the ring filled with an excited group of people and his manager Jacobs uttered the now famous line, "We wuz robbed."

Immediately after the verdict came over the loudspeaker many in the crowd voiced their disagreement loudly with cries of robbery, while others yelled excitedly, giving wild tribute for Sharkey. Even the press was divided, with Grantland Rice saying he gave Schmeling 8 rounds, Sharkey 4 and 3 even and then calling it, "one of the worst decisions in the history of the heavyweight game."[147] David F. Egan saw the fight for Jack saying, "Sharkey fought one of the most intelligent battles of his speckled career and he beat back "The Black Uhlan" with one of the prettiest exhibitions of boxing the ring has seen in many years."[148]

When the press finally caught up with an animated Sharkey in his dressing room he said, "I won the title. I won it honestly. Now I will defend it. I will be a fighting champion. I was not hurt. I am going back to Boston and there will decide on my next plans. But you can say for me that I will keep on fighting."[149]

Over in Max's dressing room Schmeling was taking the loss of his title surprisingly well. Jacobs, however, was furious. Sitting in his dressing room covered in sweat and draped in a damp towel Max tried to grin as he answered questions. "If someone beats me I don't care, I say the better man he wins and that is all right. But how can Sharkey beat me running away all the time?"[150] Jacobs, in a towering rage over what he charged was a "plot" to steal the championship tried to console Schmeling, who said, "Sharkey was only playing with his punches, he runs away all the time, never did he hurt me. Only a few times I hit him hard but I know he is hurt. I can feel

---

147 "Rice Calls Decision One of Worst Ever," by Grantland Rice, *Boston Globe*, June 22, 1932, pg.24.
148 "Jack Sharkey Wins World Title Fight," by David F. Egan, *Boston Globe*, June 22, 1932, pg.1.
149 "70,000 See Sharkey Win Decision, 2-1," *Syracuse Herald*, June 22, 1932, pg.43.
150 "Max Schmeling Takes His Defeat Quite Gracefully," by Edward Neil, *Winnipeg Free Press*, June 22, 1932, pg.7.

that he knows I am beating him, but they give him the decision. Well I am a young fellow. I have plenty of time. I fight Sharkey again. Now, I will telephone my mother in Berlin, she will be waiting."[151]

With that Jacobs took over and didn't mince words when it came to letting everyone know exactly how he felt about the decision. "I knew two weeks ago," fumed Jacobs, "that Smith was going to referee and I knew all along they were going to steal the title if he did. A few weeks ago I told newspapermen that if a certain referee went into the ring I would not let Schmeling leave his dressing room, so certain was my information. But the New York State Boxing Commission kept assuring me we would get an even break. Well, look what happened. The only mistake I made was not publishing the name of the referee two weeks ago when I knew what was coming off."[152]

After a call to his mother, Max continued with his interview saying, "I believe I won tonight. I never was so surprised in all my life as I was when Joe Humphries announced, 'Winner and new heavyweight champion, Jack Sharkey.' I think there was only one person more surprised than I and that was Jack Sharkey. Of course I would like to fight Sharkey again. I will meet him in September if Joe Jacobs can drag him into another match."[153]

Unfortunately, a third match never materialized. For Schmeling he would continue on with a storied career and life. In 1936 he would meet Joe Louis, and in one of the greatest upsets of all time he would knockout the great "Brown Bomber." But he never would regain the heavyweight title. For Sharkey, his career would continue with a controversial rematch against Primo Carnera in a fight that would go down in history as one of the greatest "alleged" fixes of all time.

---

151 Ibid.
152 Ibid.
153 "German Thinks He is Winner," by Max Schmeling, *Boston Globe*, June 22, 1932, pg.24.

CHAPTER 24
THE PASSING OF ERNIE SCHAAF

The new champion and his wife arrived home at about 7:30 p.m. on July 23 two days after the fight. The first thing they noticed as they pulled into the long driveway was dozens of reporters, photographers and fans gathered around the front of their house. As they came to a stop and got out of the car, the crowd cheered a loud welcome. Before spending time with fans and reporters Jack first greeted his kids and scolded his daughters (with a smile), for staying up late and listening to his fight on the radio. He then took some time to catch up with Dorothy's grandparents who were once again on babysitting duty.

Tired and sore, Jack sat down with fans and the media. He started off by saying he felt a thousand times better now that he was home. When asked about the championship Sharkey replied, "The championship doesn't mean a thing to me now, I suppose it will mean more in a few days when I get time to think about it. But just now I want to get to sleep. I haven't slept a wink since Tuesday morning. I had a lot of things to do in New York this morning talking for the news reels and posing for pictures."

Talking of Schmeling and the fight Jack said, "Schmeling surprised me; I mean it he had improved. I don't mean 100 percent, I mean 1,000 percent. When I first tried him out I found he was covering up well, that made me think. Then I found he was sticking out his left jab continually and that surprised me too. I didn't expect anyone to keep jabbing at me. He certainly improved and I suppose he will improve more. Of course after the fight was going along, I saw what was happening, Schmeling was leading with his left, what did you think I'd do? I wasn't going to go in because I'd have to go in and lead at the same time. I let him jab and then, when I'd feint, he'd start with his left and I'd shuffle away. Then he'd have to jab again. It was the style of fight that I fought that led me to shuffle away. And Schmeling fought the kind of a fight I wanted him to fight."[154]

The subject then turned to the radio broadcast of the fight, which many people felt gave the wrong idea that Schmeling was winning by a wide margin. Sharkey felt that the radio blow-by-blow of the fight gave the wrong impression because it was not done by professionals. In fact, Sharkey was surprised that Charles Francis Coe, a novelist and Graham McNamee an announcer were allowed to call the fight. Sharkey then explained that Francis and he had run-ins before, and Francis Coe wasn't exactly a Sharkey

---

154 "Sharkey at Home, Just Daddy," *Boston Globe*, June 23, 1932, pg.1.

fan and wouldn't give him a break. Such was the controversy over the announcing, that some people felt contributed to the controversial decision, that New York banned any but boxing experts, such as sports writers, judges, and referees from broadcasting descriptions of future fights. Wrapping up the interviews, photos and autographs, Jack was finally able to get to bed.

It would be a year before Sharkey would step back into the ring, but for the next twelve months the new champion was a very busy man. Being heavyweight champion in the 1920s meant being one of the most recognizable and sought after sports figures in the world. The heavyweight crown, at the time, was the greatest prize in all sports and the man who wore it was considered to be the greatest fighting man on the planet.

On June 29 Jack was part of a parade honoring Emilia Earhart in Boston that wound through downtown. Emilia and Jack were then guests of honor, along with other athletes, at a carnival at Braves Field put on for the benefit of the unemployed in Boston. Over 22,000 people showed up to watch wrestling, boxing, and sprint races, along with various Vaudeville acts. Last but not least was the ball game between the Boston Red Sox and the Braves, won by the Sox 6 to 3. While there, Jack was interviewed and urged people to support the charity. Afterwards he was given a thunderous applause. In all the charity raised $25,000.

After the charity event Jack and his family went on vacation at Bow Lake. While there Jack participated in the firing off of the annual Fourth of July fireworks. On August 29 Jack was a guest of honor at a Democratic rally. On September 26, he was at the Schmeling-Mickey Walker match along with Jack Dempsey, Primo Carnera, Jimmy Mclarnin and Johnny Risko. Together the fighters sat and watched as Schmeling hammered Walker to defeat in the eighth round. October 11 saw Sharkey climb into a ring for the first time since winning the title; boxing a four round exhibition against Owen Flynn. By late October, Jack was on a hunting trip to Nova Scotia with friends.

While living the life of a man of leisure, fight offers were coming in. There were talks of Jack and Primo getting together for a rematch, if Primo defeated Ernie Schaaf in their fight that was coming up in February. It was also reported that Jack was offered $100,000 to defend his title against George Godfrey in Chicago. Buckley refused, saying that Sharkey was under contract with Madison Square Garden and would only fight in New York. Jack Dempsey was also said to have offered Sharkey a fight against the winner of the Max Bear-Max Schmeling bout that was coming up in June. Buckley again refused, saying Sharkey would be glad to do business with Dempsey in the ring, but would never fight for him. Talks then circulated back to a third fight between Sharkey and Schmeling. Joe Jacobs said Max would be glad to meet Sharkey anytime, but not under the promotion of Madison Square Garden. "There is no chance to make the match with Sharkey on account of it being necessary to box under the promotion of Madison Square Garden, which I absolutely refuse to do."[155]

On February 10, 1933 at Madison Square Garden, Jack was acting as second in the corner of his good friend and stable mate Ernie Schaaf, who was facing the Italian giant Primo Carnera. Sitting ringside was Johnny Buckley, who also managed Ernie. The fight started with both men feeling each other out and at first everything seemed fine, but it wasn't. What only a few people knew was Ernie had been sick with influenza and had visited the hospital two weeks prior to the fight with flu-like symptoms. As a result of his illness he was not able to train properly. Buckley being one of the few who knew about Ernie's illness, would later state that because of the influenza Ernie had only trained 10 days. In all truth, Schaaf was in no shape to be facing a powerful man who outweighed him by 57-pounds and stood 5 inches taller.

As the fight wore on it became apparent that Ernie was fatigued and his performance was suffering. By the tenth round Ernie was visibly tired and by round twelve he was completely exhausted. The reports say that Ernie had been on the end of Carnera's long jab and had taken quite a few of the giant's hooks and smashing uppercuts throughout the fight.

The two met in the center of the ring to begin round 13. Schaaf landed a solid left early but then only pawed with his punches after that. Carnera on the other hand was landing solid blows. Out in the center of the ring the huge Italian landed a straight left jab that was deceptively hard, snapping Ernie's head back violently. Schaaf hit the canvas, landing on his left side with his right hand clutching the ropes; a dazed look on his face. Referee Cavanaugh began the count. At three Ernie's hand slipped from the ropes. At four he slowly collapsed forward completely unconscious. By five, seeing that Ernie was not going to get up, Cavanaugh waved the fight over. Within a few seconds a concerned Primo was standing over Ernie, offering his help. A moment later Primo's corner men were in the ring followed by Sharkey, Buckley and the rest of Schaaf's corner. As Ernie lay on the Garden canvas struggling for his life, the decision was announced and ring announcer Joe Humphries lifted Carnera's hand in victory. Immediately the crowd erupted with loud boos and yells of "fake" and "fix." They could not believe that the jab Primo had landed was hard enough to knockout the rugged Schaaf and they were probably right. But, what they failed to realize was that it wasn't just the final punch that felled Schaaf, it was the cumulative effect of 13-rounds of punishment, coupled with his illness that was causing his brain to swell and his body to give out.

---

155 "Poll Puts Schmeling Over Jack Sharkey," *Boston Globe*, December 29, 1932, pg.1.

In the ring, Ernie's corner tried desperately to revive their fallen fighter, but was unable to. Sharkey grabbed him under the arms and dragged him bodily to his corner, propping him up on his stool. Several frantic moments followed, but they had no luck waking Ernie. It was then that they decided to move Schaaf to his dressing room. Jack along with five others lifted Ernie out of the ring.

In Ernie's crowded dressing room medical personnel desperately tried to awaken the young fighter. After 20 minutes the New York Athletic Commission's doctor ordered Schaaf to be rushed to the hospital. A few hours later at Polyclinic Hospital, Ernie underwent an examination by Dr. William H. Walker who said Schaaf was suffering from a severe concussion. Schaaf remained at Polyclinic for several days in critical condition drifting in and out of a coma. His mother Lucy and sister, Amy Daly had hurriedly come down from Massachusetts to be at his side along with Buckley. Initially, Sharkey was there but was told that there was nothing he could do. Having already planned a vacation in Florida with his family Jack left apparently unaware of the seriousness of Schaaf's injuries.[156] His vacation didn't last long. On Monday Jack received a telegram informing him that they were going to operate on Ernie. The next morning Sharkey packed his bags and left for New York to be at Ernie's side. But, by the time he arrived it was too late.

On Monday, February 13, Ernie underwent three hours of brain surgery. A team of four noted neurosurgeons worked carefully to relieve the swelling from a deep-seated intra-cranial hemorrhage. Following the surgery Ernie showed some improvement by moving his left arm which had previously been paralyzed. A hospital bulletin stated, "The patient stood the operation well, and afterwards moved his left arm which had been paralyzed. The patient's condition, however, is still critical."[157]

By midnight of Tuesday the 14th the doctors knew that Ernie was slipping away and his death was inevitable. Before his passing Ernie woke briefly. When asked by his mother how he was feeling the young fighter answered weakly, "I'm ok, Mom." He then slipped back into a coma. At 4:10 a.m. Ernie passed away. He was 24-years-old.

On Friday the 17th friends and family members gathered at Schaaf's home in Wrentham, Massachusetts to escort his body to the cemetery in Foxboro. The town's highways were choked with traffic and public buildings flew flags at half staff as the funeral procession slowly wound its way to the church where Ernie's flag draped casket was carried inside and

---

156 "Boxer Better After Ordeal," *Boston Globe*, February 14, 1933, pg.1.
157 *Nashville Banner*, February 14, 1933, Eddie Neil.

Mass was performed. From there Ernie was taken to his final resting place at a cemetery in Foxboro.

Immediately following Ernie's death the New York boxing commission talked of starting a super heavyweight or "dreadnought" class for fighters as big as Carnera. Nobody less than 6'2" and 220-pounds would be allowed to fight in the class. The commission also barred Sharkey from defending his title against Carnera even though Jack had easily beaten "The Ambling Alp" in their first meeting. Talks of placing Carnera in a super heavyweight class were short lived. A few days later, head of the Garden, Jimmy Johnston said he was going ahead with preparations for a Sharkey-Carnera rematch "until definitely ordered otherwise by the boxing commission."

CHAPTER 25
SHARKEY-CARNERA II

On April 12, 1933 it became official. The New York boxing commission agreed to sanction a fight between Jack Sharkey and Primo Carnera set for June 29, 1933 at Madison Square Garden. Before going into serious training Jack, along with welterweight fighter George Lee and his Chestnut Hill neighbor left for Sebago Lake, Maine, on Tuesday, April 11, for a few days of fly fishing. Sharkey returned home on Saturday but turned right around and left for a trip to Nova Scotia for another week of fishing. Returning from his fishing trip Jack was refreshed. The following day he went into serious training at Jerry Buckley's gym for his first title defense. After spending two weeks of preliminary training at Buckley's, Jack left for Gus Wilson's camp in Orangeburg, New Jersey with Buckley and trainer Al Lacy in tow. "I'm leaving in better condition right now than I was for Schmeling," said Jack. "I weighed 215 when I left to train for Schmeling and right now I weigh 207. I went into the ring against Schmeling at 205, but I don't know what my weight will be against Carnera."[158]

Early on, both camps were quiet; odds on the fight were in favor of Sharkey at 8-5. On June 20, just nine days out reports were that Carnera at 261-pounds looked to be in tremendous condition.

Over at Camp Sharkey the reports were just as positive. Jack was down to 203-pounds and said to be vicious in sparring. His mood, however, was playful and he was having a good time pulling pranks. Unknown to some of the spectators that showed up daily to watch Sharkey train, Jack and his spar mates had wired several of the chairs with electricity. With the flick of a hidden button Sharkey would zap the unsuspecting victims sending them howling into the air. Another trick that Jack and his friends played was to wire a kind of skyrocket to the ignition of a car. When the key was turned the rocket would whistle, pour smoke and end with a great bang, frightening the driver.

All kidding aside, things turned deadly serious when three letters were received at Sharkey's residence. The letters threatened to kidnap and do harm to Jack's family if he did not turn over $5,000. Obviously concerned Jack, Dorothy and Buckley hastily sped home driving the 400 miles in record time to find everyone safe. Not taking any chances, Jack had his good friend Alfred Hammell, a police officer stay at his house until after the

---

[158] "Heavyweight Champion Delighted With Condition as he Prepares to Leave Boston For Training Camp," *Boston Globe*, May 23, 1933, pg.19.

fight. Following an investigation the letters were found to be "crank" letters.

With his family safe at home Jack returned to training camp where the drama continued when it was found that, Walter "Good Time Charley" Friedman (one of Primo's managers), had infiltrated Jack's training camp to get a peek at Sharkey while he trained. Once it was discovered that Walter was in the camp he was quickly asked to leave. Walter then issued a statement to the newspaper, saying, "That Sharkey looks like a big bum, it was the worst exhibition of supposedly championship boxing I've ever seen. If Carnera doesn't knock him out in eight rounds I'll retire him to the nearest circus. Carnera will win in a walk."[159] Sharkey's chief sparring partner, Hans Birkie, who had fought ten close rounds with Primo the previous summer, issued an immediate response. "Jack is a clever man. You can't hit him the same punch more than once. He is too fast, has too many methods of getting under the Italian's left hand to make Primo's only means of defense, Jack should win easily. He should really knock Carnera out."[160]

Jack took May 8 off from training as did Carnera to attend the Max Baer-Max Schmeling fight. The winner of the fight would almost certainly meet the winner of the Sharkey-Carnera fight. The bout, which turned out to be the fight of the year for 1933, was won by Baer via tenth round TKO.

June 27 was Jack's last training day. After finishing up with three rounds of shadow boxing the ex-gob looked pleased as he toweled himself off and spoke to a group of journalists. "I'm in great shape. Be sure to tell Carnera that he'd better be the same."[161]

Over at the Carnera camp Primo was finishing his lasts workout. By all accounts Primo looked good and had improved significantly since his last fight with Sharkey. Former heavyweight champion Tommy Burns watched ringside and commented, "If Carnera doesn't win the title Thursday night he's certain to do so his next time out. He's the most amazing looking fighter I've ever seen."

Cloudy conditions and a threat of rain had kept ticket sales from reaching the expected 60,000 mark. Nevertheless, by 9:30 over 40,000 fans eagerly awaited the showdown for the heavyweight championship of the world. The champion entered the ring first with a week's worth of stubble on his chin and a scowl on his face, accompanied by Tony Polazzolo, Al Lacy, Buckley and Gus Wilson. As a result of a sudden rush of money being bet on Carnera the odds on the fight had switched from favoring Jack at 6-5 to favoring Carnera. This shift in odds made Jack the first heavyweight

---

159 "Friedman Says Sharkey Sure to be Stopped," *Boston Globe*, June 26, 1933, pg.1.
160 Ibid.
161 "Sharkey Warns Carnera to be in Great Shape," *Boston Globe*, June 28, 1933, pg.23.

champion to enter the ring as an underdog. A few moments later Carnera arrived with Billy Duffy and Billy Defoe wearing a green robe and waving to the crowd. As the fighters went over last minute instruction in their respective corners, former champions Jack Dempsey, Gene Tunney and Tommy Loughran were introduced by ring announcer, Harry Balogh. A moment later referee Arthur Donavan gave the men their final instructions and with a loud clang the fight was underway.

Supremely confident Jack, at 201-pounds, opened the round at a sizzling pace bringing the fight to the 260½-pound Carnera. Jack began with stinging jabs and rights to the body and at times he would try to sneak in a left hook over Carnera's long jab. Bobbing and weaving, Jack would rush in and unleash a series of fast punches to Primo's face. The challenger, effective with his long range jab caught the champion midway through the round with a clubbing left that sent Sharkey off balance and into the ropes. Later in the round, Primo caught Jack again with a clubbing left hook that sent "The Boston Gob" spinning into the ropes. Angered, Sharkey came storming back with a determined jab and a smashing left to Primo's ribs. Near the round's end Primo, who was remarkably fast and light on his feet for a man of his size, caught Jack with an impressive right, left, right combination. It was a good round for the "man mountain."

From the second round on Jack took over with his superior boxing ability and speed. "The Boston Gob" began to find his range with his jabs and was able to slip under Primo's long left and catch the Italian with hard left hooks that visibly hurt the big man. David F. Eagan, columnist for the *Boston Globe* wrote of the second round saying, "In the second round Sharkey continued his brilliant boxing. He made the giant look like a ghastly mistake or else something that the cat sniffed at, and the crowed was in roars of laughter when Carnera missed dozens of punches."[162]

The Associated Press reported, "Right up to the last punch tonight Sharkey was fighting one of the greatest battles of his career. Bobbing, feinting, his lips in a thin snarl, eyes flashing between narrowed lids, the Boston sailor ripped into battle in flashes. He moved the giant Italian around, found his opening, and then lashed his punches-long rights to the head-left hooks to the body, straight to the mark."[163]

Round three was another good round for Sharkey. He was effective with his jabs and caught Primo on more than one occasion with looping left hooks, and rights to the body. Carnera, more and more on the defensive, was having a difficult time landing a punch on his fast, aggressive, bobbing

---

[162] "Carnera Knocks Out Sharkey in the Sixth," by David F. Egan, *Boston Globe,* June 30, 1933, pg.2.
[163] *Nashville Tennessee,* June 30, 1933, AP.

and weaving opponent. The giant did however manage to land a powerful, half push/half punch, that drove Sharkey into and bouncing off the ropes.

Carnera did better in the fourth and was able to keep the round just about even, with his long jab. At about the midpoint of the round things turned rough and Primo was warned by the referee for holding and backhanding.

In the fifth, Jack nearly toppled the giant when he landed a crashing right hook to the temple that staggered Carnera. A few moments later Jack landed another smashing right that shook Carnera's huge body and turned the giant's legs rubbery. Bravely, Carnera fought back, but again found the elusive Sharkey hard to hit. Jack continued landing head snapping jabs while sneaking in the occasional left hook. A moment before the bell clanged Jack leaped in with a hard right to Primo's face that again sent the giant reeling.

Sharkey opened round six with a snapping jab and a left hook that grazed Carnera's face; Primo grabbed and held. Separated by referee Donovan, Primo fired a right, left, but Sharkey ducked the blows and connected with a counter left hook to Primo's jaw. Primo returned fired with a jab that Jack slipped and Sharkey drove in a pounding left to Primo's body. The two men traded jabs and clinched. Primo then fired a left, right combo that Sharkey avoided by bobbing and weaving. Jack came forward and the two exchanged jabs and Jack drove in a left to Primo's belly. After a quick exchange of jabs Jack rushed in with a left, right combination that missed. A brief clinch followed, then Carnera opened up with a flurry of blows to Sharkey's head while Jack moved around bobbing and weaving trying to avoid the blows. Suddenly the champion slipped to the canvas but was up quickly as it was not ruled a knockdown. Once up, Sharkey came in with a left hook and the two spent a moment in the center of the ring looking for openings.

The champion then swarmed in and Primo opened up with lefts and rights catching Jack with a left elbow to the side of his face. Sharkey came back with a left and the two sent out light jabs. Primo then grabbed Jack in a head lock but the referee quickly stepped in and separated them. Jack then fired a hard right that only brushed Primo's face. Bobbing and weaving, Sharkey came forward and Primo missed a one, two. The two then clinched and Carnera threw a hard uppercut to Jack's face followed by a left that drove the champion back.

Primo continued to open up with punches while Sharkey bobbed to avoid the blows. Carnera landed a pushing left followed by a jab that Jack avoided. Pressing forward, Jack shot out a jab and a right that Carnera dodged. Primo then threw a straight right hand followed by a left uppercut, both blows landing solidly. Sharkey, undaunted came straight at Primo shooting out stiff jabs to his face and forcing his huge opponent back. The

Champion then exploded a hard right onto Carnera's chin that wobbled the giant and had Primo's long arms flailing wildly.

Continuing to be the aggressor, Sharkey came straight in and tried to land another hard right, but missed. Wisely, Carnera clinched and pushed Jack into the ropes. And at that moment, Carnera followed through with a powerful, uplifting uppercut that caught Sharkey square on the face, lifting his head up and back violently. Jack dropped to the canvas landing on his stomach. Immediately, the crowd rose to its feet with a deafening roar of excitement. Unable to rise, Jack moved only a little as the referee counted him out.

Immediately after the count Jack's corner men jumped into the ring and carried the fallen champion to his stool. Primo, overwhelmed with happiness ran across the ring and spoke a few words to the dazed ex-champion.

Back in his dressing room there was much back slapping and hugging. A jubilant Carnera sat grinning and answering questions in his heavily accented voice. "Was it a tough fight?" he was asked. "No," replied the new champion. "Did he hurt you?" asked one of the reporters. "No, must be careful. Very dangerous, all his punches low and with full strength," said the giant Italian as he stood and threw punches to demonstrate and then slumped back into his chair. When asked if Primo would face Max Bear next, Bill Duffy and Albert Soresi, Primo's handlers were uncertain. Neither appeared anxious to answer and said Primo had no immediate plans as to who he would face next.

Under a barrage of more questions, Primo continued, speaking in even more Italian-laced English than usual. The new champion had nothing but praise for Sharkey. "He fought much better than he did in his last fight,"[164] said the Italian, "and he hurt me much more than he did then. But he didn't reach me as often, and when I discovered that, early in the fight, I knew I could win."[165] "Jack never hurt me. I feel better all the time, stronger, and I know I was going to win after the third round. Jack's knees wobble when I hit him in the stomach. I say, 'Oh, oh, it won't be long now.' Then Mr. Duffy tell me to go get him."[166] Carnera might have been fibbing a bit when he claimed that Sharkey never hurt him during the fight, but with just over a half a minute to go in the sixth round, Carnera indeed got him.

Over in Jack's dressing room the mood was quiet, subdued and filled with uncertainty. A crossfire of questions by a crowd of newspapermen

---

164 *New York Times*, June 30, 1933.
165 *New York Times*, June 30, 1933.
166 Gayle Talbot, *Nashville Banner*, June 30, 1933.

revealed that Jack had no idea what happened. "Well this is the first time in a long while," Sharkey reflected as he thought back to Dempsey, the last man to knock the Gob out. "Is Sharkey through?" one of the press members asked Johnny Buckley. "Whatever Sharkey decides is ok with me," said Buckley. When asked if Jack would fight again the fallen champion replied, "Sure I'll fight again. Why not?" "Who would you like to fight next?" "I don't know," answered Sharkey shaking his head. One of the reporters asked Jack if Carnera had improved. Sharkey replied, "Only in the art of self-defense. I got careless and Carnera caught me with a right uppercut. I think the old blade needs sharpening."[167]

It wasn't long after Sharkey's loss to Carnera that the chatter began about the legitimacy of Carnera's knockout. Although most at ringside said it was a genuine knockout, there were some that contested that the punch never landed. In time, rumors of a fixed fight abounded and there were whispers that Jack had taken a dive. And as we shall see there are many different opinions concerning the "fix" question.

---

[167] "Sure I'll fight again" insists a dazed Sharkey, *Boston Globe*, June 30, 1933, pg.24.

CHAPTER 26
THE "FIX" QUESTION

The question of a "fix" has lingered for decades. The fight has been viewed, discussed and dissected by top boxing authorities. Some believe the knockout was legit, while others believe Sharkey took a seat. There are several factors that lend ammunition to the people that say the fight wasn't on the level. First, and perhaps the most damming evidence being that Carnera had been in a number of fights that were questionable. In fact, his managers, Leon See and Walter "Good Time Charley" Freidman admitted that some of them were set-ups. Second, despite his great size and strength, the giant Italian was not known for his one punch knockout power and Jack had a solid chin. Third, Sharkey had beaten Primo easily in their first encounter. And lastly, it's been said by some, that Sharkey was involved with the Mob during his career and maybe the Mob offered Sharkey a large amount of money to take a dive. There is even a picture of Jack with legendary gangster, Al "scarface" Capone. When asked about the picture by his grandson, Sharkey said that they were not business associates, and only had dinner together. Sharkey then added, "When Al Capone invites you to dinner, you go."

Boxing historian, Joe Page, who wrote a biography on Primo: "The Life and Career of the Heavyweight Boxing Champion, Primo Carnera" believes the fight was on the level saying, "Yes, Carnera – Sharkey II was on the level. I say this without reservation and for several reasons. First, I've never been a believer that the preponderance of Carnera's fights were actually fixed. Some have made this claim over the years, but many others, both during Primo's time and since - including me - disagree. We don't see the reason that they needed to be. Given his size, strength, conditioning and in time, improved skills, many believed that Primo had the ability to win. Sharkey attributed his loss to the fact that Carnera was a much improved fighter and that he had not given Primo credit for that improvement. Also, Sharkey was a wildly talented, but moody, irrational and inconsistent fighter. At ring time, odds makers actually had Primo a 6-5 favorite. I've watched that fight repeatedly and seen Sharkey's head snapped back again and again by a solid right uppercut. Carnera's uppercut was no new phenomenon or a one-time lucky strike."

Writing over three weeks before the championship bout, legendary New York sportswriter Hype Igoe wrote the following about Primo's abilities: "My contention is that Carnera is somewhat muscle bound. That accounts for his inability to snap a hard punch. With the uppercut, it is different. He isn't afraid to step in close and when he's in the position, he brings his right up like an elevator in a new, snappy tower building."

"Those at ringside, various newspaper reporters, the Associated Press, the International News Service and *Time Magazine* all emphasized the power of Carnera's right uppercut and its devastating effect on Sharkey. None questioned its genuineness."

"I've read a great many press reports from the era, said Page. In all, I don't see any overwhelming support for the sentiment that the fight was fixed. Yes, some pundits from the day declared Primo unworthy, but no more than claimed that Braddock or Douglas or Willard or Leon Spinks were undeserving of the title - that's boxing. Bert Sugar and many others, who were not at ringside, got this one completely wrong. In referring to the blow that transferred the championship belt, Sugar states that," "People are still looking for that punch to land. It even surprised Carnera." "I'm simply not sure how he can say this. Again, a viewing of the fight video clearly shows that the right uppercut was a legitimate shot. News reports from the time generally ran along the lines of the *New York Times*, who called the punch 'a terrific right hand uppercut to the chin which almost decapitated Sharkey and brought Carnera the title.' That's pretty amazing for a punch that hasn't yet landed."

"Sharkey's manager, Johnny Buckley, certainly saw the punch and he had no doubt that it landed. His concern was whether Carnera had a horseshoe in his glove or not. He immediately called for officials to examine the Italian's gloves. Billy Duffy having nothing to hide told Primo to leave the gloves on until they could be examined by referee Arthur Donovan and NYSAC officials. No sleep aid was found other than Primo's right fist, Sharkey – who never saw it coming – also never questioned the punch."

The Associated Press wrote in their summation by stating, "There was no question about the power behind Carnera's final thrust, the climax of a spectacular closing flurry that saw the champion flounder suddenly, lost almost complete control of his defense and crumple under the ponderous punches of the biggest man who ever scaled the world heavyweight heights. It was an uppercut that had everything Carnera could muster in his huge frame behind it and Sharkey looked 'cold' if ever a fighter did as he went down. It was his 'secret punch' Carnera exclaimed exultantly after the fight, and perhaps he was right, for Sharkey didn't see it coming and may not know yet what hit him."[168]

The New York Times ran the story of the fight on their front-page on June 29th. Writing for the Times James P. Dawson recalled the punch as, "a

---

168 *Nashville Banner*, June 30, 1933, Plan Gould (AP).

terrific right hand uppercut to the chin which almost decapitated Sharkey and brought Carnera the title."[169]

Even Walter Friedman, who claimed that a number of Primo's early fights were "mischievous" asserted that the Sharkey fight was on the level. "Every once in a while Carnera could complete a perfect punch," Friedman said. "That's what happened when he caught Sharkey with that right uppercut in the sixth round."[170]

According to renowned boxing reporter Hype Igoe of the International News Service: "I'll say that the Preem's port poke is a demoralizing dewdrop, as Jack Sharkey will attest. It was Jack who thought he could stand up and fire lefts with Carnera in their first fight. The bout didn't go far, say five rounds, before Sharkey decided that if his head was bashed back much more it might be torn loose from its moorings." Igoe continued, "It was these right hand up-see-doosies that started Jack Sharkey on his visit to the floor in the championship fight. The one that put Jack down didn't hold a candle to the two he got over on the other side of the ring, two blasting blows that were cruel in their power."

Carnera's punches were described by various sportswriters as ones, "which would have shaken the Statue of Liberty," "which would have tunneled the Eighth Avenue subway," as ones "that must have felt like a cobblestone wrapped in a leather sack."

Primo's children, who themselves are not certain about the legitimacy of some of their father's fights, have been quoted as saying about the set up claims: "Daddy told us that he never knew that. He told us that he never knew and that the decision only depended on the boxing ability of the opponents. He was too naive. We are sorry to say so, but it is like that. His relation to arranged bouts is to be found in his naivete, which came from the goodness of his heart. We do not want to sanctify him, however the importance of what he did and his honesty helped him to survive everything and everybody." They did, however, quote their father as being certain of one thing, "the world title match was not fixed." According to him, "It was too important and could not be fixed."

"For years, Jack Sharkey had to deny rumors that he had taken a dive in the championship fight with Carnera. To the day he died, he swore that the fight was on the level. But rumors have a way of living on, with or without merit. Carnera and Sharkey were however, not the only fighters of the era implicated by rumors of shady dealings. Notables such as Jack Dempsey, Gene Tunney, Jack Johnson, Kid Chocolate, Young Stribling, Max Baer,

---

[169] *New York Times*, James P. Dawson, June 30, 1933.
[170] *St. Petersburg Times*, June 30, 1967.

Jess Willard and Gene Tunney, all were at one time or another, accused of being involved in set up fights."

Sharkey's grandson, Jack Sharkey III, believes the fight to be credible saying, "I asked my grandfather about the "fix" when I was a teenager and he was adamant that he did not take a dive regardless what people thought and regardless of Primo's affiliations. I would expect a grandfather to respond to his ever curious grandson with such a response. I spent an awful a lot of time with my grandfather growing up living just 63 miles away. I had been around him long enough to know and in several situations where my grandfather spoke what was on his mind to the dismay of those confronting him. I have read a lot about my grandfather being very opinionated and after being around him a lot, I find that maybe the newspapers were not too far off. I am saying all of this because my grandfather was his own man and NO ONE told him what to do. If he did not want to do something and he had his mind made up not to do it, he was not going to do it. He would not throw any fight let alone the title. I do not believe that any threat or any bribe would have been enough to entice my grandfather to take a dive. I know he beat Carnera in a non-title fight in 1931. The fact that he lost the title to him in 1933 does not prove that he threw the fight just because he beat him in 1931."

Well respected boxing historian Mike Silver, author of one of the greatest books on boxing, The Arch of Boxing: *the Rise and Decline of the Sweet Science*, is of a different opinion.

"All you have to do is look at the way Sharkey was 'knocked out' in that fight. Carnera was physically strong and a better boxer than most people think, but he was muscle bound and never scored a legitimate one punch knockout in his life. He pushed his punches--no snap. In that last round Sharkey keeps bending low, unlike his normal style. He is waiting and inviting Carnera to throw the damn uppercut already so he can lay down! Poor Carnera is having a hard time landing the punch even when the other guy is giving him every opportunity! It's not easy for a good fighter to throw a fight against an inferior opponent and make it look convincing. When Carnera finally throws the uppercut, which you can't see land, there is no snap to the punch and Sharkey swoons like he has been hit by a sledgehammer. He straightens up and plays dead to the world. It is almost cartoonish. What malarkey! He doesn't even move or twitch while on the canvas (has to make it look good). It was a typical Carnera push-punch. It if had real KO power Sharkey's head would have snapped back and he would have collapsed straight down face first.

Carnera was mobbed up to his eyeballs. So was Sharkey. It's a no brainer as far as I am concerned. Then Sharkey comes back past his peak three years later to fight murderous hitting Joe Louis and is knocked down by tremendous punches three times (or more) and he is never knocked unconscious."

And here we have Sharkey speaking of the fight during a 1970 interview for the book, "In This Corner: *42 world champions tell their st*ories."

"Then in 1933 I lost to Carnera. I had no trouble with him in the second bout but all of a sudden, and I can't convince anybody of this, even my own wife had her doubts, I think I see Schaaf in front of me, the next thing I know I lost the championship of the world. During the process of the fight I visualized Schaaf there, I saw him, and I stayed there long enough to get knocked out. I saw Schaaf, a vision.

Carnera's style and his reach, you've got to find a way to get to him. Well, I did that the first time. The second time I realized I'd do the same thing again, but I didn't give the guy credit that he might improve. He handled me with ease. He picked me up bodily and placed me over near the ropes. Those arms of his were like limbs of a tree and when he put them in front of him there was nothing to hit. I had trouble physically. I had no trouble, physically fit and everything and I boxed the guy before. I come out the round I got knocked out, I looked and I see a vision of Ernie Schaaf. There's no pain, just a feeling of turmoil, momentum, constant Buzzsaw going around, like you're in a dream. Of course, when you snap out of it, that's when the shame comes. You know you've lost. The Carnera fight, as I remember it, I snapped out of it and I more or less was ready to start crying. They figured, like most of his bouts had been more or less, well, I won't say what I should say, but skeptical, in other words, dubious. Like I say I can convince you, but I can't convince two hundred million people. What could I get doing what I did? The prestige and the honor there is in the Championship of the world, what could I get? Even my own manager accused me. What could I get? I've got everything I want financially and all that, what good is anymore?"[171]

And lastly, at 85-years-old Jack gave an interview to *Boxing Illustrated*. When asked about taking a dive, Jack responded, "I'd never have done anything like that, I'm Lithuanian and I was raised Catholic. I was raised to be honest. I was on top of the world, why would I purposefully lose?" When asked what it was like to lose the title Jack replied, "It's a terrible, terrible feeling," said the old man shaking his head slowly, struggling to maintain his composure. "You devalue yourself, you don't want to see anyone, you just wanna to hide."[172]

Despite Sharkey denial of a "fix" until his dying day, the question still remains a subject of interest and debate to this day.

---

171 *In This Corner: 42 World Champions Tell Their Stories*, by Peter Heller. pg.159.
172 "The Life Story of Jack Sharkey Boxing's Tragic Figure," *Boxing Illustrated*, by Jim Brady. Pg.91.

CHAPTER 27
THE KINGFISH AND LOUGHRAN

When Jack fought Primo in 1933 he was only 31-years-old and by all accounts had fought very well, up to the point of being knocked out. But the truth was, Jack was on the down-slide and quickly losing interest in boxing. He was not fighting as often as he once did and the grind of training camp and being away from his family was becoming wearisome. Jack had also started to spend a lot more time hunting and fishing and was extremely passionate about fly fishing. In addition, Sharkey and Buckley had purchased a bar together, and not just any bar. This one had the distinction of having the longest bar in the United States, measuring in at an incredible 146 feet. The tavern, named "Jack Sharkey's Ringside Café," was located at 156 Canal Street, less than two blocks from the Boston Garden and was a popular hangout. At times it was so smoky that the end of the bar was impossible to see through the smoky haze and as many as a dozen bartenders served drinks. Nevertheless, despite his declining interest in boxing; Jack wasn't quite ready to hang'em up, just yet.

By July 1, 1933 reports were coming out that Jack wanted another shot at Carnera and would be willing to fight Max Baer to prove that he was the outstanding challenger. Hearing that Sharkey was looking for an opponent, Jack "Doc" Kearns was reported to have offered Sharkey $25,000 for a rematch with Mickey Walker. Other talks centered on Jack possibly facing Schmeling in a third fight if he were to whip Max Baer.

By July 10, Buckley had everything taken care of. Jack's first comeback fight would be against Kingfish Levinsky, slated for September 15, 1933 at Comiskey Park in Chicago.

Kingfish Levinsky was born Harris Krakow in 1910 and was one of boxing's colorful characters. He got his alias because he was a member of the Krakow fish-selling family of Maxwell Street in Chicago's old Jewish ghetto where he worked as a fish peddler. Outside of the ring he was a clown, inside he was one of the most feared fighters of his time; a wild free swinging brawler with a powerful punch. During the Depression racked 1930s a fighter had to be something special to separate fans from what little money they had. Fans gladly paid to watch Sharkey, Bear and Loughran. Around the Chicago area they tore down the gates to watch the swaggering Kingfish.

Reporters and publicity men loved Kingfish because he made hilariously good copy. Everything about "The King" was eccentric, especially the way he butchered the English language with quotes like, "Dat broad spitted in my eye."[173] Nearly everyone who came in contact with Levinsky liked him, and enjoyed hearing him talk. Even years after retiring other pugs would egg the King into telling stories just to hear the funny way he would tell them. One story about his days as a wrestler went, "I got mad at this gorilla I'm rasslin' so I belts him on the chin and knocks him dead. The referee insults me so I belt him too. Then the cops come into the ring and take me away. Next day I'm banned in the state for life. So I quit, da hell wit em."[174]

A month after signing to meet Kingfish, Jack also agreed to a rematch with Tommy Loughran. The fight was scheduled just 12 days after his fight with Levinsky. Evidently, Jack was thinking his tune-up fight with the "The King" would be an easy victory and get him back into the heavyweight mix; his official prediction was a knockout within five rounds. The boisterous Kingfish confidently declared, "I'll knock him out. You know me, the King can punch. Beside, Sharkey is an old man, anyway."[175] The Associated Press predicted that the fight would be entertaining, saying, "The fight between 'Kingfish' a free swinging walloper, and Jack Sharkey, a scientific boxer, promises to be a rollicking affair as long as it lasts."

After a postponement of three days because of bad weather the two finally met on September 18. In what turned out to be a jaw dropping shocker, Sharkey a 9 to 5 favorite lost a lopsided 10-round decision to the ex-fish peddler and came close to being stopped in the opening seconds of the fight. The wild swinging Levinsky came out fast and rocked Sharkey with the first right hand punch that he landed. A moment later he caught Jack again with a smashing right hand that had the ex-champion dazed and on his back. Shaken and bewildered, Jack was up at the count of seven and in serious trouble. It took all of his ring experience and savvy, along with a lot of holding to make it through the round.

In the second, still shaken, Jack had to survive another ferocious, whirlwind attack by Levinsky. Again the "King" got in a hard, right hand blast to the jaw that had Sharkey on the verge of going down. Once again Jack called on his vast experience and skill to help him survive the round. For the remainder of the fight, with the exception of rounds 4, 6 and 7, (some accounts had Jack winning only round 7) Levinsky kept up his wild, two-fisted attack and had "The Boston Gob" on the defensive for most of the fight. When it was over Levinsky was awarded a majority decision and Jack's hopes of another chance at the heavyweight title were slipping away.

---

173 "The King Was A Clown," by Stanley Weston, *Ring magazine*, 1956, pg.66.
174 Ibid.
175 "Sharkey Confident of Stopping Rival," *Boston Globe*, September 15, 1933, pg.25.

Nine days later, on September 27, Sharkey climbed into the ring with Loughran. Even with the loss to Levinsky a win over the highly rated "Philadelphia Phantom" would get Jack right back into contention. When asked what would happen if he were to lose another fight Jack responded, "If Tommy is victorious I'd be crowded out of the top ten. I guess I'm going to have to whip him so decisively they'll have to put me up there at the top again."[176]

The rematch with Loughran turned out to be a much different fight than their first battle. Tommy courageously stood up to Jack and his vicious body bombardment and boxed his way out of one trying moment after another. In the tenth Tommy shocked the crowd when he dropped Sharkey to his knees with a right hand smash to the chin. Not known for his knockout punch, the blow may well have been the hardest Loughran ever threw.

The next morning the *Boston Globe* read, "It was a far more thrilling duel than their first meeting in the Yankee Stadium four years ago, when a chance at the heavyweight championship hung in the balance. A punching fury that night, Sharkey caught Loughran in a corner in the third round and felled him with an overhand right to the temple. Tommy went down, came up at five, and wandered aimlessly about the ring seeking a chair. Lou Magnolia, the referee halted that one right there. But tonight a 31-year-old Loughran had the guile to evade an identical punch in almost the same moment of the same round in the corresponding corner, the endurance to stand up under Sharkey's terrific body battering and the courage to keep going after the sailor's first real punch, a left hook to the head, opened a gash in his right brow.

Loughran's margin was desperately close and many of the critics counting the astonishing knockdown as merely an incident in one round gave Sharkey an edge over the route. But, narrow and controversial though the margin was, it was enough to count the Bostonian sailorman, knocked out of his championship by Primo Carnera in June, walloped by King Levinsky in Chicago 10 days ago, out of the major heavyweight picture."[177]

When it was over Tommy was awarded a razor thin decision. The two judges, Al Voice and Herman Weingert were divided with Al voting for Sharkey and Herman giving it to Tommy. Referee "Spud" Murphy scored the rounds even, giving Tommy six and Sharkey six and calling three even. But his deciding vote went to Tommy because of the knockdown. For Tommy it was sweet revenge. For Jack it looked like the end of the road for his boxing career.

---

176 "Jack Sharkey In Shape For Bout," *Boston Globe*, September 27, 1933, pg.1.
177 "Loughran Jab Edges Sharkey," *Boston Globe*, September 28, 1933, pg.1.

A few days later Jack was back home at his Chestnut Hill estate being interviewed. "I was not greatly surprised at the decision in Loughran's favor. It is customary for the hometown officials to favor the local fighters and when they awarded Loughran the decision it was the natural thing to expect. As for myself I knew and felt when the 15th round was over that I had won the fight. After the decision was made public I felt the same way and there is no reason why I shouldn't continue to feel so. There is nothing I can do about the verdict."[178] As to his future plans Jack said he hadn't had much time to think about them. His first thoughts were on a hunting trip he had planned for next week and that he was just happy to be home with his wife and kids after being gone for over three weeks.

For the next two years Jack would be out of the ring. But his career wasn't quite over and neither was the controversy.

---

178 "Loughran Jab Edges Sharkey," *Boston Globe*, September 28, 1933, pg.1.

CHAPTER 28
COMEBACK

After his loss to Loughran, Jack was eliminated as a top contender. Most fans and members of the press felt that he was a shot fighter. Although he had not made an official announcement, Jack was seriously considering retirement. To clear his mind Sharkey went on a hunting and fishing trip. While Jack was on vacation, Buckley was busy trying to put together a fight with either Art Laskey or Max Baer. In fact, Los Angeles promoter Lou Daro was in Boston and the two had discussed a possible match, but when Buckley asked for a guarantee on the Laskey fight, Lou hesitated to promise anything. Buckley then suggested a match with Baer. Lou liked the idea, but said he would have to talk to Ancil Hoffman, Baer's manager.

While contemplating retirement Jack kept busy with guest appearances, fishing and vacations. On July 7, 1934 Jack, along with Babe Ruth was a guest of honor at a General Motors car show at the Boston Garden. On September 12, the ex-champ was a referee for the weekly wrestling show at the Mechanics Building in Boston. The show featured a battle royal of four gigantic wrestlers. As part of the show Sharkey became involved in the melee and knocked out a couple of the wrestlers with "well timed" uppercuts. The match was eventually declared a draw and everyone, including the 6,000 fans, had a good time.

While being semi retired there were a number of big fights that took place. The first was Max Schmeling's draw with Paulino Uzcudun. Following the Schmeling fight, Primo Carnera took on Max Baer for the heavyweight championship of the world on June 14, 1934. Jack and his wife Dorothy sat ringside as Max Bear handed the Italian giant a terrible beating, knocking him down 11 time and taking his crown.

By January 1935 the hot topic was a possible Sharkey-Baer fight. The two, along with former champion Jack Dempsey, had met a couple of times in Boston, after Max won the title, and the subject had come up. It was reported that Jack had been offered a guarantee of $50,000 to face Baer.

Even with a promise of big money, Jack didn't seem to be in a hurry to get back into the ring. He was enjoying spending time with his family, running his bar, fly fishing and making guest appearances.

On April 16, 1935 Sharkey was featured at the first "World's Championship Guides' Tournament." The tournament featured fly-fishing competitions, as well as canoe races and rescue. The event also featured log rolling as well as other hunting and camping related events. Initially only there as a guest, Jack was persuaded to try his skills in the fly casting competition. Debonair as ever, the ex-champ stepped up to the microphone saying to the large audience that he was only here to practice for a fishing trip to Sebago, but would give it his best. With a fly-cast of 91' Sharkey walked away with the first place trophy.

Two months after Sharkey's fly-casting victory, on June 13, 1935, Max Baer lost his heavyweight title on his first defense to Jimmy Braddock. The fight went down in history as one of the greatest upsets of all time and one of the greatest comebacks in boxing history. Given almost no chance against Max and his thunderous right hand, Braddock, an 8 to 1 underdog defied the odds and won the title. What made Jimmy's victory so amazing was that just a little over a year prior he and his family were penniless, living on welfare and suffering through the Great Depression. Before the Depression, Jimmy had been to the top of the world and had fought for the light heavyweight championship against Tommy Loughran. Following his losing effort against Tommy, Braddock spent the next five years losing more fights than he won and working whatever jobs he could find. Coupled with the Depression, a scarcity of jobs and a losing record, Jimmy eventually had to go on relief to feed his family and was considered completely washed up.

A few days after the fight Sharkey was interviewed and said, "When I get ready to come back I'll tell the newspaper myself. I am not planning on fighting again. I guess Johnny Buckley was so enthused over the outcome of the Baer-Braddock bout figuring that I might be able to beat both of them; he thought I'd resume boxing. I don't think I could get money enough to make my comeback worthwhile."[179] Four months later Sharkey ended his retirement when he signed to fight Eddie "Unknown" Winston.

After being out of the ring for two years and two months Jack met Winston at the Boston Garden on November 22, 1935. Over 12,000 curious fans showed up to see the return of "The Boston Gob." The fight turned out to be a memorable one, but for all the wrong reasons. Stepping into the ring Jack looked fit at 196-pounds. Two months of intense training, that included six weeks of road word and chopping logs followed by intense sparring at Gus Wilson's Gym, had obviously paid off.

When the bell clanged Jack came out and swung a right uppercut that missed by a half a foot. Continuing to press the action Jack waded into Winston, but found that his timing was off and he was missing the majority of his punches.

Just past the minute mark, Winston backed Sharkey to the ropes with a flurry of body punches. Bouncing off the ropes, Sharkey landed what appeared to be a grazing left hook followed by a right under the heart. Although the punches didn't appear hard, surprisingly, Winston went down.

---

179 "Not to Fight Again, Says Sharkey," *Boston Globe*, June 22, 1935, pg.1.

On the canvas he looked around for a second then turned over on his face and laid there for about half a minute. Instantly the crowd sensed that Winston was putting on an act and began to boo loudly. Cries of "fix" and "fake" were heard all over the arena. A large number of irate fans crowded around the ring screaming obscenities and demanding that the fight be refought. Even Sharkey, surprised at the quick ending, agreed to a restart. After being lifted bodily to his corner Winston was attended to by his seconds. Several minutes passed while referee Johnny Martin, who wanted to disqualify Winston for not trying, and Commissioner Kelly discussed the situation. Eventually it was decided that the fight would be refought.

The next day the *Boston Globe* had this to say about the ending of the match. "Jack came out for the resumption of the fight as he had for its initial opening. He threw no wild punches this time. In fact he didn't have to for Winston made but a feeble attempt at protecting himself. The first round was all Sharkey. Winston hardly even feinting a punch.

In the second session Winston made his best showing of the bout. He showed that he could reach the squire with a long left and that he could poke his right home to Sharkey's stomach. However, Eddie fought only in flashes and never once followed up the many openings that he had.

The second finish came somewhat like the first. Winston was on the offensive when suddenly Sharkey shot a right uppercut that didn't travel a foot and Winston went down under it. He remained down for eight and when he got up on his feet a second time Sharkey nailed him with a left hook. Winston went down again and remained in a horizontal position for the required 10 seconds."[180]

A few moments later Jack's hand was raised in victory while Winston floundered around as if he couldn't believe the fight was over. The crowd, angry over the whole ordeal went nuts with insults and yells of "fake" and "fix."

Subsequent to the fight there was a full investigation by the state boxing commission headed by Daniel J. Kelly, Peter Carr, Paul Kirk and referee Johnny Martin. Subsequent to a viewing of the fight and lengthy deliberations they decided to suspend Winston for a year for "not giving his best effort." As for Sharkey he was cleared, except in Rhode Island. Charles Reynolds, chief of the state bureau of athletics suspended Sharkey from practicing his fist wares in Rhode Island stating that, "I do not believe that his comeback in the ring game will add anything to boxing."[181] Furthermore, Reynolds added that if the Sharkey-Winston match had been staged in Rhode Island one knockout would have been enough. "There

---

180 "Sharkey Twice KO's Winston," *Boston Globe*, November 23, 1935, pg.1.
181 "Jack Sharkey is Barred From Rhode Island Rings," *Boston Globe*, December 4, 1935, pg.22.

would have been no need for a second and I doubt very much if either would have been paid for that first one."[182]

A few weeks after the Winston fight in early December, Jack's comeback was in serious trouble. Having injured his elbow during his fight with Winston, Sharkey had to undergo surgery to repair the damage. Initially when he started his comeback Jack wanted to fight once a month to sharpen himself and get a fight with Joe Louis. At this point it would be weeks before Jack could resume training. Moreover, the doctors were unsure if the injury would heal with no problems or continue to plague Sharkey.

By January 15, 1936 it was reported that Jack had made a complete recovery from his surgery, and felt great in his first training session. He announced that he planned on continuing his comeback and had a match set up against Tony Shucco for February 7, 1936.

Going into the fight Jack was the favorite. Tony, a tough brawler with a respectable record of 68-9-6 was a talented and somewhat underrated fighter. During his career he defeated such notables as Maxie Rosenbloom, Jimmy Braddock and Al Gainer. The general feeling about the fight was that Sharkey, the more polished and skillful of the two, would be able to handle Tony with little trouble.

Advantages in skill notwithstanding, Jack lost a close but unanimous decision. Round one started slowly with Tony fighting out of a crouch and Jack boxing smartly. Throughout the round Tony landed a higher volume of punches, but Jack, who was physically stronger and carried a 15-pound weight advantage, landed the more damaging blows. The round was seen as mostly even. With a steady supply of punches that piled up the points Tony took rounds two, three and four. In the fifth, Jack made a comeback and out fought Tony. Moments before the bell rang ending the round Jack caught Tony with a hard left hook that split Tony's right eyebrow open causing blood to flow freely.

Having wounded his opponent, Jack tore out for round six. With stiff jabs and right crosses he took the round and turned Tony's face into a crimson mess. At one point Sharkey wobbled Tony with a stiff jab and a head snapping uppercut that sent a shower of blood flying across the ring and had his fans on their feet howling.

Jack continued to bring the fight to Tony in round seven and was extremely accurate landing a number of crisp combinations. By the round's end Jack's pinpoint accuracy had opened a cut over Shucco's left eye and had his nose and mouth bleeding as well. Sharkey started round eight strong but began to fade towards the mid-point. Although Sharkey wasn't as

---

[182] Ibid.

impressive as he had been in the preceding rounds, Shucco was unable to score effectively as he had in the earlier rounds.

Tony caught his second wind in the ninth while Jack was tiring fast. With an aggressive two-fisted, swarming attack Tony carried the round by a wide margin. Tony kept up his busy pace in round ten and finished the fight strong. Fatigued from sweeping round five, six and seven, Jack was unable to mount an effective counter offensive.

Moments later Tony was given the hard won decision much to the delight of his many fans. Along with the cheers for Tony were boos from those that believed Jack should have gotten the nod. Although famous for his after-bout tantrums, Sharkey took the defeat graciously, calmly saying afterwards, "I was satisfied with my performance and I hope the bout was a satisfactory one for those who paid to see it. I found in the bout that I was able to travel ten rounds with a much younger and speedy opponent. My condition was just what I expected it to be and I see no reason for retiring. I'll fight anybody that the boxing commission will name for me; and if they won't name one for me I'll fight some prominent opponent in my next bout."[183]

That next opponent would be a rematch with Shucco set for April 14, 1936. It was reported that Sharkey took his training a little more seriously for this fight. Even going as far as to bring in top notch sparring partners, Don Petrin and Fred Fiducia who were reported to be giving Jack the kind of workouts he needed to get into top shape.

Jack's performance in the rematch was much better and the fight proved to be more exciting than the first one. But despite a better effort, Sharkey only managed to walk away with a draw.

Full of confidence, Tony came out fast, landing a hard left to Sharkey's ribs. Jack countered with a right to Tony's jaw and Shucco fired right back with a left and right to the body. Compared to his speedy, aggressive opponent, Sharkey appeared a trifle slow; as a result the round belonged to Tony. Much like the first round, Tony took the second as well by out landing Jack and forcing the action. Jack woke up in the third and landed jolting lefts and rights to Tony's jaw that had him in trouble and hanging on. It was decidedly Jack's round. In the fourth Tony lost some of his confidence as Jack continued to come on strong. Near the end of the round Tony made up some ground by landing a straight left that shook Sharkey and sent him back on his heels. It looked as if Jack were trying to end the fight in the fifth as he tried to land big haymakers but found his speedy opponent hard to hit. The round was about even.

---

183 "Shucco Outpoints Sharkey," *Boston Globe*, by Hy Hurwitz, February 8, 1936, pg.1.

Sharkey switched his attack in the sixth and began working Tony's body. When he thought the time was right he swung a right to the jaw but missed. Jack carried a slight edge throughout and even helped Tony to his feet when he slipped and fell. The act of good sportsmanship got him a lusty cheer from the crowd. Both fighters landed their share of hard shots in the seventh. Moments before the round ended, Sharkey landed a pulverizing left hook that stunned Tony and sent him to his knees. Up at the count of four the bell rang a second later. Saved from a possible knockout, Tony staggered to his corner where he dropped heavily onto his stool.

Recovered from his knockdown, Tony came out with a whirlwind of blows to begin round eight. Not backing down, Sharkey met Tony's aggressive attack with a couple of hard left hooks that had Tony holding and hanging on for most of the round.

After a minute's rest Tony fought well in the ninth as Jack was noticeably tiring. The tenth saw both men, obviously exhausted from the fast pace, fight well and the round was about even. When it was over both judges, Frank Bowman and Jim Carrig decided it was a draw. Referee Johnny Brassil cast his vote for Sharkey. However, a few days later Johnny recanted saying there had been a mistake and that he had actually given the fight to Tony. This made no difference though, since both judges had it a draw.

After the announcement, the majority of the crowd voiced their disappointment with the decision. A disgruntled Sharkey leaned over the ropes and said to the newspapermen seated in press row, "I would have to come to Boston to get such a decision."[184]

Believing along with most people who watched the fight that he was robbed, Jack's decision to continue his comeback was an easy one. Just a few days later he was signed to fight Phil Brubaker with the winner being promised a fight with rising contender, and star, Joe Louis.

Six days before Sharkey climbed into the ring with Phil one of the greatest upsets of all time played out to the disbelief of millions. On June 19, 1936 Joe Louis, the heir apparent to the heavyweight championship and hero to millions of black Americans, was knocked out in the 12th round by Max Schmeling. The defeat was a crushing one to Louis, but a valuable lesson to the young Bomber who admitted to not taking his training seriously and going into the fight in less than top condition.

While everyone was recovering from the shock of Louis's defeat, Jack touched gloves with Brubaker on June 25, 1936 at Boston's Fenway Park.

---

184 "Jack Sharkey and Tony Shucco Battle to a Draw in Return Engagement in Boston Garden Ring," *Boston Globe*, by James C. O'Leary, April 15, 1936, pg.24.

Before 8,000 fans Jack showed his mettle in a fierce, bloody battle against a tough opponent who was eight years younger.

Sharkey came out boxing beautifully in round one, jabbing Phil at will and making him look like an amateur while Phil tried to block Jack's punches and counter. At about the halfway point Phil shot a hard right that landed flush on Sharkey's jaw and followed up quickly with a left, right that wobbled "The Boston Gob." Stunned, Jack grasped the ropes to steady himself but fell to the canvas for a one count. When he stood up his nose was a blood covered mess and blood flowed freely from a cut under his right eye. Seeing that Jack was hurt, Phil went on the attack, but Jack, wise in ring warfare hung tough and lasted out the round.

Coming out for the second, Phil swarmed into Sharkey trying to finish him. A right hook bounced off Jack's body followed by two lefts to the chin, but Jack kept his head and began to jab away at Phil with quick lefts. Towards the end of the round Phil forced Sharkey against the ropes with a right uppercut. Stubbornly, Sharkey fought his way off the ropes, but was hammered again with a hard right and a left to the belly just as the bell rang.

Looking to make up some ground in round three, Jack sprang from his corner and set a blistering pace. When the round ended Phil's nose was pouring blood and he was clinching and puffing hard. For the full minute between rounds, Phil's corner men worked on their fighter's nose bleed. Eventually they stopped the flow of blood by spraying a coagulant into Phil's nose.

Phil backed Sharkey to the ropes with a short left, right to the head to start round four. With Sharkey's back against the ropes, Phil opened up with a barrage of punches. Jack, bobbing and weaving, battled back savagely and drove Phil away with a hard left hook. He then hammered away at Phil's body until Phil had to clinch. Jack then smashed Phil with a right cross to the jaw, followed by another right that instantly caused Phil's eye to swell closed. Just before the bell, Jack feinted a left hook and sent in a fast right hand that visibly rocked the younger man.

The fifth was Jack's round all the way through, thanks to his left hook that found its mark frequently.

Sharkey came out for round six full of confidence, but got a little careless and was rocked by some big shots. He tried to strike back with some hard left hooks but was hit under the heart by a vicious right hand counter. At some point during a ferocious exchange of wild punches, Jack's left eye was torn open; a few seconds later the bell ended the round. Bloody but unbowed Sharkey headed for his corner.

The action slowed a little in the seventh and both fighters were somewhat cautious at the start. Following a solid jab from Phil, Jack's left eye began to bleed profusely. Phil took advantage of the damaged eye with a steady stream of hard jabs. At the midpoint of the round Sharkey threw a sneaky right that caught Phil solidly and sent him staggering back and nearly dropping him to the canvas. Seeing his opponent hurt, Jack moved in and pounded Phil's body with hard lefts and rights. Despite being staggered, Phil fought back hard until the bell ended a close round.

Phil edged the eighth round but Jack came back and out boxed him throughout the ninth and tenth, showing amazing stamina and determination. When the bell signaled the end both warriors wearily went to their respective corners. It had been a rough and tumble fight and each bore the cuts and bruises of a fierce battle. In the end, despite being knocked down and busted up, Jack out-punched, out-boxed and out-smarted his rival. With a roar of acclaim from the crowd he was awarded the hard won decision. "The Boston Gob's" path was now clear for the final fight of his illustrious career, a battle with "The Brown Bomber."

CHAPTER 29
THE BROWN BOMBER

By July of 1936, reports were coming out that Mike Jacobs' 20th century boxing club, team Sharkey and team Louis had reached an agreement for a fight. After Joe's unexpected defeat at the hands of Schmeling, team Louis felt that Sharkey, the aging ex-champion, was the perfect opponent to restore Joe's shaken confidence. There were many however, who felt that Sharkey, even though he was 33-years-old and on the down side, was too shrewd a campaigner. And that maybe Joe should take on someone a little softer for his first fight back. Full of confidence as usual, Jack felt that he could repeat Max Schmeling's knockout.

Louis began training at Pompton Lakes, New Jersey. Deadly serious after his defeat, Joe's camp was closed to the public and only members of his immediate party and press were allowed to have a peek. Conversely, Jack's camp in Orangeburg, New Jersey was open to the public at a few cents per head. On July 17, Tom Sharkey, the fighter that Jack borrowed half his ring name from, visited Sharkey's training site. Having watched both Louis and Jack spar, the old battler predicted that Louis would win by knockout, if Sharkey did not foul. The old contender then added, "I could lick both these fellows in one evening in less than ten rounds when I was in my prime." He then said that present day fighters don't know the method of training or have teachers equal to those in the old days. "Fighters now train at nightclubs and go stale from playing golf, not from road work."[185]

Reports coming out of Sharkey's camp were positive, saying that Jack's condition and his sparring were impressive. Sports writer Hy Hurwitz was at Sharkey's camp and said, "Jack looked and acted in fine fighting shape. He slashed away at a trio of sparring partners with a determination that left one with the impression that it would take a superman to whip him."[186] During Hy's visit Max Schmeling showed up and watched Jack workout. Schmeling was impressed with Jack, saying in thickly accented German, "It shows that age doesn't matter but goot living. If you liff goot you'll be in goot shape. I feel better, stronger today than five years back. Jack surprised me. I didn't think he'd be in the shape he is. Goot living, that's the answer."[187]

---

[185] "Tom Sharkey Predicts Knockout For Louis If Sharkey Doesn't Foul Out," *Boston Globe*, August 4, 1936 pg.10.
[186] "Sharkey Surprises Critics by Fine Fighting Condition," by Hy Hurwitz, *Boston Globe*, August 13, 1936, pg.1.
[187] Ibid.

On August 18, 1936, Jack Sharkey climbed into the ring at Yankee Stadium for the final fight of his colorful career. After the instruction from referee Arthur Donavan the two fighters returned to their respective corners and disrobed.

With a clang of the bell they came out jabbing. Pressing forward, Louis missed a big right hand and they went into a clinch. Separated by Donavan, Joe caught Sharkey with jolting rights then forced him back against the ropes with two lefts and ripping, right uppercuts that slammed into Jack's face. Sharkey then jabbed and missed a right as they fell into a clinch. Catching Sharkey on the ropes Joe connected with a right and then missed a left as Sharkey grabbed. Pushing Sharkey back, Joe jabbed but Sharkey blocked the blows with his gloves. The former champion then landed several light rights in close and danced away, keeping his jab in Joe's face. Louis answered back with a hard right to the body that made Jack's knees quiver just as the bell sounded.

They came out moving and jabbing to begin round two. Jack tried to keep Louis away by sticking his jab in his face, but it was no use. Pressing forward, Louis opened up with a left that missed but caught Jack with a jolting one-two. Sharkey retaliated with a counter left hook to Joe's face and Louis shot back a snapping jab that ripped open a bloody cut above Jack's left eye. "The Brown Bomber" then moved in and battered Sharkey with a fast combination of powerful lefts and rights to the chin, followed by a sizzling right that dropped Jack for a count of nine. As soon as Sharkey was up, Louis, one the deadliest finishers of all time, moved in for the kill. A crushing left followed by a right to the ribs once again sent Jack down for a count of nine. Back on his feet, Louis tore into Jack with blindingly fast lefts and rights. Desperately Jack hung on under the bombardment as another crushing left hook sent him reeling. Summoning all his remaining strength, Jack fought back bravely and hung tough until the bell signaled the round's end.

There was no escape for Jack in the third. Louis started methodically, but Jack came out fast with a hard left that forced him back. Louis then came in, jabbed twice and sent Jack sprawling to the canvas with two stinging rights to the chin. The crowd was on its feet screaming as "The Boston Gob," looking dazed, gamely struggled to his feet at the count of nine. Cleared to continue by Donavan, Joe, using his left, measured Sharkey with deadly precision. He then sent in a right and a vicious left that caught Jack flush on the side of his face and shook his entire body. Louis continued his attack with a hook to the body, a left hook to the head, a right uppercut and a left hook followed by a crushing right that sent Jack down again. Visibly dazed, Jack sat for a moment, pulled out his mouthpiece and once again struggled to his feet. By the time he was up,

Donavan had seen enough and waved the fight over. Battered, bloodied and beaten, Sharkey was helped to his corner by the referee.

In his dressing room a few minutes after the fight Jack showed no bitterness, but was disappointed with his performance. Sitting with Polazzolo, Al Lacy and Buckley, Sharkey chugged water and iced his swollen eye. While he worked his jaw opened and closed to make sure it was ok, Dr. William Walker, New York Boxing commissioner doctor, examined Sharkey's eye. Talking with the press Jack said, "I got clipped somewhere along there and I can't remember much of what happened after that"[188] When asked if Louis' punches hurt, Jack replied, "Hurt? Sure he hurts. There's no use talking about that, you don't get knocked down without getting hurt. All I have to say is the better man won tonight. I said two years ago when I couldn't beat Primo Carnera, that youth must be served. Youth was served tonight. Good luck to him."[189] Jack continued after some more questions with, "Give the other guy credit. I've been around this racket for long enough to know that all the fights can't end in a draw. He's a good fighter, better than I am. Whether he'll be as good as I was tonight at 34 remains to be seen." When asked if he was aiming to retire, Jack responded with a string of profane expletives. "Retiring?" he repeated. "I'm not retiring, I'm retired."[190]

In the end it was a gutsy performance by Jack against a prime Louis. Ten months later Joe would win the heavyweight title from Jimmy Braddock. From there he would go on to become arguably the greatest heavyweight champion in history, holding the crown for 12-years and making 25 successful title defenses.

A day after the fight Victor O. Jones of the *Boston Globe* wrote a fitting tribute to Sharkey saying, "The old squire fell with his boots on and gave everything he had before, after getting up twice, he was finally counted out by referee Arthur Donavan in the second minute of the third round."[191]

---

188 "Sharkey Says Louis' Blows Hurt, Doesn't Remember Much," by Victor O. Jones, *Boston Daily Globe*, August 19, 1936,pg.21.
189 Ibid.
190 Ibid.
191 Ibid.

CHAPTER 30
GONE FISHING

It didn't take Jack long to rethink his retirement. Just a month after his loss to Louis, reports were coming out that "The Boston Gob" was looking for a fight. "I am going to sign articles to meet Al McCoy at the Garden next month. I still have a few good fights under my belt. Meanwhile, I am getting into condition, training every day and refereeing wrestling matches."[192] Despite the talks of another fight, however, Jack's bout with Louis would be his last. After nearly 13-years in the ring and a career that took him from sailor to heavyweight champion of the world, Jack was done. He ended his career at 34-years-old with a record of 37 wins, 13 losses, with 13 knockouts and 3 draws; along with 2 newspaper decisions: winning 1 and losing 1.

Following his boxing career, Jack turned his attention to his love of fly fishing and running his bar, where he received frequent visitors. Freddy Corcoran, a sports promoter and amateur golfer who was hugely influential in making the game of golf more popular in America, caught up with Jack at his ringside bar. During their conversation Freddy asked Jack who hit harder Louis or Dempsey? "Tell me," asked Eddie. "Who hit you the hardest, Dempsey or Louis?"

"Well I was at my peak when I met Dempsey, and on my way out when I fought Louis. When Dempsey hit me it was just like someone dumped a load of concrete over my head. I've felt that punch for 13-years. I never thought a man could hit so hard. When Dempsey hits you one good one that's enough and the show is over. Louis hit me about 13 times and put me down several times. I don't think Louis has the paralyzing punch that Dempsey has."

Then Jack was asked what would have happened if they had met each other at his peak?

"Well," he ventured, "Louis can be hit. So can Dempsey, but if Dempsey hits you once it would be curtains. Put'em both in a telephone booth, and see which one would come out. Dempsey would beat any man he could hit."[193]

When World War II broke out Jack, along with baseball great, "Lefty" Gomez and Freddy Corcoran went on a 25,000 mile, three month tour of Africa and Italy. The three entertained thousands of troops with stories, and

---

[192] "Sharkey Not Done With Ring-Expects," *Boston Globe,* September 15, 1936, pg.22.
[193] "Dempsey Hits Harder Than Louis, Sharkey Tells Corcoran," *Boston Globe*, October 20, 1939, pg.23.

watched moving pictures of the 1943 World Series, boxing matches and golf tournaments. While overseas, Jack also refereed over 50 boxing matches including the AMT championships and visited hospitals to cheer up wounded soldiers.

After the war Jack continued to remain popular as a referee and guest speaker and along with Dorothy enjoyed watching his children grow into young adults. Jack's son, Jack Sharkey, Jr. played high school hockey and was a standout player. During a championship game Jack Junior scored an important goal in Newton High's 3-1 upset victory against Medford in the Greater Boston quadruple hockey scramble before two thousand fans at Madison Square Garden.

By the early 1950s Jack and Dorothy had sold their mansion in Chestnut Hill and moved into her parents' beautiful three story Victorian style house in Epping, New Hampshire. Their children were by now young adults and starting lives of their own. Jack's son, after finishing college became a civil engineer for the state of Massachusetts. His daughter Marylyn an artist and author and his daughter Dorothy worked for a pathologist.

It was during the 1950s that Jack became involved with the Boston sportsman show which was geared around hunting, fishing and camping. Jack, along with his long time fishing buddy, baseball great, Ted Williams was part of the fly fishing exhibitions. Side by side the two expert fishermen would headline the shows and make appearances all over Boston, New England and New York at different venues. The shows had a carnival type atmosphere that featured events like knife throwing, log rolling, a boxing kangaroo and a seal named Sharkey that performed tricks. Moreover, the newest camping, fishing, and hunting related gear was on full display. Together the two sports personalities were instrumental in bringing in thousands of people and were paid quite well; between $5,000 and $10,000 per appearance. Their fly fishing techniques were all the rage at the shows throughout the 1950s and into the 70s, as were their fly casting duels which were typically the highlight of the events.

At one show at the Mechanics Building in Boston over 22,000 eager fans showed up to watch Jack, who often called Ted "Marblehead" and Ted, who typical refered to Sharkey as "Bush" face off. Sharkey, wearing his ever present fishing cap covered in colorful handmade flies, battled it out with Ted in a fierce fly casting distance competition, won by Ted. Oftentimes the two sportsman were joined by Mickey Mantle, Florence Chadwick, and Jackie Robinson. During a show in New York in 1965, Jack was asked if he preferred fly fishing to boxing. "It doesn't pay as much," he replied "but then the fish don't hit back."

When not on tour with the sportsman show Jack was either fishing or hunting, usually over a hundred days a year. When at home, the ex-champ said if he gets bored he grabs a hammer and fixes things around the house.

In January 1963 Sharkey was interviewed by *Boston Globe* columnist Hy Hurwitz. Having just turned 60-years-old Jack was in fine spirits and shape and didn't look his age. During the interview Jack said, "I weigh 210 or 212, I've been like this for almost thirty years. I could take a few pounds off any time if I had to but my weight is ideal for my size and age, I was 60 in October."[194] When asked about his diet Jack replied, "I stick to liquids one day and eat solids the next. I seldom eat breakfast. When I'm on my liquid day I'll drink all sorts of juices about every hour or two. On my solid day I'll eat salads for lunch, without any dressing and one good meal in the evening. But the big secret is to not gorge yourself. That's what too many people seem to be doing. I'd rather eat six times a day, but eat lightly than to gorge myself once or twice a day."[195] When asked about exercise Jack responded, "I do a lot of fast walking. And up around my home in Epping I get out and hunt. But before I go to bed at night, I'll do some bending forward and backward. Maybe 10 times each way. And in the morning before I get out of bed, I'll do some pushups. All this has helped me keep in shape."[196]

On August 6, 1963 Jack's ex manager Johnny Buckley passed away at St. Elizabeth hospital after a long illness, he was 74-years-old. Jack, along with several fighters, including welterweight Lou Brouillard and middleweight Paul Pender were in attendance at the funeral. In addition, a number of newspapermen and boxing commissioner Thomas Rawson as well as Buckley's two daughters and sons were there accompanied by dozens of friends and family members.

On August 8, 1971 Jack's greatest rival, Jimmy Maloney, passed away at the age of 68. Two years later in 1973, Jack's beloved wife Dorothy passed away from lung cancer. After nearly 50-years of marriage Jack was devastated; he had loved Dorothy deeply. She was laid to rest at a cemetery located about a mile from their Epping home. After her death Jack would walk or drive to the cemetery daily to visit her grave. He would continue to do this without missing a day for the next 15-years.

In 1976 Jack was 73-years-old. The years had been kind to Sharkey. He was in great health and sharp as a tack mentally, and unlike most ex-fighters he was well off financially. Jack had invested the bulk of his more than one million dollars that he made during his career, as well as the thousands he profited from his bar and tournament appearances. The ex-champ lived alone but had frequent visits from his kids and fourteen grandkids as well as the occasional writer wanting to interview him for a magazine article or

---

194 "Dieting, Bending Keep Sharkey Trim, Alert," by Hy Hurwitz, *Boston Globe*, January 22, 1963, pg.32.
195 Ibid.
196 Ibid.

book. During one interview Jack was asked about his thoughts on boxing to which he replied, "Now the referee breaks the fighters up constantly, when I was fighting all the good action took place in the clinches."[197]

On September 11, 1980 Jack, along with 350 sport legends from Boston was honored at a banquet. The 77-year-old Sharkey stood before the assembled mass of people and said, "In pursuing my career I had many ups and downs, but a lot of the time I was down more than up. A lot of the time I forgot to duck. I'm grateful to have the opportunity to be standing here before you, because half the time I was on the floor."[198] Following his speech he was given a heartfelt round of applause.

Throughout the 1980s Jack continued to live alone in Epping. Most days were spent smoking his pipe, making fishing flies, working around the house, fishing and giving occasional interviews to visiting reporters who still remembered him.

By 1990 Jack had gotten to where he could no longer live on his own and was moved to a retirement home where he spent about the last five years of his life. He passed away on August 17, 1994 at the age of 91, from respiratory failure. Prior to his death he was the oldest living former champion. Following a modest funeral attended by friends and family members Jack was laid to rest beside his wife Dorothy.

With his passing there were a few articles in the papers and boxing magazines that gave tributes to the ex-champ, but these were written by people who never knew Jack or had actually seen him fight live. The best tributes given to Sharkey may well have come years before by two men who knew Jack personally. Damon Runyon the great newspaperman and author wrote of Sharkey in 1933 saying, "Erratic, emotional, with the ring temperament of a grand opera prima donna. The Lithuanian nearly always leaves behind him in his fights some strange and untoward happenstance. Yet back of his peculiar ring personality is the staid disposition of a man who loves his fireside and his kids, and who is happiest when he is far removed from the roar of the mob. I think that ultimately Sharkey will be rated as a great fighter, yet he has been one of the strangest characters that ever poked his nose between the ropes. The real Sharkey is a likeable chap."

Nat Fleisher founder and editor of *Ring Magazine* said of Sharkey: "He had boxing skill, cleverness, perfect jabs and a heart that only a top-notcher possesses."

Just a few months before Jack's death, he was inducted into the International Boxing Hall of Fame. It was an honor that no doubt Sharkey felt he deserved and was proud to receive. Although he was too frail to

---

197 "Jack Sharkey at 76," *Boston Globe*, February 13, 1979, pg.2.
198 "City Pays Tribute to Great Athletes," by Steve Marantz, *Boston Globe*, September 11, 1980, pg. 46.

attend the ceremony, Jack was well represented by his son, Jack Sharkey Jr., his grandson, Jack Sharkey III, and great grandson Jack Sharkey IV. In the Hall "The Boston Gob" has his place alongside the greatest fighters of all time. Within those hallowed walls the spirit and memory of Jack Sharkey will live on for generations to come, and like Sharkey once said, "it's nice to be remembered and hell to be forgotten."

Bibliography

Dempsey, Jack and Piattelli Dempsey, Barbara. *Dempsey*, Harper & Row Publishing, 1977.

Goodwen, David. *Jack Sharkey: Yankee Magazine*, September 1983.

Heller, Peter. *In This Corner: 42 world champions tell their stories*, Da Capo press, 1973.

Margolick, David. Beyond Glory: *Joe Louis and Max Schmeling and a world on the brink*, Vintage books, Random House, 2005.

Montville, Leigh. *Ted Williams*: The Biography of an American Hero, Doubleday Publishing, 2004.

Page, Joseph S. Primo Carnera: *The Life and Career of the Heavyweight Boxing Champion*, McFarland Publishing, 2011.

Jack Sharkeys's Professional Record:
Won 37 Lost 13 Drew 3 with 13 Knockouts.
Newspaper Decisions: Won 1, Lost 1.

1924

Jan 29	Billy Muldoon	Boston	W TKO 1
Feb 8	Pat Hence	Boston	W DQ 2
Feb 26	Dan Lucas	Boston	W KO 2
Mar 18	Eddie Record	Boston	L PTS 10
Apr 25	Eddie Record	Boston	W KO 7
Jun 23	Floyd Johnson	Boston	W PTS 10
Jul 15	Homer Smith	Boston	W PTS 10
Jul 23	Al Roberts	Rhode Island	W PTS 10
Aug 20	Young Jack Johnson	Maine	W NWS 6
Aug 29	Quinton Rojas	Boston	L KO 9
Nov 5	Jimmy Maloney	Boston	L PTS 10
Dec 15	Charley Weinert	New Jersey	L NWS 12

1925

Jan 8	Jack De Mave	New York	W PTS 10
Jan 20	Sully Montgomery	Boston	W UD 10
Feb 10	Charley Weinert	Boston	L PTS 10
Apr 6	George Cook	Boston	W SD 10
Jun 5	Jimmy Maloney	Boston	W DQ 9
Jul 31	Emilio Solomon	Boston	W PTS 10

1925 continued

Aug 17	Bud Gorman	Boston	L	PTS	10
Sep 17	Johnny Risko	Boston	W	PTS	10
Dec 11	Jimmy Maloney	Boston	W	PTS	10

1926

Jan 18	Mexican Joe Lawson	Connecticut	W	KO	2
Feb 12	Eddie Huffman	New York	W	PTS	10
Apr 1	Emilio Solomon	Boston	W	PTS	10
Apr 19	Pat McCarthy	Boston	W	PTS	10
Jun 25	Bud Gorman	Boston	W	DQ	1
Sep 13	Orlando Riverberi	New Jersey	W	TKO	1
Sep 21	George Godfrey	Boston	W	PTS	10
Oct 12	Harry Wills	New York	W	DQ	13
Dec 15	Homer Smith	New York	W	TKO	7

1927

Mar 3	Mike McTigue	New York	W	TKO	12
May 20	Jimmy Maloney	New York	W	TKO	5
Jul 21	Jack Dempsey	New York	L	KO	7

1928

Jan 13	Tom Heeney	New York	D	SD	12
Mar 12	Johnny Risko	New York	L	SD	15
Apr 30	Jack Delaney	New York	W	KO	1

| Jun 21 | Leo Gates | Missouri | W | KO | 3 |
| Dec 10 | Arthur DeKuh | Boston | W | PTS | 10 |

1929

Jan 25	KO Christner	New York	W	MD	10
Feb 27	Young Stribling	Florida	W	PT	10
Sep 26	Tommy Loughran	New York	W	KO	3

1930

| Feb 27 | Phil Scott | Florida | W | TKO | 3 |
| Jun 12 | Max Schmeling | New York | L | DQ | 4 |

1931

| Jul 22 | Mickey Walker | New York | D | PTS | 15 |
| Oct 12 | Primo Carnera | New York | W | UD | 15 |

1932

| Jun 21 | Max Schmeling | New York | W | SD | 15 |

1933

Jun 29	Primo Carnera	New York	L	KO	6
Sep 18	King Levinsky	Chicago	L	UD	10
Sep 27	Tommy Loughran	Philadelphia	L	SD	15

1935

| Nov 22 | Unknown Winston | Boston | W | KO | 2 |

1936

Feb 7	Tony Shucco	Boston	L	UD	10
Apr 14	Tony Shucco	Boston	D	PTS	10
Jun 25	Phil Brubaker	Boston	W	UD	10
Aug 8	Joe Louis	New York	L	KO	3

Index

Arcel, Ray, 60
Astor Hotel, 78
Balogh, Harry, 193
Barnes, Harold, 171
Barry, Dave, 141
Batchelder, Roger, 65, 144, 146
Battling Siki, 70
Bear, Max, 161, 187, 195, 206
Berlenbach, Paul, 70, 72, 145, 177
Bird, Artie, 176
Birkie, Hans, 192
Bowman, Frank, 211
Braddock, James J., "The Cinderella man" 161, 198, 207, 209, 216
Brando, Marlin, 59
Brassil, Johnny, 35, 37, 38, 40, 43, 45, 153, 211
Brennan, Bill, 15
Brisbane, Arthur, 171
Britton, Jack, 176
Brouillard, Lou, 219
Brubaker, Phil, 211, 226
Bruen, Frank, 175
Buckley, Jerry, 85, 191
Buckley, John Francis, 12, 15, 17, 19, 30, 40, 42, 47, 53, 55, 58, 60, 62, 64, 65, 68, 74, 75, 84-87, 90, 91, 103, 104, 116, 135, 137-140, 146, 152, 153, 157, 160, 163, 166, 169, 171, 175, 182, 187-189, 191, 192, 196, 198, 202, 206, 207, 216, 219
Buckley, Nellie, 12
Buelow, Arthur, 173
Burns, Tommy, 192
Campolo, Victorio, 175
Canavan, Chick, 35
Capone, Al, "Scarface" 125, 178
Carnera, Primo, 4, 5, 59, 104, 117, 118, 161, 175, 176, 179, 180-182, 185, 187, 188, 190-204, 206, 216, 222, 225
Carpentier, George, 168, 181
Carr, Peter, 208
Carrig, Jim, 211
Carroll, Dan, 74, 75, 92
Carter, Carl, 49, 51
Chadwick, Florence, 127, 218
Chicago Cardinals, 24
Clements, William, 68
Coe, Charles Francis, 186
Collins, Mike, 152
Color line, 13, 57
Cook, George, 30-32, 34, 41, 49, 223
Corcoran, Freddy, 217
Crowley, Jim, 127, 170, 172
Daly, Amy (Schaaf), 189
Daro, Lou, 206
Dawson, James P., 198, 199
De Forest, Jimmy, 146
De Lahoya, Oscar, 23
De Mave, Jack, 23, 46, 223
Defoe, Billy, 193
DeKuh, Arthur, 153, 225
Delaney, Jack, 3, 69, 71, 75, 77, 140, 143, 145-150, 159, 224
Dempsey, Edna, 89
Dempsey, John, 89
Dempsey, William Harris, "The Manassas Mauler" 3, 11, 13-17, 23-25, 35, 40, 41, 46, 48, 55-60, 66, 68, 70, 71, 74, 76, 78, 79, 84-93, 103, 110, 134-141, 143-145, 148, 150, 151, 154, 155, 157, 158, 160, 168, 176, 181, 187, 193, 196, 199, 206, 217, 222, 224
Donavan, Arthur, 118, 193, 215, 216
Donelan, Charles, 51

Dorgan, Ted, 76
Dorgan, Thomas A., 70
Duffy, Bill, 104, 193, 198
Eagle, George, 35
Earhart, Emilia, 187
Egan, David F., 67, 146, 149, 150, 160, 178, 184, 193
Ernie, Frank, 70
Fadil. Nick, 60
Fairbanks, Douglas, 13
Farley, James A., 139, 175
Fiducia, Fred, 210
Field, Walter, 155
Firpo, Angel, 16
Fleisher, Nat, 220
Flournoy, Frank, 26
Flowers, Theodore, "Tiger" 70, 177
Flynn, Leo, 89, 91
Flynn, Owen, 187
Fralich, William, 152
Frankford Yellow Jackets, 24
Friedman, Abe, 49, 145
Friedman, Charley, 192, 199
Fugazy, Herbert, 70
Fugazy, Jack, 58
Fulton, Fred, 15, 88
Gainer, Al, 209
Gains, Leo, 92
Gallico, Paul, 172
Gans, Joe, 70
Gates, Leo, 91, 151, 225
Genaro, Frankie, 60
Gibbons, Tom, 46
Gibbons, Tommy, 30, 41
Godfrey, George, 55
Goldman, Charley, 60
Goodwin, Tom, 26, 49-51, 74, 150
Gorman, Bud, 3, 46-48, 54, 55, 224
Graziano, Rocky, 59
Greb, Harry, 17, 161, 177
Griffiths, Tuffy, 163
Hagler, Marvin, "Marvelous" 13
Haley, Patsy, 61, 172
Hallahan, John, 172
Hallahan, Johnny, 52
Hansen, Knute, 71
Heeney, Tom, 112, 140, 141, 143, 144, 146, 151, 152, 160, 224
Hench, Pat, 12
Herman, Jack, 41, 92
Hine, Paul H., 40
Hoffman, Ancil, 206
Huffman, Eddie, 53, 224
Humphries, Joe, 134, 184, 185, 188
Hurley, Joseph, 40
Hurwitz, Hy, 210, 214, 219
Igoe, Hype, 197, 199
Jack Sharkey's Ringside Café, 202
Jack, Beau, 59
Jacobs, Joe, 163, 168, 173, 185, 187
Jacobs, Mike, 77, 214
Jeanette, Joe, 57
Jefferies, James J., 54, 92
Jim Toland's gymnasium, 21
Johnson, Floyd, 223
Johnson, Jack, 17, 18, 57, 199, 223
Johnston, Jimmy, 104, 164, 190
Jones, John, 157
Jones, Victor O., 216
Julian, Toney, 43
Kearns, Jack, 91, 93, 176, 202
Kelly, Daniel J., 208
Kelly, George F., 184
Kelly, Harry, 34, 51, 90, 137, 145
Kelly, Joe, 34
Kelly's Boxing Gym, 12
Kid Lavigne, 70
Kid Navarro, 57
Kieran, John, 181
Kirby, Tim, 76

Kirby, Tom, 49
Kirk, Paul, 208
Klein, Isaac, 152
Krakow, Harris, 4, 22, 88, 179, 202-204, 225
Lacey, Al, 158
Langford, Sam, 13, 55, 57
Larson, Wolf, 17
Laskey, Art, 206
Lawson, Bob, 23
Lawson, George, 42
Lawson, Joe, 53, 224
Lee, George, 191
Leonard, Benny, 59, 77, 90-92, 138, 169, 171, 172, 183
Lewis, George, 43
Lewis, Jerry, 59
Lindbergh, Charles A., 134
Loughran, Thomas Patrick, "The Phantom of Philly" 70, 148, 158, 160, 161, 177, 193, 203, 207, 225
Loughran, Tommy, 4, 161, 162, 163, 202, 204, 205, 206
Louis, Joseph, "The Brown Bomber" 59, 108, 185, 200, 209, 211, 222, 226
Lucas, Charley, 33
Lucas, Dan, 14, 223
Lyons, Jack, 35
Mackey, Richard, 91
Madison Square Garden, 23, 71, 85, 87, 89, 93, 141, 143, 145, 160, 173, 181, 187, 188, 191, 218
Magnolia, Lou, 79, 159, 160, 162, 164, 204
Maloney, Jimmy, "Dynamite" 3, 17, 20, 21, 23, 29, 30, 33-38, 40-43, 48-53, 55, 61, 68-71, 73-87, 92, 111, 145, 146, 149, 150, 158, 160, 181, 219, 223, 224
Manolina, George, 35

Mantle, Mickey, 218
Marciano, Rocky, "The Rock" 13, 59
Martin, Dean, 59
Martin, Johnny, 55, 208
Marty Fitzpatrick's gym, 42
Matheson, Charles F., 139
Matison, Charles, 184
McCarthy, Pat, 53, 54, 74, 224
McCormick, Boyo, 35
McCoy, Al, 217
McCreary, Jim, "Battling" 12, 14, 21, 23, 24, 34
McFadden, George, 69
McKirdy, Bob, 152
McLean, Alex, 30
McMullin, Eddie, 90
McNamee, Graham, 186
McTigue, Michael Francis, 3, 69-73, 75, 77, 157, 161, 176, 177, 224
McVey, Sam, 57
Melio, Al, 43
Mello, Al, 35, 150
Miami Beach Kennel Club, 157
Miske, Billy, 17, 88
Montgomery, James, 23-25, 41, 69, 223
Morris, Carl, 88
Moulden, Billy, 11
Muldoon, William, 58
Newman, Paul, 59
Norris, Jim, 77
O'Conner, Joe, 31
O'Grady, Martin, 60
O'Reagan, Mickey, 10
O'Sullivan, Jack, 134, 138
Orlando Reverberi, 55, 56, 224
Orsini, Dominic, 176
Page, Joe, 5, 117, 118, 197
Pender, Paul, 219
Pep, Willy, 59
Persson, Harry, 69, 70

Petrin, Don, 210
Phipps, Catis, 51
Piana, Amilcare, 180
Pike, Mary Van Keuren, 67
Polazzolo, Tony, 90, 105, 116, 152, 158, 159, 163, 166, 184, 192, 216
Quill, Frankie, 43
Rawson, Thomas, 219
Record, Eddie, 14, 20, 223
Renault, Jack, 3, 28, 29, 41
Reverberi, Orlando, 55
Reynolds, Charles, 208
Rice, Grantland, 90, 137, 158, 178, 184
Rickard, George Lewis, 4, 23, 26, 41, 57, 68, 70, 71, 74-76, 78, 85-87, 89, 90, 92, 93, 138, 139, 142-144, 146, 151, 152, 154, 155, 160
Risko, Johnny, 3, 47, 48, 74, 75, 143-145, 148, 152, 158, 160, 161, 168, 169, 177, 187, 224
RMS *Majestic*, 167
Roberts, Al, 17, 223
Robinson, Ray, "Sugar" 59
Rojas, Quinton Romero, 15, 18-22, 24, 28, 43, 47, 223
Rosenbloom, Maxie, "Slappsie" 179, 209
Runyon, Damon, 177, 220
Ruth, George Herman Jr., 14, 177, 206
Saavedra, Clemente, 43
Schaaf, Ernie, 4, 10, 76, 102, 151, 152, 163, 187, 188, 189, 201
Schmeling, Maximillian Adolph Otto Siegfried, 4, 106, 115, 116, 158, 160, 162-164, 167-177, 179, 180, 182-184, 185-188, 191, 192, 202, 206, 211, 214, 222, 225

Scott, Phil, 4, 152, 163, 168, 173, 175, 225
See, Leon, 181, 197
Shade, Dave, 176
Sharkey, Jack III, 3, 5, 6, 94, 95-103, 105, 106, 120, 122, 124, 126-130, 200, 221
Sharkey, Jack IV, 6, 128, 221
Sharkey, Jack Jr., 218
Sharkey, Tom, 11, 54, 214
Shucco, Tony, 209, 211, 226
Silver, Mike, 5, 200
Skinner, Archie, 34, 43
Smith, Ed, 181
Smith, Eddie, 22
Smith, Homer, 3, 17, 68, 223, 224
Solomon, Emilio, 3, 41, 42, 43, 44-46, 53, 54, 70, 223, 224
Spellman, Martin, 140
Spinks, Leon, 198
Squires, Vince E., 154
Stillman, Lou, 59, 60
Stone, Ad, 28
Stone, Jack, 60
Stribling, William Lawrence, Jr., 4, 41, 46, 114, 154-159, 161, 163, 175, 177, 183, 199, 225
Sugar, Bert Randolph, 198
Sullivan, Jack, "Twin" 12, 21
Sullivan, John L., 13, 17, 41, 168
Tate, Bill, 60
Taylor, Estelle, 56, 87
Taylor, Walter, 75
The Great Depression, 163, 202, 207
Trumbull, Walter, 175, 178, 179, 183
Tunney, Gene, 17, 29, 40, 41, 56, 58, 66, 68, 71, 75, 85, 90, 134, 140, 141, 143, 146, 150, 151, 172, 193, 199
Tyson, Mike, 88
U.S.S. Denver, 10, 11

Urban, Johnny, 91
Uzcudun, Paulino, 55, 70, 71, 74-76, 78, 92, 140, 151, 160, 161, 168, 169, 179, 181, 206
Voice, Al, 204
Walcott, Joe, 13, 59, 72
Walker, Edward Patrick, (Mickey) "The Toy Bull Dog" 70, 112, 176-180, 183, 187, 202, 225
Walker, William, 216
Walker, William H., 189
Wallace, Sam, 23
Weinert, Charley, 3, 21-23, 25-28, 40, 41, 223
Weingert, Herman, 204
Willard, Jess, 15, 79, 88, 200
Williams, Feab S., 55, 56, 187, 224
Williams, Theodore Samuel, "Ted" 120, 218, 222
Wills, Harry Coleman, "The Black Panther" 29, 35, 40, 41, 57-68, 113, 146, 154, 224
Wilson, Gus, 145, 169, 191, 192, 207
Winston, Eddie, "Unknown" 207-209, 225
Wiswell, George, 40
World War One, 9, 30, 35, 157
Wright, Bearcat, 177
Yankee Stadium, 74, 76, 79, 86, 134, 146, 160, 161, 168, 170, 183, 204, 215
Zukauskas, Agnes, 7
Zukauskas, Joseph Paul, 8-11, 40, 75, 168, 222

www.ingramcontent.com/pod-product-compliance
Lightning Source LLC
Chambersburg PA
CBHW032023230426
43671CB00005B/180